FILM FORM

ALSO BY SERGEI EISENSTEIN

The Film Sense

SERGEI EISENSTEIN

Film Form

ESSAYS IN FILM THEORY,
edited and translated by
JAY LEYDA

A Harvest/HBJ Book
Harcourt Brace Jovanovich, Publishers
San Diego   New York   London

Requests for permission to make copies
of any part of the work should be mailed to:
Permissions Department,
Harcourt Brace Jovanovich, Publishers, 8th Floor,
Orlando, Florida 32887.

ISBN 0-15-630920-3 (Harvest/HBJ : pbk.)

Printed in the United States of America

N O P Q R

CONTENTS

INTRODUCTION

THE COMPILATION of this book of essays was one of its author's last tasks. Though too weak in his last two years of life to resume film work, Eisenstein was too strong to relax his theoretical activity. His fatal attack, on the night of February 10, 1948, interrupted him at work; when he was found the next morning, before him were his last words—an unfinished essay on color, its use in the unfinished *Ivan the Terrible*. It is precisely because he was so far from being finished, as film-maker or theoretician, that we feel his loss so deeply.

A great artist leaves his work behind him, but a contemplation of Eisenstein's completed work does little to ease the shock of his death, for all these films pointed to further work in which his heroic and tireless expansion of the film medium would push beyond all the limits that lesser artists have set around it. Each step forward by Eisenstein promised a hundred following unexpected steps, and death at the age of forty-nine leaves many steps untaken.

As a great teacher he left an even richer heritage: from his students and the large body of his theory we can expect further fruit, even beyond our generation. It was said of Bach, "Only he who knows much can teach much," and we can be eternally grateful that Eisenstein's immense knowledge was poured not only into six finished films but also, directly and indirectly, into an incalculable number of pupils.

A steady source for his imagination, as artist and as teacher, lay in his consciousness of the artist's real influence in society, an influence to be fully realized only within an equally powerful sense of responsibility to society. This dual pull determined his every decision: in esthetics, for example, it made

vii

him impatient with every lean towards surface naturalism—
for he could see the unwillingness, the laziness, ignorance and
often opportunism behind such an evasion of the difficult but
central problem. The film artist's job was to learn his principles from a profound investigation of all arts and all levels
of life, to measure these principles against an unfaltering understanding of himself, and if he then did anything less than
create—with bold, living works that moved their audiences to
excitement and understanding—he was neither good artist nor
positive member of society. In film, with all its easy satis-
factions, there was more temptation to skirt this primary issue
than in any other art, but once Eisenstein chose cinema as
the supremely expressive medium, he undertook to wage upon
it, as upon a battlefield, a perpetual war against the evils of
dishonesty, satisfaction, superficiality. He fought with the
arrogance of an assured artist—he knew how much we all
needed him, whether we admitted it or not. His aim was a
poetry possible only to films, a realism heightened by *all* the
means in the film-artist's power. Though both he and the
surrealists would have denied his relation to the term, this
was sur-realism—but the dynamic aim and accomplishment of
Sergei Eisenstein need no category or label.

To challenge laziness and naturalism puts the challenger at
a disadvantage: it attaches "anti-natural" labels to the challenger's principles and practice, and forces him to prove, in
works, that they can be affective beyond those works whose
"simplicity" is essentially negative. The affective test was
passed by each of Eisenstein's films; the principles were stub-
bornly enunciated in writing that in sheer quantity outdoes
the public thinking of any film-maker. He admitted to being
neither a smooth nor a talented writer, and was dependent on
the energy of his ideas and the clarity of their expression; he
employed circumstantial as well as poetic proof—and he drew
on the world for his illustrations. His "right way," swerving
sharply from standard thinking, or rather, standard non-think-
ing about films, forced his theoretical writing to combine
polemic, rhetoric, self-defense, essay, gallery tour, analysis,

lecture, sermon, criminal investigation, chalk-talk—and to be
as valid for the local, immediate problem, as for the general,
lasting issue. A many-sided, never-ending education stocked
his armory of illustration: criticized for distortion, he would
point to the "purposeful distortion" employed by a Sharaku
or a Flaubert; accused of "unlifelike theories" he would hold
up precedents from the fields of philology and psychology;
accusations of "leftism" and "modernism" brought out de-
fenses by Milton, Pushkin, El Greco that not only solidified
his argument, but gave it a fresh dimension, and stimulated
the reader to investigate these neglected riches.

His first readers were always, as were his first audiences,
his fellow film-makers and his students, furnishing, even in
their maintenance of opposite views, a body of encourage-
ment and stimulation that would be hard to equal outside
that electric Moscow-Leningrad-Kiev circuit of film-enthusi-
asts. His foreign readers have been variously handicapped, by
an unavoidable remoteness from this stimulating atmosphere
and by a remoteness from the issues under discussion there,
that motivated a great deal of Eisenstein's combative writing;
but the greatest handicap for his readers (and professionally
interested spectators) abroad was the distortion, by misuse,
imitation, and misinterpretation, of his basic terms and concepts. To read, for example, about "montage" through the dis-
torting haze of superficiality with which this term has been
brought into our studios, has not aided an understanding of
Eisenstein's theoretical writing. In recent years, however, general information on Eisenstein's theories has tended to escape
these earlier prejudices and apings, and it seems that his films
and writings alike will be now examined with more profit in
this country than during his lifetime. It is hoped that this second volume of his writing to appear in English * will contribute to this profit and comprehension.

Of his hundreds of essays, this group was selected to show
certain key-points in the development of his film theory and,

---

* *The Film Sense*, his first book, originally appeared in 1942; the revised edition in 1947.

in particular, of his analysis of the sound-film medium. Despite the existence of *Alexander Nevsky* and *Ivan the Terrible*, the study of Eisenstein's theories usually finds its illustrations in his "silent" films. This almost makes more poignant the revelation in these essays of his long planning and contemplation of sound as an *essential* element in his vision of the total film, and he was fully aware of the apparent strangeness that he "should resemble the last to arrive at the wedding." Yet the still restless couple—sight and sound—has lost its most hopeful conciliator and advisor in Eisenstein's death, for no sound-film program has achieved either the solidity of his "Statement" of 1928 and his "Achievement" of 1939 or the adventure of his plans for *An American Tragedy* (discussed in "A Course in Treatment"). The sure simplicity of audio-visual experiment in *Nevsky* and the grand experiment in heroic style of *Ivan the Terrible, Part I* have not yet been properly gauged for their instructional virtues, and the rich fund of discussion of the sound-film in these essays must be added to the sum of his completed films to gain a rounded view on his intellectually mature grasp of the film medium.

Some of these essays have been previously available, sometimes in inadequate English renderings; the relation of the present texts to these earlier translations is indicated at the end of the volume.

Generous assistance on all levels has been given this book by Esther and Harold Leonard, by Jane and Gordon Williams, by Sergei Bertensson, Richard Collins, Robert Payne, and other friends. John Winge made the new translation from Eisenstein's German manuscript (lent by the Museum of Modern Art Film Library) of "A Dialectic Approach to Film Form," and the frames chosen by Eisenstein for its illustration were prepared for reproduction here by Irving Lerner. I am particularly grateful to the Hon. Ivor Montagu whose long association with the personality and ideas of the author produced translations so conscientious and scrupulous that a minimum of adjustment has been necessary in adding them to this collection. The library staffs that contributed their talents so patiently were those of the University of California at Los Angeles, the Los Angeles Public Library, the Beverly Hills Public Library, Columbia University, the Museum of Modern Art, and the American-Russian Institute.

JAY LEYDA

FILM FORM

THROUGH THEATER TO CINEMA

IT IS interesting to retrace the different paths of today's cinema workers to their creative beginnings, which together compose the multi-colored background of the Soviet cinema. In the early 1920s we all came to the Soviet cinema as something not yet existent. We came upon no ready-built city; there were no squares, no streets laid out; not even little crooked lanes and blind alleys, such as we may find in the cinemetropolis of our day. We came like bedouins or gold-seekers to a place with unimaginably great possibilities, only a small section of which has even now been developed.

We pitched our tents and dragged into camp our experiences in varied fields. Private activities, accidental past professions, unguessed crafts, unsuspected eruditions—all were pooled and went into the building of something that had, as yet, no written traditions, no exact stylistic requirements, nor even formulated demands.

Without going too far into the theoretical debris of the specifics of cinema, I want here to discuss two of its features. These are features of other arts as well, but the film is particularly accountable to them. *Primo:* photo-fragments of nature are recorded; *secundo:* these fragments are combined in various ways. Thus, the shot (or frame), and thus, montage.

Photography is a system of reproduction to fix real events and elements of actuality. These reproductions, or photo-reflections, may be combined in various ways. Both as reflections and in the manner of their combination, they permit any degree of distortion—either technically unavoidable or deliberately calculated. The results fluctuate from exact naturalistic

3

combinations of visual, interrelated experiences to complete alterations, arrangements unforeseen by nature, and even to abstract formalism, with remnants of reality.

The apparent arbitrariness of matter, in its relation to the *status quo* of nature, is much less arbitrary than it seems. The final order is inevitably determined, consciously or unconsciously, by the social premises of the maker of the film-composition. His class-determined tendency is the basis of what seems to be an arbitrary cinematographic relation to the object placed, or found, before the camera.

We should like to find in this two-fold process (the fragment and its relationships) a hint as to the specifics of cinema, but we cannot deny that this process is to be found in other art mediums, whether close to cinema or not (and which art is not close to cinema?). Nevertheless, it is possible to insist that these features are specific to the film, because film-specifics lie not in the process itself but in the degree to which these features are intensified.

The musician uses a scale of sounds; the painter, a scale of tones; the writer, a row of sounds and words—and these are all taken to an equal degree from nature. But the immutable fragment of actual reality in these cases is narrower and more neutral in meaning, and therefore more flexible in combination, so that when they are put together they lose all visible signs of being combined, appearing as one organic unit. A chord, or even three successive notes, seems to be an organic unit. Why should the combination of three pieces of film in montage be considered as a three-fold collision, as impulses of three successive images?

A blue tone is mixed with a red tone, and the result is thought of as violet, and not as a "double exposure" of red and blue. The same unity of word fragments makes all sorts of expressive variations possible. How easily three shades of meaning can be distinguished in language—for example: "a window without light," "a dark window," and "an unlit window."

Now try to express these various nuances in the composition of the frame. Is it at all possible?

If it is, then what complicated context will be needed in order to string the film-pieces onto the film-thread so that the black shape on the wall will begin to show either as a "dark" or as an "unlit" window? How much wit and ingenuity will be expended in order to reach an effect that words achieve so simply?

The frame is much less independently workable than the word or the sound. Therefore the mutual work of frame and montage is really an enlargement in scale of a process microscopically inherent in all arts. However, in the film this process is raised to such a degree that it seems to acquire a new quality.

The shot, considered as material for the purpose of composition, is more resistant than granite. This resistance is specific to it. The shot's tendency toward complete factual immutability is rooted in its nature. This resistance has largely determined the richness and variety of montage forms and styles—for montage becomes the mightiest means for a really important creative remolding of nature.

Thus the cinema is able, more than any other art, to disclose the process that goes on microscopically in all other arts.

The minimum "distortable" fragment of nature is the shot; ingenuity in its combinations is montage.

Analysis of this problem received the closest attention during the second half-decade of Soviet cinema (1925-1930), an attention often carried to excess. Any infinitesimal alteration of a fact or event before the camera grew, beyond all lawful limit, into whole theories of documentalism. The lawful necessity of combining these fragments of reality grew into montage conceptions which presumed to supplant all other elements of film-expression.

Within normal limits these features enter, as elements, into any style of cinematography. But they are not opposed to nor can they replace other problems—for instance, the problem of *story*.

To return to the double process indicated at the beginning of these notes: if this process is characteristic of cinema, finding its fullest expression during the second stage of Soviet cinema, it will be rewarding to investigate the creative biographies of film-workers of that period, seeing how these features emerged, how they developed in pre-cinema work. All the roads of that period led towards one Rome. I shall try to describe the path that carried me to cinema principles.

Usually my film career is said to have begun with my production of Ostrovsky's play, *Enough Simplicity in Every Sage*, at the Proletcult Theatre (Moscow, March 1923). This is both true and untrue. It is not true if it is based solely on the fact that this production contained a short comic film made especially for it (not separate, but included in the montage plan of the spectacle). It is more nearly true if it is based on the character of the production, for even then the elements of the specifics mentioned above could be detected.

We have agreed that the first sign of a cinema tendency is one showing events with the least distortion, aiming at the factual reality of the fragments.

A search in this direction shows my film tendencies beginning three years earlier, in the production of *The Mexican* (from Jack London's story). Here, my participation brought into the theater "events" themselves—a purely cinematographic element, as distinguished from "reactions to events"—which is a purely theatrical element.

This is the plot: A Mexican revolutionary group needs money for its activities. A boy, a Mexican, offers to find the money. He trains for boxing, and contracts to let the champion beat him for a fraction of the prize. Instead he beats up the champion, winning the entire prize. Now that I am better acquainted with the specifics of the Mexican revolutionary struggle, not to mention the technique of boxing, I would not think of interpreting this material as we did in 1920, let alone using so unconvincing a plot.

The play's climax is the prize-fight. In accordance with the most hallowed Art Theatre traditions, this was to take place backstage (like the bull-fight in *Carmen*), while the actors on stage were to show excitement in the fight only they can see, as well as to portray the various emotions of the persons concerned in the outcome.

My first move (trespassing upon the director's job, since I was there in the official capacity of designer only) was to propose that the fight be brought into view. Moreover I suggested that the scene be staged in the center of the auditorium to re-create the same circumstances under which a real boxing match takes place. Thus we dared the concreteness of factual events. The fight was to be carefully planned in advance but was to be utterly realistic.

The playing of our young worker-actors in the fight scene differed radically from their acting elsewhere in the production. In every other scene, one emotion gave rise to a further emotion (they were working in the Stanislavsky system), which in turn was used as a means to affect the audience; but in the fight scene the audience was excited directly.

While the other scenes influenced the audience through intonation, gestures, and mimicry, our scene employed realistic, even textural means—real fighting, bodies crashing to the ring floor, panting, the shine of sweat on torsos, and finally, the unforgettable smacking of gloves against taut skin and strained muscles. Illusionary scenery gave way to a realistic ring (though not in the center of the hall, thanks to that plague of every theatrical enterprise, the fireman) and extras closed the circle around the ring.

Thus my realization that I had struck new ore, an actual-materialistic element in theater. In *The Sage*, this element appeared on a new and clearer level. The eccentricity of the production exposed this same line, through fantastic contrasts. The tendency developed not only from illusionary acting movement, but from the physical fact of acrobatics. A gesture expands into gymnastics, rage is expressed through a somersault, exaltation through a *salto-mortale*, lyricism on "the mast

of death." The grotesque of this style permitted leaps from one
type of expression to another, as well as unexpected inter-
twinings of the two expressions. In a later production, *Listen,
Moscow* (summer 1923), these two separate lines of "real
doing" and "pictorial imagination" went through a synthesis
expressed in a specific technique of acting.

These two principles appeared again in Tretiakov's *Gas
Masks* (1923-24), with still sharper irreconcilability, broken so
noticeably that had this been a film it would have remained, as
we say, "on the shelf."

What was the matter? The conflict between material-
practical and fictitious-descriptive principles was somehow
patched up in the melodrama, but here they broke up and
we failed completely. The cart dropped to pieces, and its
driver dropped into the cinema.

This all happened because one day the director had the
marvelous idea of producing this play about a gas factory—
in a real gas factory.

As we realized later, the real interiors of the factory had
nothing to do with our theatrical fiction. At the same time
the plastic charm of reality in the factory became so strong
that the element of actuality rose with fresh strength—took
things into its own hands—and finally had to leave an art
where it could not command.

Thereby bringing us to the brink of cinema.

But this is not the end of our adventures with theater work.
Having come to the screen, this other tendency flourished,
and became known as "typage." This "typage" is just as
typical a feature of this cinema period as "montage." And
be it known that I do not want to limit the concept of "typage"
or "montage" to my own works.

I want to point out that "typage" must be understood as
broader than merely a face without make-up, or a substitution
of "naturally expressive" types for actors. In my opinion,
"typage" included a specific approach to the events embraced
by the content of the film. Here again was the method of
least interference with the natural course and combinations of

events. In concept, from beginning to end, *October* is pure "typage."

A typage tendency may be rooted in theater; growing out of the theater into film, it presents possibilities for excellent stylistic growth, in a broad sense—as an indicator of definite affinities to real life through the camera.*

And now let us examine the second feature of film-specifics, the principles of montage. How was this expressed and shaped in my work before joining the cinema?

In the midst of the flood of eccentricity in *The Sage*, including a short film comedy, we can find the first hints of a sharply expressed montage.

The action moves through an elaborate tissue of intrigue. Mamayev sends his nephew, Glumov, to his wife as guardian. Glumov takes liberties beyond his uncle's instructions and his aunt takes the courtship seriously. At the same time Glumov begins to negotiate for a marriage with Mamayev's niece, Turussina, but conceals these intentions from the aunt, Mamayeva. Courting the aunt, Glumov deceives the uncle; flattering the uncle, Glumov arranges with him the deception of the aunt.

Glumov, on a comic plane, echoes the situations, the overwhelming passions, the thunder of finance, that his French prototype, Balzac's Rastignac, experiences. Rastignac's type in Russia was still in the cradle. Money-making was still a sort of child's game between uncles and nephews, aunts and their gallants. It remains in the family, and remains trivial. Hence, the comedy. But the intrigue and entanglements are already present, playing on two fronts at the same time—with

* Eisenstein has said that one might define typage as a modern development of the *Commedia dell'arte*—with its seven stock figures multiplied into infinity. The relationship lies not in numbers, but in audience conditioning. Upon entrance of Pantalone or the Captain, his mask tells the audience immediately what to expect of this figure. Modern film typage is based on the need for presenting each new figure in our first glimpse of him so sharply and completely that further use of this figure may be as a known element. Thus new, immediate conventions are created. An amplification of this approach is given in the author's comments on Lavater, on page 127.—EDITOR.

both hands—with dual characters . . . and we showed all this with an intertwined montage of two different scenes (of Mamayev giving his instructions, and of Glumov putting them into execution). The surprising intersections of the two dialogues sharpen the characters and the play, quicken the tempo, and multiply the comic possibilities.

For the production of *The Sage* the stage was shaped like a circus arena, edged with a red barrier, and three-quarters surrounded by the audience. The other quarter was hung with a striped curtain, in front of which stood a small raised platform, several steps high. The scene with Mamayev (Shtraukh) took place downstage while the Mamayeva (Yanukova) fragments occurred on the platform. Instead of changing scenes, Glumov (Yezikanov) ran from one scene to the other and back—taking a fragment of dialogue from one scene, interrupting it with a fragment from the other scene—the dialogue thus colliding, creating new meanings and sometimes wordplays. Glumov's leaps acted as *caesurae* between the dialogue fragments.

And the "cutting" increased in tempo. What was most interesting was that the extreme sharpness of the eccentricity was not torn from the context of this part of the play; it never became comical just for comedy's sake, but stuck to its theme, sharpened by its scenic embodiment.

Another distinct film feature at work here was the new meaning acquired by common phrases in a new environment. Everyone who has had in his hands a piece of film to be edited knows by experience how neutral it remains, even though a part of a planned sequence, until it is joined with another piece, when it suddenly acquires and conveys a sharper and quite different meaning than that planned for it at the time of filming.

This was the foundation of that wise and wicked art of re-editing the work of others, the most profound examples of which can be found during the dawn of our cinematography,

when all the master film-editors—Esther Schub,* the Vas-
siliyev brothers, Benjamin Boitler, and Birrois—were engaged
in reworking ingeniously the films imported after the revolution.

I cannot resist the pleasure of citing here one montage
tour de force of this sort, executed by Boitler. One film bought
from Germany was *Danton,* with Emil Jannings. As released
on our screens, this scene was shown: Camille Desmoulins is
condemned to the guillotine. Greatly agitated, Danton rushes
to Robespierre, who turns aside and slowly wipes away a
tear. The sub-title said, approximately, "In the name of freedom I had to sacrifice a friend. . . ." Fine.

But who could have guessed that in the German original,
Danton, represented as an idler, a petticoat-chaser, a splendid
chap and the only positive figure in the midst of evil characters, that this Danton ran to the evil Robespierre and . . .
spat in his face? And that it was this spit that Robespierre
wiped from his face with a handkerchief? And that the title
indicated Robespierre's hatred of Danton, a hate that in the
end of the film motivates the condemnation of Jannings-Dan-
ton to the guillotine?!

Two tiny cuts reversed the entire significance of this scene!

Where did my montage experiment in these scenes of *The
Sage* come from?

There was already an "aroma" of montage in the new
"left" cinema, particularly among the documentalists. Our
replacement of Glumov's diary in Ostrovsky's text with a
short "film-diary" was itself a parody on the first experiments
with newsreels.

* Schub, long a familiar name to world-documentalists, is known
abroad only by the film exhibited in America as *Cannons and Tractors.*
The first time Eisenstein ever joined together two pieces of "real film"
was while assisting Esther Schub in the re-editing of Lang's *Dr. Mabuse.*
This was shortly after the production of *The Sage.* The Vassiliyevs'
Chapayev establishes their place in cinema history.—EDITOR.

I think that first and foremost we must give the credit to
the basic principles of the circus and the music-hall—for which
I had had a passionate love since childhood. Under the influence of the French comedians, and of Chaplin (of whom we
had only heard), and the first news of the fox-trot and jazz,
this early love thrived.

The music-hall element was obviously needed at the time
for the emergence of a "montage" form of thought. Harle-
quin's parti-colored costume grew and spread, first over the
structure of the program, and finally into the method of the
whole production.

But the background extended more deeply into tradition.
Strangely enough, it was Flaubert who gave us one of the
finest examples of cross-montage of dialogues, used with the
same intention of expressive sharpening of idea. This is the
scene in *Madame Bovary* where Emma and Rodolphe grow
more intimate. Two lines of speech are interlaced: the speech
of the orator in the square below, and the conversation of the
future lovers:

Monsieur Derozerays got up, beginning another speech . . .
praise of the Government took up less space in it; religion and
agriculture more. He showed in it the relations of these two, and
how they had always contributed to civilization. Rodolphe with
Madame Bovary was talking dreams, presentiments, magnetism.
Going back to the cradle of society, the orator painted those fierce
times when men lived on acorns in the heart of woods. Then they
had left off the skins of beasts, had put on cloth, tilled the soil,
planted the vine. Was this a good, and in this discovery was there
not more of injury than of gain? Monsieur Derozerays set himself
this problem. From magnetism little by little Rodolphe had come
to affinities, and while the president was citing Cincinnatus and
his plough, Diocletian planting his cabbages, and the Emperors of
China inaugurating the year by the sowing of seed, the young
man was explaining to the young woman that these irresistible
attractions find their cause in some previous state of experience.

"Thus we," he said, "why did we come to know one another?
What chance willed it? It was because across the infinite, like

two streams that flow but to unite, our special bents of mind had driven us towards each other."

And he seized her hand; she did not withdraw it.

"For good farming generally!" cried the president.

"Just now, for example, when I went to your house."

"To Monsieur Bizat of Quincampoix."

"Did I know I should accompany you?"

"Seventy francs."

"A hundred times I wished to go; and I followed you—I remained."

"Manures!"

"And I shall remain to-night, to-morrow, all other days, all my life!" [1]

And so on, with the "pieces" developing increasing tension.

As we can see, this is an interweaving of two lines, thematically identical, equally trivial. The matter is sublimated to a monumental triviality, whose climax is reached through a continuation of this cross-cutting and word-play, with the significance always dependent on the juxtaposition of the two lines.

Literature is full of such examples. This method is used with increasing popularity by Flaubert's artistic heirs.

Our pranks in regard to Ostrovsky remained on an "avant garde" level of an indubitable nakedness. But this seed of montage tendencies grew quickly and splendidly in *Patatra*, which remained a project through lack of an adequate hall and technical possibilities. The production was planned with "chase tempos," quick changes of action, scene intersections, and simultaneous playing of several scenes on a stage that surrounded an auditorium of revolving seats. Another even earlier project attempted to embrace the entire theater building in its composition. This was broken up during rehearsals and later produced by other hands as a purely theatrical conception. It was the Pletnëv play, *Precipice*, which Smishlayev and I worked on, following *The Mexican*, until we disagreed on principles and dissolved our partnership. (When I returned

[1] See Sources, pp. 268-272.

to Proletcult a year later, to do *The Sage*, it was as a director, although I continued to design my own productions.)

Precipice contains a scene where an inventor, thrilled by his new invention, runs, like Archimedes, about the city (or perhaps he was being chased by gangsters—I don't remember exactly). The task was to solve the dynamics of city streets, as well as to show the helplessness of an individual at the mercy of the "big city." (Our mistaken imaginings about Europe naturally led us to the false concept of "urbanism.")

An amusing combination occurred to me, not only to use running scenery—pieces of buildings and details (Meyerhold had not yet worked out, for his *Trust D. E.*, the neutral polished shields, *murs mobiles*, to unify several places of action)—but also, possibly under the demands of shifting scenery, to connect these moving decorations with people. The actors on roller skates carried not only themselves about the stage, but also their "piece of city." Our solution of the problem—the intersection of man and milieu—was undoubtedly influenced by the principles of the cubists. But the "urbanistic" paintings of Picasso were of less importance here than the need to express the dynamics of the city—glimpses of façades, hands, legs, pillars, heads, domes. All of this can be found in Gogol's work, but we did not notice that until Andrei Belyi enlightened us about the special cubism of Gogol.[2] I still remember the four legs of two bankers, supporting the façade of the stock-exchange, with two top-hats crowning the whole. There was also a policeman, sliced and quartered with traffic. Costumes blazing with perspectives of twirling lights, with only great rouged lips visible above. These all remained on paper—and now that even the paper has gone, we may become quite pathetically lyrical in our reminiscences.

These close-ups cut into views of a city become another link in our analysis, a film element that tried to fit itself into the stubborn stage. Here are also elements of double and multiple exposure—"superimposing" images of man onto images of buildings—all an attempt to interrelate man and his milieu in a single complicated display. (The fact that the film *Strike* was full of this sort of complexity proves the "infantile malady of leftism" existing in these first steps of cinema.)

Out of mechanical fusion, from plastic synthesis, the attempt evolves into thematic synthesis. In *Strike*, there is more than a transformation into the technique of the camera. The composition and structure of the film as a whole achieves the effect and sensation of uninterrupted unity between the collective and the milieu that creates the collective. And the organic unity of sailors, battleships, and sea that is shown in plastic and thematic cross-section in *Potemkin* is not by trickery or double-exposure or mechanical intersection, but by the general structure of the composition. But in the theater, the impossibility of the *mise-en-scène* unfolding throughout the auditorium, fusing stage and audience in a developing pattern, was the reason for the concentrated absorption of the *mise-en-scène* problems within the scenic action.

The almost geometrically conventional *mise-en-scène* of *The Sage* and its formal sequel, *Listen, Moscow*, becomes one of the basic elements of expression. The montage intersection eventually became too emphatically exact. The composition singled out groups, shifted the spectator's attention from one point to another, presented close-ups, a hand holding a letter, the play of eyebrows, a glance. The technique of genuine *mise-en-scène* composition was being mastered—and approaching its limits. It was already threatened with becoming the knight's move in chess, the shift of purely plastic contours in the already non-theatrical outlines of detailed drawings.

Sculptural details seen through the frame of the *cadre*, or shot, transitions from shot to shot, appeared to be the logical way out for the threatened hypertrophy of the *mise-en-scène*. Theoretically it established our dependence on *mise-en-scène* and montage. Pedagogically, it determined, for the future, the approaches to montage and cinema, arrived at through the mastering of theatrical construction and through the art of *mise-en-scène.** Thus was born the concept of *mise-en-cadre*. As the *mise-en-scène* is an interrelation of people in action, so the *mise-en-cadre* is the pictorial composition of mutually dependent *cadres* (shots) in a montage sequence.

In *Gas Masks* we see all the elements of film tendencies meeting. The turbines, the factory background, negated the last remnants of make-up and theatrical costumes, and all elements appeared as independently fused. Theater accessories in the midst of real factory plastics appeared ridiculous. The element of "play" was incompatible with the acrid smell of gas. The pitiful platform kept getting lost among the real platforms of labor activity. In short, the production was a failure. And we found ourselves in the cinema.

Our first film opus, *Strike* [1924-25], reflected, as in a mirror, in reverse, our production of *Gas Masks*. But the film floundered about in the flotsam of a rank theatricality that had become alien to it.

At the same time, the break with the theater in principle was so sharp that in my "revolt against the theater" I did away with a very vital element of theater—the story.

At that time this seemed natural. We brought collective and mass action onto the screen, in contrast to individualism and the "triangle" drama of the bourgeois cinema. Discarding the individualist conception of the bourgeois hero, our films of this period made an abrupt deviation—insisting on an understanding of the mass as hero.

No screen had ever before reflected an image of collective action. Now the conception of "collectivity" was to be pictured. But our enthusiasm produced a one-sided representation of the masses and the collective; one-sided because collectivism means the maximum development of the individual within the collective, a conception irreconcilably opposed to bourgeois individualism. Our first mass films missed this deeper meaning.

* As indicated in "A Course in Treatment," the first two years of Eisenstein's course for directors at the State Cinema Institute emphasize a thorough study of *theater* principles.—EDITOR.

Still, I am sure that for its period this deviation was not only natural but necessary. It was important that the screen be first penetrated by the general image, the collective united and propelled by one wish. "Individuality within the collective," the deeper meaning, demanded of cinema today, would have found entrance almost impossible if the way had not been cleared by the general concept.

In 1924 I wrote, with intense zeal: "Down with the story and the plot!" Today, the story, which then seemed to be almost "an attack of individualism" upon our revolutionary cinema, returns in a fresh form, to its proper place. In this turn towards the story lies the historical importance of the third half-decade of Soviet cinematography (1930-1935).

And here, as we begin our fourth five-year period of cinema, when abstract discussions of the epigones of the "story" film and the embryones of the "plotless" film are calming down, it is time to take an inventory of our credits and debits.

I consider that besides mastering the elements of filmic diction, the technique of the frame, and the theory of montage, we have another credit to list—the value of profound ties with the traditions and methodology of literature. Not in vain, during this period, was the new concept of film-language born, film-language not as the language of the film-critic, but as an expression of cinema thinking, when the cinema was called upon to embody the philosophy and ideology of the victorious proletariat.

Stretching out its hand to the new quality of literature—the dramatics of subject—the cinema cannot forget the tremendous experience of its earlier periods. But the way is not back to them, but forward to the synthesis of all the best that has been done by our silent cinematography, towards a synthesis of these with the demands of today, along the lines of story and Marxist-Leninist ideological analysis. The phase of monumental synthesis in the images of the people of the epoch of socialism—the phase of socialist realism.

[1934]

THE UNEXPECTED

> Hark! the voice of a pheasant
> Has swallowed the wide field
> At a gulp.
>
> YAMEI [1]

> Givochini, the famous comedian of the
> Malii Theatre, was once forced to substitute
> at the last moment for the popular Moscow
> basso, Lavrov, in an opera, *The Amorous
> Bayaderka*. But Givochini had no singing
> voice. His friends shook their heads sympa-
> thetically. "How can you possibly sing the
> role, Vasili Ignatyevich?" Givochini was not
> disheartened. Said he, happily, *"Whatever
> notes I can't take with my voice, I'll show
> with my hands."* [2]

WE HAVE been visited by the Kabuki theater—a wonderful manifestation of theatrical culture.*

Every critical voice gushes praise for its splendid crafts-manship. But there has been no appraisal of what constitutes its wonder. Its "museum" elements, though indispensable in estimating its value, cannot alone afford a satisfactory esti-mate of this phenomenon, of this wonder. A "wonder" must promote cultural progress, feeding and stimulating the intellec-tual questions of our day. The Kabuki is dismissed in plati-tudes: "How musical!" "What handling of objects!" "What plasticity!" And we come to the conclusion that there is nothing to be learned, that (as one of our most respected critics has announced) there's nothing new here: Meyerhold

---

* In its European tour during 1928 a troupe of Kabuki actors, headed by Ichikawa Sadanji, performed in Moscow and Leningrad; in the latter city the magazine *Zhizn Iskusstva* devoted to this visit an issue (19 August 1928), to which Eisenstein contributed this essay.

has already plundered everything of use from the Japanese theater!

Behind the fulsome generalities, there are some real attitudes revealed. Kabuki is conventional! How can such conventions move Europeans! Its craftsmanship is merely the cold perfection of form! And the plays they perform are *feudal!*—What a nightmare!

More than any other obstacle, it is this conventionalism that prevents our thorough use of all that may be borrowed from the Kabuki.

But the conventionalism that we have learned "from books" proves in fact to be a conventionalism of extremely interesting relationships. The conventionalism of Kabuki is by no means the stylized and premeditated mannerism that we know in our own theater, artificially grafted on outside the technical requirements of the premise. In Kabuki this conventionalism is profoundly logical—as in any Oriental theater, for example, in the Chinese theater.

Among the characters of the Chinese theater is "the spirit of the oyster"! Look at the make-up of the performer of this rôle, with its series of concentric touching circles spreading from the right and left of his nose, graphically reproducing the halves of an oyster shell, and it becomes apparent that this is quite "justified." This is neither more nor less a convention than are the epaulettes of a general. From their narrowly utilitarian origin, once warding off blows of the battle-axe from the shoulder, to their being furnished with hierarchic little stars, the epaulettes are indistinguishable in principle from the blue frog inscribed on the forehead of the actor who is playing the frog's "spirit."

Another convention is taken directly from life. In the first scene of *Chushingura* (*The Forty-Seven Ronin*), Shocho, playing a married woman, appears without eyebrows and with blackened teeth. This conventionalism is no more unreal than the custom of Jewish women who shear their heads so that the ears remain exposed, nor of that among girls joining the Komsomol who wear red kerchiefs, as some sort of "form."

In distinction from European practice, where marriage has been made a guard against the risks of freer attachments, in ancient Japan (of the play's epoch) the married woman, once the need had passed, destroyed her attractiveness! She removed her eyebrows, and blackened (and sometimes extracted) her teeth.

Let us move on to the most important matter, to a conventionalism that is explained by the specific world-viewpoint of the Japanese. This appears with particular clarity during the direct *perception* of the performance, to a peculiar degree that no description has been able to convey to us.

And here we find something totally unexpected—a junction of the Kabuki theater with these extreme probings in the theater, where theater is transformed into cinema.* And where cinema takes that latest step in its development: the *sound* film.

The sharpest distinction between Kabuki and our theater is— if such an expression may be permitted—in a *monism of ensemble*.

We are familiar with the emotional ensemble of the Moscow Art Theatre—the ensemble of a unified collective "re-experience"; the parallelism of ensemble employed in opera (by orchestra, chorus, and soloists); when the settings also make their contribution to this parallelism, the theater is designated by that dirtied word "synthetic"; the "animal" ensemble finally has its revenge—that outmoded form where the whole stage clucks and barks and moos a naturalistic imitation of the life that is led by the "assisting" human beings.

The Japanese have shown us another, extremely interesting form of ensemble—*the monistic ensemble*. Sound—movement— space—voice here *do not accompany* (nor even parallel) each other, but function *as elements of equal significance*.

The first association that occurs to one in experiencing

---

* It is my conviction that cinema is *today's level* of theater. That theater in its older form has died and continues to exist only by inertia. [The author's commentary of eleven years later on this viewpoint can be found in "Achievement," p. 191.—EDITOR.]

Kabuki is *soccer*, the most collective, ensemble sport. Voice, clappers, mimic movement, the narrator's shouts, the folding screens—all are so many backs, half-backs, goal-keepers, forwards, passing to each other the dramatic ball and driving towards the goal of the dazed spectator.

It is impossible to speak of "accompaniments" in Kabuki— just as one would not say that, in walking or running, the right leg "accompanies" the left leg, or that both of them accompany the diaphragm!

Here a single monistic sensation of theatrical "provocation" takes place. The Japanese regards each theatrical element, not as an incommensurable unit among the various categories of affect (on the various sense-organs), but as a single unit of *theater*.

. . . the patter of Ostuzhev no more than the pink tights of the prima-donna, a roll on the kettledrums as much as Romeo's soliloquy, the cricket on the hearth no less than the cannon fired over the heads of the audience.[3]

Thus I wrote in 1923, placing a sign of equality between the elements of every category, establishing theoretically the basic *unity of theater*, which I then called "attractions."

The Japanese in his, of course, instinctive practice, makes a fully one hundred per cent appeal with his theater, just as I then had in mind. Directing himself to the various organs of sensation, he builds his summation to a grand *total* provocation of the human brain, without taking any notice *which* of these several paths he is following.*

In place of *accompaniment*, it is the naked method of *transfer* that flashes in the Kabuki theater. Transferring the basic affective aim from one material to another, from one category of "provocation" to another.

In experiencing Kabuki one involuntarily recalls an American novel about a man in whom are transposed the hearing

* Not even what is *eaten* in this theater is accidental! I had no opportunity to discover if it is ritual food eaten. Do they eat whatever happens to be there, or is there a definite menu? If the latter, we must also include in the ensemble the sense of taste!

and seeing nerves, so that he perceives light vibrations as sounds, and tremors of the air—as colors: he *hears light* and *sees sound*. This is also what happens in Kabuki! We actually "hear movement" and "see sound."

An example: Yuranosuke leaves the surrendered castle. And moves from the depth of the stage towards the extreme foreground. Suddenly the background screen with its gate painted in natural dimensions (close-up) is folded away. In its place is seen a second screen, with a tiny gate painted on it (long shot). This means that he has moved even further away. Yuranosuke continues on. Across the background is drawn a brown-green-black curtain, indicating: the castle is now hidden from his sight. More steps. Yuranosuke now moves out on to the "flowery way." This further removal is emphasized by . . . the *samisen*,* that is—by sound!!

First removal—steps, i.e., a *spatial* removal by the actor.

Second removal—a flat *painting:* the change of backgrounds.

Third removal—an *intellectually*-explained indication: we understand that the curtain "effaces" something visible.

Fourth removal—*sound!*

Here is an example of pure cinematographic method from the last fragment of *Chushingura:*

After a short fight ("for several feet") we have a "break"— an empty stage, a landscape. Then more fighting. Exactly as if, in a film, we had cut in a piece of landscape to create a mood in a scene, here is cut in an empty nocturnal snow landscape

---

* ". . . samisen music depends almost completely on rhythm, rather than melody, to interpret emotion. Sound is inexhaustible, and by groupings of sounds in changing rhythms the samisen musicians gain the effects they desire. . . . Ripple-clang-bang; smoothness, roughness, villainy, tranquillity; falling snow, a flight of birds, wind in the tree-tops; skirmish and fray, the peace of moonlight, the sorrow of parting, the rapture of spring; the infirmity of age, the gladness of lovers—all these and much more the samisen expresses to those who are able to look beyond the curtain that shuts this musical world away from Western ears because of its baffling conventions of sound rather than melody."
—KINCAID.[4]

(on an empty stage). And here after several feet, two of the "forty-seven faithful" observe a shed where the villain has hidden (of which the spectator is already aware). Just as in cinema, within such a sharpened dramatic moment, some brake has to be applied. In *Potemkin*, after the preparation for the command to "Fire!" on the sailors covered by the tarpaulin, there are several shots of "indifferent" parts of the battleship before the final command is given: the prow, the gun-muzzles, a life-preserver, etc. A brake is applied to the action, and the tension is screwed tighter.

The moment of the discovery of the hiding-place must be accentuated. To find the *right* solution for this moment, this accent must be shaped from the *same* rhythmic material—a return to the same nocturnal, empty, snowy landscape . . .

But now there are people on the stage! Nevertheless, the Japanese do find the right solution—and it is a *flute* that enters triumphantly! And you *see* the same snowy fields, the same echoing emptiness and night, that you *heard* a short while before, when you *looked* at the empty stage . . .

Occasionally (and usually at the moment when the nerves seem about to burst from tension) the Japanese double their effects. With their mastery of the equivalents of visual and aural images, they suddenly give *both*, "squaring" them, and brilliantly calculating the blow of their sensual billiard-cue on the spectator's cerebral target. I know no better way to describe that combination, of the moving hand of Ichikawa Ennosuke as he commits hara-kiri—*with* the sobbing sound offstage, *graphically* corresponding with the movement of the knife.

There it is: "Whatever notes I can't take with my voice, I'll show with my hands!" But here it was taken by the voice *and* shown with the hands! And we stand benumbed before such a perfection of—montage.

We all know those three trick questions: What shape is a winding staircase? How would you describe "compactly"?

What is a "surging sea"? One can't formulate intellectually analyzed answers to these. Perhaps Baudouin de Courtenay * knows, but we are forced to answer with gestures. We show the difficult concept of "compactly" with a clenched fist, and so on.

And what is more, such a description is *fully satisfactory*. We also are slightly Kabuki! But not sufficiently!

In our "Statement" on the sound film † we wrote of a contrapuntal method of combining visual and aural images. To possess this method one must develop in oneself a new *sense: the capacity of reducing visual and aural perceptions to a "common denominator."*

This is possessed by Kabuki to perfection. And we, too—crossing in turn the successive Rubicons flowing between theater and cinema and between cinema and sound-cinema—must also possess this. We can learn the mastery of this required new sense from the Japanese. As distinctly as impressionism owes a debt to the Japanese print, and post-impressionism to Negro sculpture, so the sound film will be no less obliged to the Japanese.

And not to the Japanese theater, alone, for these fundamental features, in my opinion, profoundly penetrate all aspects of the Japanese world-view. Certainly in those incomplete fragments of Japanese culture accessible to me, this seems a penetration to their very base.

We need not look beyond Kabuki for examples of identical perceptions of naturalistic three-dimensionality and flat painting. "Alien?" But it is necessary for this pot to boil in its own way before we can witness the completely satisfactory resolution of a waterfall made of vertical lines, against which a silver-paper serpentine fish-dragon, fastened by a thread, swims desperately. Or, folding back the screen-walls of a strictly cubist tea-house "of the vale of fans," a hanging backdrop is disclosed, a "perspective" gallery racing obliquely down its

---

* A professor in comparative philology at the University of St. Petersburg.
† This "Statement" is printed in Appendix A.

center. Our theater design has never known such decorative cubism, nor such primitivism of painted perspective. Nor, moreover, such *simultaneity*—here, apparently, pervading everything.

Costume. In the Dance of the Snake Odato Goro enters, bound with a rope that is also expressed, through transfer, in the robe's pattern of a flat rope-design, and her sash, as well, is twisted into a three-dimensional rope—a *third* form.

Writing. The Japanese masters an apparently limitless quantity of hieroglyphs. Hieroglyphs developed from conventionalized features of objects, put together, express concepts, i.e., the picture of a concept—an ideogram. Alongside these exists a series of Europeanized phonetic alphabets: the Manyō kana, hiragana, and others. But the Japanese writes *all* letters, employing both forms at once! It is not considered remarkable to compose sentences of hieroglyph *pictures* concurrently with the *letters* of several absolutely opposed alphabets.

Poetry. The *tanka* is an almost untranslatable form of lyrical epigram of severe dimension: 5, 7, 5 syllables in the first strophe (*kami-no-ku*) and 7, 7 syllables in the second (*shimo-no-ku*).* This must be the most uncommon of all poetry, in both form and content. When written, it can be judged both pictorially and poetically. Its writing is valued no less as calligraphy than as a poem.

And content? One critic justly says of the Japanese lyric: "A Japanese poem should be sooner *seen* [i.e., *represented* visually.—S.E.] than *heard*."⁶

APPROACH OF WINTER

They leave for the East
A flying bridge of magpies
A stream across the sky . . .
The tedious nights
Will be trimmed with hoar-frost.

* "The measure of the classical stanza is known as the *shichigoto,* or seven-and-five movement, which all Japanese believe to echo the divine pulse-beat of the race."—BRYAN.⁵

Across a bridge of magpies in flight, it seems that Yakamochi (who died in 785) departs into the ether.

CROW IN THE SPRING MIST

The crow perched there
Is half-concealed
By the kimono of fog . . .
As is a silken songster
By the folds of the sash.

The anonymous author (ca. 1800) wishes to express that the crow is as incompletely visible through the morning mist as is the bird in the pattern of the silk robe, when the sash is wound around the robed figure.

Strictly limited in its number of syllables, calligraphically charming in description and in comparison, striking in an incongruity that is also wonderfully near (crow, half-hidden by the mist, and the patterned bird, half-hidden by the sash), the Japanese lyric evidences an interesting "*fusion*" of images, which appeals to the most varied senses. This original archaic "pantheism" is undoubtedly based on a *non-differentiation of perception—a well-known absence of the sensation of "perspective."* It could not be otherwise. Japanese history is too rich in historical experience, and the burden of feudalism, though overcome politically, still runs like a red thread through the *cultural* traditions of Japan. Differentiation, entering society with its transition to capitalism and bringing in its wake, as a consequence of economic differentiation, differentiated perceptions of the world,—is not yet apparent in many cultural areas of Japan. And the Japanese continue to think "feudally," i.e., undifferentiatedly.

This is found in children's art. This also happens to people cured of blindness where all the objects, far and near, of the world, do not exist in space, but crowd in upon them closely.

In addition to Kabuki, the Japanese also showed us a film, *Karakuri-musume.* But in this, non-differentiation, brought to such brilliant unexpectedness in Kabuki, is realized *negatively*.

Karakuri-musume is a melodramatic farce. Beginning in the manner of Monty Banks, it ends in incredible gloom, and for long intervals is criminally torn in both directions.

The attempt to tie these opposing elements together is generally the hardest of tasks.

Even such a master as Chaplin, whose fusion of these opposing elements in *The Kid* is unsurpassed, was unable in *The Gold Rush* to balance these elements. The material slid from plane to plane. But in *Karakuri-musume* there is a complete smash-up.

As ever the echo, the unexpected junction, is found only at polar extremes. The archaism of non-differentiated sense "provocations" of Kabuki on one side, and on the other—the acme of *montage thinking*.

Montage thinking—the height of differentiatedly sensing and resolving the "organic" world—is realized anew in a mathematic faultlessly performing instrument-machine.

Recalling the words of Kleist, so close to the Kabuki theater, which was born from marionettes:

. . . [grace] appears best in that human bodily structure which has no consciousness at all, or has an infinite consciousness—that is, in the mechanical puppet, or in the god.[7]

Extremes meet. . . .

Nothing is gained by whining about the soullessness of Kabuki or, still worse, by finding in Sadanji's acting a "confirmation of the Stanislavsky theory"! Or in looking for what "Meyerhold hasn't yet stolen"!

Let us rather—*hail the junction of Kabuki and the sound-film!*

[1928]

THE CINEMATOGRAPHIC PRINCIPLE
AND THE IDEOGRAM

IT IS a weird and wonderful feat to have written a pamphlet on something that in reality does not exist. There is, for example, no such thing as a cinema without cinematography. And yet the author of the pamphlet preceding this essay * has contrived to write a book about the *cinema* of a country that has no *cinematography*. About the cinema of a country that has, in its culture, an infinite number of cinematographic traits, strewn everywhere with the sole exception of—its cinema.

This essay is on the cinematographic traits of Japanese culture that lie outside the Japanese cinema, and is itself as apart from the preceding pamphlet as these traits are apart from the Japanese cinema.

Cinema is: so many corporations, such and such turnovers of capital, so and so many stars, such and such dramas.

Cinematography is, first and foremost, montage.

The Japanese cinema is excellently equipped with corporations, actors, and stories. But the Japanese cinema is completely unaware of montage. Nevertheless the principle of montage can be identified as the basic element of Japanese representational culture.

Writing—for their writing is primarily representational.

The hieroglyph.

The naturalistic image of an object, as portrayed by the skilful Chinese hand of Ts'ang Chieh 2650 years before our era,

* Eisenstein's essay was originally published as an "afterword" to N. Kaufman's pamphlet, *Japanese Cinema* (Moscow, 1929).

becomes slightly formalized and, with its 539 fellows, forms the first "contingent" of hieroglyphs. Scratched out with a stylus on a slip of bamboo, the portrait of an object maintained a resemblance to its original in every respect.

But then, by the end of the third century, the brush is invented. In the first century after the "joyous event" (A.D.)— paper. And, lastly, in the year 220—India ink.

A complete upheaval. A revolution in draughtsmanship. And, after having undergone in the course of history no fewer than fourteen different styles of handwriting, the hieroglyph crystallized in its present form. The means of production (brush and India ink) determined the form.

The fourteen reforms had their way. As a result:

In the fierily cavorting hieroglyph *ma* (a horse) it is already impossible to recognize the features of the dear little horse sagging pathetically in its hindquarters, in the writing style of Ts'ang Chieh, so well-known from ancient Chinese bronzes.

But let it rest in the Lord, this dear little horse, together with the other 607 remaining *hsiang cheng* symbols—the earliest extant category of hieroglyphs.

The real interest begins with the second category of hieroglyphs—the *huei-i*, i.e., "copulative."

The point is that the copulation (perhaps we had better say, the combination) of two hieroglyphs of the simplest series is to be regarded not as their sum, but as their product, i.e., as a value of another dimension, another degree; each, separately, corresponds to an *object*, to a fact, but their combination corresponds to a *concept*. From separate hieroglyphs has been fused—the ideogram. By the combination of two "depictables" is achieved the representation of something that is graphically undepictable.

For example: the picture for water and the picture of an eye signifies "to weep"; the picture of an ear near the drawing of a door = "to listen";

a dog + a mouth = "to bark";
a mouth + a child = "to scream";
a mouth + a bird = "to sing";
a knife + a heart = "sorrow," and so on.[1]

But this is—montage!

Yes. It is exactly what we do in the cinema, combining shots that are *depictive*, single in meaning, neutral in content—into *intellectual* contexts and series.

This is a means and method inevitable in any cinematographic exposition. And, in a condensed and purified form, the starting point for the "intellectual cinema."

For a cinema seeking a maximum laconism for the visual representation of abstract concepts.

And we hail the method of the long-lamented Ts'ang Chieh as a first step along these paths.

We have mentioned laconism. Laconism furnishes us a transition to another point. Japan possesses the most laconic form of poetry: the *haikai* (appearing at the beginning of the thirteenth century and known today as "haiku" or "hokku") and the even earlier *tanka* (mythologically assumed to have been created along with heaven and earth).

Both are little more than hieroglyphs transposed into phrases. So much so that half their quality is appraised by their calligraphy. The method of their resolution is completely analogous to the structure of the ideogram.

As the ideogram provides a means for the laconic imprinting of an abstract concept, the same method, when transposed into literary exposition, gives rise to an identical laconism of pointed imagery.

Applied to the collision of an austere combination of symbols this method results in a dry definition of abstract concepts. The same method, expanded into the luxury of a group of already formed verbal combinations, swells into a splendor of *imagist* effect.

The concept is a bare formula; its adornment (an expansion by additional material) transforms the formula into an image—a finished form.

Exactly, though in reverse, as a primitive thought process—imagist thinking, displaced to a definite degree, becomes transformed to conceptual thinking.

But let us turn to examples.

The *haiku* is a concentrated impressionist sketch:

> A lonely crow
>   On leafless bough,
>   One autumn eve.
>
> BASHŌ

> What a resplendent moon!
>   It casts the shadow of pine boughs
>   Upon the mats.
>
> KIKAKU

> An evening breeze blows.
>   The water ripples
>   Against the blue heron's legs.
>
> BUSON

> It is early dawn.
>   The castle is surrounded
>   By the cries of wild ducks.
>
> KYOROKU [2]

The earlier *tanka* is slightly longer (by two lines):

> O mountain pheasant
> long are the feathers trail'st thou
> on the wooded hill-side—
> as long the nights seem to me
> on lonely couch sleep seeking.
>
> HITOMARO[?] [3]

From our point of view, these are montage phrases. Shot lists. The simple combination of two or three details of a material kind yields a perfectly finished representation of another kind—psychological.

And if the finely ground edges of the intellectually defined concepts formed by the combined ideograms are blurred in these poems, yet, in *emotional quality*, the concepts have blossomed forth immeasurably. We should observe that the emotion is directed towards the reader, for, as Yone Noguchi has said, "it is the readers who make the *haiku's* imperfection a perfection of art." [4]

It is uncertain in Japanese writing whether its predominating aspect is as a system of characters (denotative), or as an independent creation of graphics (depictive). In any case, born of the dual mating of the depictive by method, and the denotative by purpose, the ideogram continued both these lines (not consecutive historically but consecutive in principle in the minds of those developing the method).

Not only did the denotative line continue into literature, in the *tanka*, as we have shown, but exactly the same method (in its depictive aspect) operates also in the most perfect examples of Japanese pictorial art.

Sharaku—creator of the finest prints of the eighteenth century, and especially of an immortal gallery of actors' portraits. The Japanese Daumier. Despite this, almost unknown to us. The characteristic traits of his work have been analyzed only in our century. One of these critics, Julius Kurth, in discussing the question of the influence on Sharaku of sculpture, draws a parallel between his wood-cut portrait of the actor Nakayama Tomisaburō and an antique mask of the semi-religious Nō theater, the mask of a Rozo.

The faces of both the print and the mask wear an *identical expression*. . . . Features and masses are similarly arranged although the mask represents an old priest, and the print a young woman. This relationship is striking, yet these two works are otherwise totally dissimilar; this in itself is a demonstration of Sharaku's originality. While the carved mask was constructed according to fairly accurate anatomical proportions, the proportions of the portrait print are simply impossible. The space between the eyes comprises a width that makes mock of all good sense. The nose is almost twice as long in relation to the eyes as any normal nose would dare to be, and the chin stands in no sort of relation to the mouth; the brows, the mouth, and every feature—is hopelessly misrelated. *This observation may be made in all the large heads by Sharaku.* That the artist was unaware that all these proportions are false is, of course, out of the question. It was with a full awareness that he repudiated normalcy, and, while the drawing of the separate features depends on severely concentrated naturalism, their proportions have been subordinated to purely intellectual considerations. *He set up the essence of the psychic expression as the norm for the proportions of the single features.*[5]

Is not this process that of the ideogram, combining the independent "mouth" and the dissociated symbol of "child" to form the significance of "scream"?

Is this not exactly what we of the cinema do temporally, just as Sharaku in simultaneity, when we cause a monstrous disproportion of the parts of a normally flowing event, and suddenly dismember the event into "close-up of clutching hands," "medium shots of the struggle," and "extreme close-up of bulging eyes," in making a montage disintegration of the event in various planes? In making an eye twice as large as a man's full figure?! By combining these monstrous incongruities we newly collect the disintegrated event into one whole, but in *our* aspect. According to the treatment of our relation to the event.

The disproportionate depiction of an event is organically natural to us from the beginning. Professor Luriya, of the Psychological Institute in Moscow, has shown me a drawing by a child of "lighting a stove." Everything is represented in passably accurate relationship and with great care. Firewood. Stove. Chimney. But what are those zigzags in that huge central rectangle? They turn out to be—matches. Taking into account the crucial importance of these matches for the depicted process, the child provides a proper scale for them.*

The representation of objects in the actual (absolute) proportions proper to them is, of course, merely a tribute to

* It is possible to trace this particular tendency from its ancient, almost pre-historical source (". . . in all ideational art, objects are given size according to their importance, the king being twice as large as his subjects, or a tree half the size of a man when it merely informs us that the scene is out-of-doors. Something of this principle of size according to significance persisted in the Chinese tradition. The favorite disciple of Confucius looked like a little boy beside him and the most important figure in any group was usually the largest." 6) through the highest development of Chinese art, parent of Japanese graphic arts: ". . . natural scale always had to bow to pictorial scale . . . size according to distance never followed the laws of geometric perspective but the needs of the design. Foreground features might be diminished to avoid obstruction and overemphasis, and far distant objects, which were too minute to count pictorially, might be enlarged to act as a counterpoint to the middle distance or foreground." 7

orthodox formal logic. A subordination to an inviolable order of things.

Both in painting and sculpture there is a periodic and invariable return to periods of the establishment of absolutism. Displacing the expressiveness of archaic disproportion for regulated "stone tables" of officially decreed harmony.

Absolute realism is by no means the correct form of perception. It is simply the function of a certain form of social structure. Following a state monarchy, a state uniformity of thought is implanted. Ideological uniformity of a sort that can be developed pictorially in the ranks of colors and designs of the Guards regiments . . .

Thus we have seen how the principle of the hieroglyph—"denotation by depiction"—split in two: along the line of its purpose (the principle of "denotation"), into the principles of creating literary imagery; along the line of its method of realizing this purpose (the principle of "depiction"), into the striking methods of expressiveness used by Sharaku.*

And, just as the two outspreading wings of a hyperbola meet, as we say, at infinity (though no one has visited so distant a region!), so the principle of hieroglyphics, infinitely splitting into two parts (in accordance with the function of symbols), unexpectedly unites again from this dual estrangement, in yet a fourth sphere—in the theater.

Estranged for so long, they are once again—in the cradle period of the drama—present in a *parallel* form, in a curious dualism.

The *significance* (denotation) of the action is effected by the reciting of the *Jōruri* by a voice behind the stage—the *representation* (depiction) of the action is effected by silent marionettes on the stage. Along with a specific manner of movement this archaism migrated into the early Kabuki the-

---

* It has been left to James Joyce to develop in *literature* the depictive line of the Japanese hieroglyph. Every word of Kurth's analysis of Sharaku may be applied, neatly and easily, to Joyce.

ater, as well. To this day it is preserved, as a partial method, in the classical repertory (where certain parts of the action are narrated from behind the stage while the actor mimes).

But this is not the point. The most important fact is that into the technique of acting itself the ideographic (montage) method has been wedged in the most interesting ways.

However, before discussing this, let us be allowed the luxury of a digression—on the matter of the shot, to settle the debated question of its nature, once and for all.

A shot. A single piece of celluloid. A tiny rectangular frame in which there is, organized in some way, a piece of an event.

"Cemented together, these shots form montage. When this is done in an appropriate rhythm, *of course!*"

This, roughly, is what is taught by the old, old school of film-making, that sang:

> "Screw by screw,
> Brick by brick . . ."

Kuleshov, for example, even writes with a brick:

If you have an idea-phrase, a particle of the story, a link in the whole dramatic chain, then that idea is to be expressed and accumulated from shot-ciphers, just like bricks.[8]

"The shot is an element of montage. Montage is an assembly of these elements." This is a most pernicious make-shift analysis.

Here the understanding of the process as a whole (connection, shot-montage) derives only from the external indications of its flow (a piece cemented to another piece). Thus it would be possible, for instance, to arrive at the well-known conclusion that street-cars exist in order to be laid across streets. An entirely logical deduction, if one limits oneself to the external indications of the functions they performed during the street-fighting of February, 1917, here in Russia. But the materialist conception of history interprets it otherwise.

The worst of it is that an approach of this kind does actually lie, like an insurmountable street-car, across the potentialities of formal development. Such an approach overrules dialectical development, and dooms one to mere evolutionary "perfecting," in so far as it gives no bite into the dialectical substance of events.

In the long run, such evolutionizing leads either through refinement to decadence or, on the other hand, to a simple withering away due to stagnation of the blood.

Strange as it may seem, a melodious witness to both these distressing eventualities, simultaneously, is Kuleshov's latest film, *The Gay Canary* [1929].

The shot is by no means an *element* of montage.

The shot is a montage *cell*.

Just as cells in their division form a phenomenon of another order, the organism or embryo, so, on the other side of the dialectical leap from the shot, there is montage.

By what, then, is montage characterized and, consequently, its cell—the shot?

By collision. By the conflict of two pieces in opposition to each other. By conflict. By collision.

In front of me lies a crumpled yellowed sheet of paper. On it is a mysterious note:

"Linkage—P" and "Collision—E."

This is a substantial trace of a heated bout on the subject of montage between P (Pudovkin) and E (myself).

This has become a habit. At regular intervals he visits me late at night and behind closed doors we wrangle over matters of principle. A graduate of the Kuleshov school, he loudly defends an understanding of montage as a *linkage* of pieces. Into a chain. Again, "bricks." Bricks, arranged in series to *expound* an idea.

I confronted him with my viewpoint on montage as a *collision*. A view that from the collision of two given factors *arises* a concept.

From my point of view, linkage is merely a possible *special* case.

Recall what an infinite number of combinations is known in physics to be capable of arising from the impact (collision) of spheres. Depending on whether the spheres be resilient, non-resilient, or mingled. Amongst all these combinations there is one in which the impact is so weak that the collision is degraded to an even movement of both in the same direction.

This is the one combination which would correspond with Pudovkin's view.

Not long ago we had another talk. Today he agrees with my point of view. True, during the interval he took the opportunity to acquaint himself with the series of lectures I gave during that period at the State Cinema Institute. . . .

So, montage is conflict.

As the basis of every art is conflict (an "imagist" transformation of the dialectical principle). The shot appears as the *cell* of montage. Therefore it also must be considered from the viewpoint of *conflict*.

Conflict within the shot is potential montage, in the development of its intensity shattering the quadrilateral cage of the shot and exploding its conflict into montage impulses *between* the montage pieces. As, in a zigzag of mimicry, the *mise-en-scène* splashes out into a spatial zigzag with the *same* shattering. As the slogan, "All obstacles are vain before Russians," bursts out in the multitude of incident of *War and Peace*.

If montage is to be compared with something, then a phalanx of montage pieces, of shots, should be compared to the series of explosions of an internal combustion engine, driving forward its automobile or tractor: for, similarly, the dynamics of montage serve as impulses driving forward the total film.

Conflict within the frame. This can be very varied in character: it even can be a conflict in—the story. As in that "prehistoric" period in films (although there are plenty of instances in the present, as well), when entire scenes would be photographed in a single, uncut shot. This, however, is outside the strict jurisdiction of the film-form.

These are the "cinematographic" conflicts within the frame:
Conflict of graphic directions.

> (*Lines—either static or dynamic*)

Conflict of scales.
Conflict of volumes.
Conflict of masses.

> (*Volumes filled with various intensities of light*)

Conflict of depths.

And the following conflicts, requiring only one further impulse of intensification before flying into antagonistic pairs of pieces:

Close shots and long shots.

Pieces of graphically varied directions. Pieces resolved in volume, with pieces resolved in area.

Pieces of darkness and pieces of lightness.

And, lastly, there are such unexpected conflicts as:

Conflicts between an object and its dimension—and conflicts between an event and its duration.

These may sound strange, but both are familiar to us. The first is accomplished by an optically distorted lens, and the second by stop-motion or slow-motion.

The compression of all cinematographic factors and properties within a single dialectical formula of conflict is no empty rhetorical diversion.

We are now seeking a unified system for methods of cinematographic expressiveness that shall hold good for all its elements. The assembly of these into series of common indications will solve the task as a whole.

Experience in the separate elements of the cinema cannot be absolutely measured.

Whereas we know a good deal about montage, in the theory of the shot we are still floundering about amidst the most academic attitudes, some vague tentatives, and the sort of harsh radicalism that sets one's teeth on edge.

To regard the frame as a particular, as it were, molecular case of montage makes possible the direct application of montage practice to the theory of the shot.

And similarly with the theory of lighting. To sense this as a collision between a stream of light and an obstacle, like the impact of a stream from a fire-hose striking a concrete object, or of the wind buffeting a human figure, must result in a usage of light entirely different in comprehension from that employed in playing with various combinations of "gauzes" and "spots."

Thus far we have one such significant principle of conflict: *the principle of optical counterpoint.*

And let us not now forget that soon we shall face another and less simple problem in counterpoint: *the conflict in the sound film of acoustics and optics.*

Let us return to one of the most fascinating of optical conflicts: the conflict between the frame of the shot and the object!

The camera position, as a materialization of the conflict between organizing logic of the director and the inert logic of the object, in collision, reflects the dialectic of the camera-angle.

In this matter we are still impressionistic and lacking in principle to a sickening degree. Nevertheless, a sharpness of principle can be had in the technique of this, too. The dry quadrilateral, plunging into the hazards of nature's diffuseness . . .

And once again we are in Japan! For the cinematographic method is used in teaching drawing in Japanese schools.

What is our method of teaching drawing? Take any piece of white paper with four corners to it. Then cram onto it, usually even without using the edges (mostly greasy from the long drudgery!), some bored caryatid, some conceited Corinthian capital, or a plaster Dante (not the magician performing at the Moscow Hermitage, but the other one—Alighieri, the comedy writer).

The Japanese approach this from a quite different direction:

Here's the branch of a cherry-tree.[9] And the pupil cuts out from this whole, with a square, and a circle, and a rectangle—compositional units:

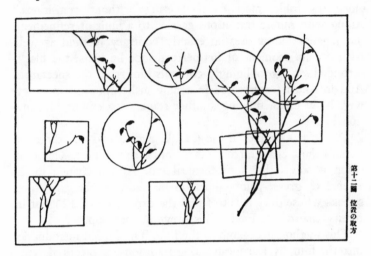

第十二圖　位置の取方

He frames a shot!

These two ways of teaching drawing can characterize the two basic tendencies struggling within the cinema of today. One—the expiring method of artificial spatial organization of an event in front of the lens. From the "direction" of a sequence, to the erection of a Tower of Babel in front of the lens. The other—a "picking-out" by the camera: organization by means of the camera. Hewing out a piece of actuality with the ax of the lens.

However, at the present moment, when the center of attention is finally beginning, in the intellectual cinema, to be transferred from the materials of cinema, as such, to "deductions and conclusions," to "slogans" based on the material, both schools of thought are losing distinction in their differences and can quietly blend into a synthesis.

Several pages back we lost, like an overshoe in a street-car, the question of the theater. Let us turn back to the question of methods of montage in the Japanese theater, particularly in acting.

The first and most striking example, of course, is the purely cinematographic method of "acting without transitions." Along with mimic transitions carried to a limit of refinement, the Japanese actor uses an exactly contrary method as well. At a certain moment of his performance he halts; the black-shrouded *kurogo* obligingly conceals him from the spectators. And lo!—he is resurrected in a new make-up. And in a new wig. Now characterizing another stage (degree) of his emotional state.

Thus, for example, in the Kabuki play *Narukami*, the actor Sadanji must change from drunkenness to madness. This transition is solved by a mechanical cut. And a change in the arsenal of grease-paint colors on his face, emphasizing those streaks whose duty it is to fulfill the expression of a higher intensity than those used in his previous make-up.

This method is organic to the film. The forced introduction into the film, by European acting traditions, of pieces of "emotional transitions" is yet another influence forcing the cinema to mark time. Whereas the method of "cut" acting makes possible the construction of entirely new methods. Replacing one changing face with a whole scale of facial types of varying moods affords a far more acutely expressive result than does the changing surface, too receptive and devoid of organic resistance, of any single professional actor's face.

In our new film [*Old and New*] I have eliminated the intervals between the sharply contrasting polar stages of a face's expression. Thus is achieved a greater sharpness in the "play of doubts" around the new cream separator. Will the milk thicken or no? Trickery? Wealth? Here the psychological process of mingled faith and doubt is broken up into its two extreme states of joy (confidence) and gloom (disillusionment). Furthermore, this is sharply emphasized by light—illumination in no wise conforming to actual light conditions. This brings a distinct strengthening of the tension.

Another remarkable characteristic of the Kabuki theater is

the principle of "disintegrated" acting. Shocho, who played the leading female rôles in the Kabuki theater that visited Moscow, in depicting the dying daughter in *Yashaō* (*The Mask-Maker*), performed his rôle in pieces of acting completely detached from each other: Acting with only the right arm. Acting with one leg. Acting with the neck and head only. (The whole process of the death agony was disintegrated into solo performances of each member playing its own rôle: the rôle of the leg, the rôle of the arms, the rôle of the head.) A breaking-up into shots. With a gradual shortening of these separate, successive pieces of acting as the tragic end approached.

Freed from the yoke of primitive naturalism, the actor is enabled by this method to fully grip the spectator by "rhythms," making not only acceptable, but definitely attractive, a stage built on the most consecutive and detailed flesh and blood of naturalism.

Since we no longer distinguish in principle between questions of shot-content and montage, we may here cite a third example:

The Japanese theater makes use of a slow tempo to a degree unknown to our stage. The famous scene of hara-kiri in *Chushingura* is based on an unprecedented slowing down of all movement—beyond any point we have ever seen. Whereas, in the previous example, we observed a disintegration of the transitions between movements, here we see disintegration of the process of movement, viz., slow-motion. I have heard of only one example of a thorough application of this method, using the technical possibility of the film with a compositionally reasoned plan. It is usually employed with some purely pictorial aim, such as the "submarine kingdom" in *The Thief of Bagdad*, or to represent a dream, as in *Zvenigora*. Or, more often, it is used simply for formalist jackstraws and unmotivated camera mischief as in Vertov's *Man with the Movie-Camera*. The more commendable example appears to be in Jean Epstein's *La chute de la Maison Usher*—at least according to the press reports. In this film, normally acted emotions filmed with a speeded-up camera are said to give unusual emotional pressure by their unrealistic slowness on the screen. If it be borne in mind that the effect of an actor's performance on the audience is based on its identification by each spectator, it will be easy to relate both examples (the Kabuki play and the Epstein film) to an identical causal explanation. The intensity of perception increases as the didactic process of identification proceeds more easily along a disintegrated action.

Even instruction in handling a rifle can be hammered into the tightest motor-mentality among a group of raw recruits if the instructor uses a "break-down" method.

The most interesting link of the Japanese theater is, of course, its link with the sound film, which can and must learn its fundamentals from the Japanese—the reduction of visual and aural sensations to a common physiological denominator.*

So, it has been possible to establish (cursorily) the permeation of the most varied branches of Japanese culture by a pure cinematographic element—its basic nerve, montage.

And it is only the Japanese cinema that falls into the same error as the "leftward drifting" Kabuki. Instead of learning how to extract the principles and technique of their remarkable acting from the traditional feudal forms of their materials, the most progressive leaders of the Japanese theater throw their energies into an adaptation of the spongy shapelessness of our own "inner" naturalism. The results are tearful and saddening. In its cinema Japan similarly pursues imitations of the most revolting examples of American and European entries in the international commercial film race.

To understand and apply her cultural peculiarities to the cinema, this is the task of Japan! Colleagues of Japan, are you really going to leave this for us to do?

[1929]

* Discussed in the preceding essay.—EDITOR.

A DIALECTIC APPROACH TO FILM FORM

> In nature we never see anything isolated, but
> everything in connection with something else
> which is before it, beside it, under it, and
> over it.
>
> GOETHE [1]

> According to Marx and Engels the dialectic
> system is only the conscious reproduction of
> the dialectic course (substance) of the external
> events of the world.[2]

Thus:

The projection of the dialectic system of things
into the brain
into creating abstractly
into the process of thinking
yields: dialectic methods of thinking;
dialectic materialism—   PHILOSOPHY.

And also:

The projection of the same system of things
while creating concretely
while giving form
yields: ART.

The foundation for this philosophy is a *dynamic* concept
of things:

Being—as a constant evolution from the interaction of two
contradictory opposites.

Synthesis—arising from the opposition between thesis and
antithesis.

45

A dynamic comprehension of things is also basic to the same degree, for a correct understanding of art and of all art-forms. In the realm of art this dialectic principle of dynamics is embodied in

CONFLICT

as the fundamental principle for the existence of every artwork and every art-form.

For art is always conflict:
(1) according to its social mission,
(2) according to its nature,
(3) according to its methodology.

According to its social mission *because:* It is art's task to make manifest the contradictions of Being. To form equitable views by stirring up contradictions within the spectator's mind, and to forge accurate intellectual concepts from the dynamic clash of opposing passions.

According to its nature *because:* Its nature is a conflict between natural existence and creative tendency. Between organic inertia and purposeful initiative. Hypertrophy of the purposive initiative—the principles of rational logic—ossifies art into mathematical technicalism. (A painted landscape becomes a topographical map, a painted Saint Sebastian becomes an anatomical chart.) Hypertrophy of organic naturalness—of organic logic—dilutes art into formlessness. (A Malevich becomes a Kaulbach, an Archipenko becomes a waxworks side-show.)

Because the limit of organic form (the passive principle of being) is *Nature*. The limit of rational form (the active principle of production) is *Industry*. At the intersection of Nature and Industry stands *Art*.

The logic of organic form *vs.* the logic of rational form yields, in collision,

the dialectic of the art-form.

The interaction of the two produces and determines Dynamism. (Not only in the sense of a space-time continuum, but also in the field of absolute thinking. I also regard the inception of new concepts and viewpoints in the conflict between customary conception and particular representation as dynamic—as a dynamization of the inertia of perception—as a dynamization of the "traditional view" into a new one.)

The quantity of interval determines the pressure of the tension. (See in music, for example, the concept of intervals. There can be cases where the distance of separation is so wide that it leads to a break—to a collapse of the homogeneous concept of art. For instance, the "inaudibility" of certain intervals.)

> *The spatial form of this dynamism is expression.*
> *The phases of its tension: rhythm.*

This is true for every art-form, and, indeed, for every kind of expression.

Similarly, human expression is a conflict between conditioned and unconditioned reflexes. (In this I cannot agree with Klages, who, *a*) does not consider human expression dynamically as a process, but statically as a result, and who, *b*) attributes everything in motion to the field of the "soul," and only the hindering element to "reason." [3] ["Reason" and "Soul" of the idealistic concept here correspond remotely with the ideas of conditioned and unconditioned reflexes.])

This is true in every field that can be understood as an art. For example, logical thought, considered as an art, shows the same dynamic mechanism:

. . . the intellectual lives of Plato or Dante or Spinoza or Newton were largely guided and sustained by their delight in the sheer beauty of the rhythmic relation between law and instance, species and individual, or cause and effect. [4]

This holds in other fields, as well, e.g., in speech, where all its sap, vitality, and dynamism arise from the irregularity of the part in relation to the laws of the system as a whole.

In contrast we can observe the sterility of expression in such artificial, totally regulated languages as Esperanto.

It is from this principle that the whole charm of poetry derives. Its rhythm arises as a conflict between the metric measure employed and the distribution of accents, over-riding this measure.

The concept of a formally static phenomenon as a dynamic function is dialectically imaged in the wise words of Goethe:

> *Die Baukunst ist eine ertarrte Musik.*
> (Architecture is frozen music.) [5]

Just as in the case of a homogeneous ideology (a monistic viewpoint), the whole, as well as the least detail, must be penetrated by a sole principle. So, ranged alongside the conflict of *social conditionality*, and the conflict of *existing nature*, the *methodology* of an art reveals this same principle of conflict. As the basic principle of the rhythm to be created and the inception of the art-form.

Art is always conflict, according to its methodology.

Here we shall consider the general problem of art in the specific example of its highest form—film.

Shot and montage are the basic elements of cinema.

Montage

has been established by the Soviet film as the nerve of cinema.

To determine the nature of montage is to solve the specific problem of cinema. The earliest conscious film-makers, and our first film theoreticians, regarded montage as a means of description by placing single shots one after the other like building-blocks. The movement within these building-block shots, and the consequent length of the component pieces, was then considered as rhythm.

A completely false concept!

This would mean the defining of a given object solely in relation to the nature of its external course. The mechanical process of splicing would be made a principle. We cannot describe such a relationship of lengths as rhythm. From this comes metric rather than rhythmic relationships, as opposed to one another as the mechanical-metric system of Mensendieck is to the organic-rhythmic school of Bode in matters of body exercise.

According to this definition, shared even by Pudovkin as a theoretician, montage is the means of *unrolling* an idea with the help of single shots: the "epic" principle.

In my opinion, however, montage is an idea that arises from the collision of independent shots—shots even opposite to one another: the "dramatic" principle.*

A sophism? Certainly not. For we are seeking a definition of the whole nature, the principal style and spirit of cinema from its technical (optical) basis.

We know that the phenomenon of movement in film resides in the fact that two motionless images of a moving body, following one another, blend into an appearance of motion by showing them sequentially at a required speed.

This popularized description of what happens as a *blending* has its share of responsibility for the popular miscomprehension of the nature of montage that we have quoted above.

Let us examine more exactly the course of the phenomenon we are discussing—how it really occurs—and draw our conclusion from this. Placed next to each other, two photographed immobile images result in the appearance of movement. Is this accurate? Pictorially—and phraseologically, yes.

But mechanically, it is not. For, in fact, each sequential element is perceived not *next* to the other, but on *top* of the other. For the idea (or sensation) of movement arises from the process of superimposing on the retained impression of the object's first position, a newly visible further position of the object. This is, by the way, the reason for the phenomenon of spatial depth, in the optical superimposition of two planes in stereoscopy. From the superimposition of two elements of the same dimension always arises a new, higher dimension. In the case of stereoscopy the superimposition of two nonidentical

---

* "Epic" and "dramatic" are used here in regard to methodology of form—not to *content* or *plot!*

two-dimensionalities results in stereoscopic three-dimensionality.

In another field: a concrete word (a denotation) set beside
a concrete word yields an abstract concept—as in the Chinese
and Japanese languages,* where a material ideogram can indicate a transcendental (conceptual) result.

The incongruence in contour of the first picture—already
impressed on the mind—with the subsequently perceived second picture engenders, in conflict, the feeling of motion. Degree of incongruence determines intensity of impression, and
determines that tension which becomes the real element of authentic rhythm.

Here we have, temporally, what we see arising spatially on a
graphic or painted plane.

What comprises the dynamic effect of a painting? The eye
follows the direction of an element in the painting. It retains
a visual impression, which then collides with the impression
derived from following the direction of a second element. The
conflict of these directions forms the dynamic effect in appre-
hending the whole.

I. It may be purely linear: Fernand Léger, or Suprematism.

II. It may be "anecdotal." The secret of the marvelous mobil-
ity of Daumier's and Lautrec's figures dwells in the fact that
the various anatomical parts of a body are represented in spatial circumstances (positions) that are temporally various, disjunctive. For example, in Toulouse-Lautrec's lithograph of
Miss Cissy Loftus, if one logically develops position A of the
foot, one builds a body in position A corresponding to it.
But the body is represented from knee up already in position
A + a. The cinematic effect of joined motionless pictures is
already established here! From hips to shoulders we can see
A + a + a. The figure comes alive and kicking!

III. Between I and II lies primitive Italian futurism—such as
in Balla's "Man with Six Legs in Six Positions"—for II obtains

* See discussion in preceding essay.

its effect by retaining natural unity and anatomical correctness, while I, on the other hand, does this with purely elementary elements. III, although destroying naturalness, has not yet pressed forward to abstraction.

IV. The conflict of directions may also be of an ideographic kind. It was in this way that we have gained the pregnant characterizations of a Sharaku, for example. The secret of his extremely perfected strength of expression lies in the anatomical and *spatial disproportion* of the parts—in comparison with which, our I might be termed *temporal disproportion*.

Generally termed "irregularity," this *spatial disproportion* has been a constant attraction and instrument for artists. In writing of Rodin's drawings, Camille Mauclair indicated one explanation for this search:

The greatest artists, Michelangelo, Rembrandt, Delacroix, all, at a certain moment of the upthrusting of their genius, threw aside, as it were, the ballast of exactitude as conceived by our simplifying reason and our ordinary eyes, in order to attain the fixation of ideas, the synthesis, the *pictorial handwriting* of their dreams.[6]

Two experimental artists of the nineteenth century—a painter and a poet—attempted esthetic formulations of this "irregularity." Renoir advanced this thesis:

Beauty of every description finds its charm in variety. Nature abhors both vacuum and regularity. For the same reason, no work of art can really be called such if it has not been created by an artist who believes in irregularity and rejects any set form. Regularity, order, desire for perfection (which is always a false perfection) destroy art. The only possibility of maintaining taste in art is to impress on artists and the public the importance of irregularity. Irregularity is the basis of all art.[7]

And Baudelaire wrote in his journal:

That which is not slightly distorted lacks sensible appeal; from which it follows that irregularity—that is to say, the unexpected, surprise and astonishment, are an essential part and characteristic of beauty.[8]

Upon closer examination of the particular beauty of irregularity as employed in painting, whether by Grünewald or by Renoir, it will be seen that it is a disproportion in the relation of a detail in one dimension to another detail in a different dimension.

The spatial development of the relative size of one detail in correspondence with another, and the consequent collision between the proportions designed by the artist for that purpose, result in a characterization—a definition of the represented matter.

Finally, color. Any shade of a color imparts to our vision a given rhythm of vibration. This is not said figuratively, but purely physiologically, for colors are distinguished from one another by their number of light vibrations.

The adjacent shade or tone of color is in another rate of vibration. The counterpoint (conflict) of the two—the retained rate of vibration against the newly perceived one—yields the dynamism of our apprehension of the interplay of color.

Hence, with only one step from visual vibrations to acoustic vibrations, we find ourselves in the field of music. From the domain of the spatial-pictorial—to the domain of the temporal-pictorial—where the same law rules. For counterpoint is to music not only a form of composition, but is altogether the basic factor for the possibility of tone perception and tone differentiation.

It may almost be said that in every case we have cited we have seen in operation the same *Principle of Comparison* that makes possible for us perception and definition in every field.

In the moving image (cinema) we have, so to speak, a synthesis of two counterpoints—the spatial counterpoint of graphic art, and the temporal counterpoint of music.

Within cinema, and characterizing it, occurs what may be described as:

visual counterpoint

In applying this concept to the film, we gain several leads to the problem of film grammar. As well as a *syntax* of film

1. GRAPHIC CONFLICT

2. CONFLICT OF PLANES

3. CONFLICT OF VOLUMES

4. SPATIAL CONFLICT

5.

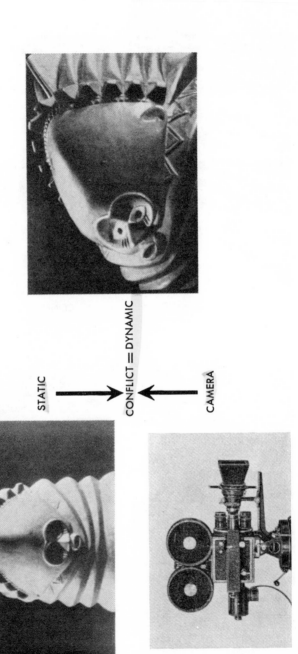

STATIC → CONFLICT = DYNAMIC ← CAMERA

7.

[from *Potemkin*]

6.

[from *October*]

ARTIFICIALLY PRODUCED IMAGES OF MOTION

a. Logical

8.

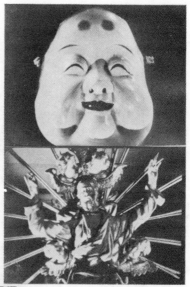

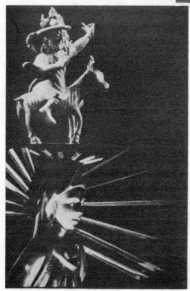

9.

ARTIFICIALLY PRODUCED IMAGES OF MOTION
b. Illogical

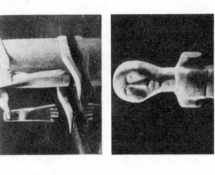

10.

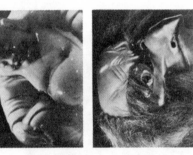

INTELLECTUAL DYNAMIZATION

manifestations, in which visual counterpoint may determine a whole new system of forms of manifestation. (Experiments in this direction are illustrated in the preceding pages by fragments from my films.)

For all this, the *basic premise* is:

> *The shot is by no means an element of montage.*
> *The shot is a montage cell (or molecule).*

In this formulation the dualistic division of

Sub-title and shot
and
Shot and montage

leaps forward in analysis to a dialectic consideration as three different phases of one homogeneous task of expression, its homogeneous characteristics determining the homogeneity of their structural laws.

Inter-relation of the three phases:

Conflict within a thesis (an abstract idea)—*formulates* itself in the dialectics of the sub-title—*forms* itself spatially in the conflict within the shot—and *explodes* with increasing intensity in montage-conflict among the separate shots.

This is fully analogous to human, psychological expression. This is a conflict of motives, which can also be comprehended in three phases:

1. Purely verbal utterance. Without intonation—expression in speech.

2. Gesticulatory (mimic-intonational) expression. Projection of the conflict onto the whole expressive bodily system of man. Gesture of bodily movement and gesture of intonation.

3. Projection of the conflict into space. With an intensification of motives, the zigzag of mimic expression is propelled into the surrounding space following the same formula of distortion. A zigzag of expression arising from the spatial division caused by man moving in space. *Mise-en-scène.*

This gives us the basis for an entirely new understanding of the problem of film form.

We can list, as examples of types of conflicts within the form—characteristic for the conflict within the shot, as well as for the conflict between colliding shots, or, montage:

1. Graphic conflict (see Figure 1).
2. Conflict of planes (see Figure 2).
3. Conflict of volumes (see Figure 3).
4. Spatial conflict (see Figure 4).
5. Light conflict.
6. Tempo conflict, and so on.*

Nota bene: This list is of principal features, of *dominants*. It is naturally understood that they occur chiefly as complexes.

For a transition to montage, it will be sufficient to divide any example into two independent primary pieces, as in the case of graphic conflict, although all other cases can be similarly divided:

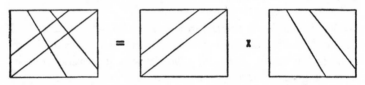

Some further examples:

7. Conflict between matter and viewpoint (achieved by spatial distortion through camera-angle) (see Figure 5).
8. Conflict between matter and its spatial nature (achieved by *optical distortion* by the lens).
9. Conflict between an event and its temporal nature (achieved by *slow-motion* and *stop-motion*)
   and finally
10. Conflict between the whole *optical* complex and a quite different sphere.

Thus does conflict between optical and acoustical experience produce:

sound-film,

* Further details on this film grammar of conflicts are given in the preceding essay, pp. 39-40.—EDITOR.

which is capable of being realized as

audio-visual counterpoint.

Formulation and investigation of the phenomenon of cinema as forms of conflict yield the first possibility of devising a homogeneous system of *visual dramaturgy* for all general and particular cases of the film problem.

Of devising a *dramaturgy of the visual film-form* as regulated and precise as the existing *dramaturgy of the film-story.*

From this viewpoint on the film medium, the following forms and potentialities of style may be summed up as a film syntax, or it may be more exact to describe the following as:

a tentative film-syntax.

We shall list here a number of potentialities of dialectical development to be derived from this proposition: The concept of the moving (time-consuming) image arises from the superimposition—or counterpoint—of two differing immobile images.

I. Each *moving fragment of montage.* Each photographed piece. Technical definition of the phenomenon of movement. *No composition as yet.* (A running man. A rifle fired. A splash of water.)

II. *An artificially produced image of motion.* The basic optical element is used for deliberate compositions:

A. *Logical*

Example 1 (from *October*): a montage rendition of a machine-gun being fired, by cross-cutting details of the firing.

Combination A: a brightly lit machine-gun. A different shot in a low key. Double burst: graphic burst + light burst. Close-up of machine-gunner.

Combination B (see Figure 6): Effect almost of double exposure achieved by *clatter* montage effect. Length of montage pieces—two frames each.

Example 2 (from *Potemkin*): an illustration of instantaneous action. Woman with pince-nez. Followed immediately—without transition—by the same woman with shattered pince-nez and bleeding eye: impression of a shot hitting the eye (see Figure 7).

B. *Illogical*

Example 3 (from *Potemkin*): the same device used for pictorial symbolism. In the thunder of the *Potemkin's* guns, a marble lion leaps up, in protest against the bloodshed on the Odessa steps (see Figure 8). Composed of three shots of three stationary marble lions at the Alupka Palace in the Crimea: a sleeping lion, an awakening lion, a rising lion. The effect is achieved by a correct calculation of the length of the second shot. Its superimposition on the first shot produces the first action. This establishes time to impress the second position on the mind. Superimposition of the third position on the second produces the second action: the lion finally rises.

Example 4 (from *October*): Example 1 showed how the firing was manufactured symbolically from elements outside the process of firing itself. In illustrating the monarchist *putsch* attempted by General Kornilov, it occurred to me that his militarist *tendency* could be shown in a montage that would employ religious details for its material. For Kornilov had revealed his intention in the guise of a peculiar "Crusade" of Moslems (!), his Caucasian "Wild Division," together with some Christians, against the Bolsheviki. So we intercut shots of a Baroque Christ (apparently exploding in the radiant beams of his halo) with shots of an egg-shaped mask of Uzume, Goddess of Mirth, completely self-contained. The temporal conflict between the closed egg-form and the graphic star-form produced the effect of an instantaneous *burst*—of a bomb, or shrapnel (see Figure 9).* (Figure 10, showing the opportunity for tendentious—or ideological—expressiveness of such materials, will be discussed below.)

Thus far the examples have shown *primitive-physiological*

---

* Examples of more primitive effects belong here also, such as simple cross-cutting of church spires, angled in mutual opposition.

cases—employing superimposition of optical motion *exclusively*.

III. *Emotional* combinations, not only with the visible elements of the shots, but chiefly with chains of psychological associations. *Association montage*. As a means for pointing up a situation emotionally.

In Example 1, we had two successive shots A and B, identical in subject. However, they were not identical in respect to the position of the subject within the frame:

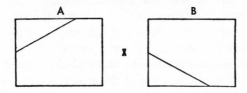

producing *dynamization in space*—an impression of spatial dynamics:

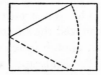

The degree of difference between the positions A and B determines the tension of the movement.

For a new case, let us suppose that the subjects of Shots A and B are not *identical*. Although the associations of the two shots are identical, that is, associatively identical.

This *dynamization of the subject*, not in the field of space but of psychology, i.e., *emotion*, thus produces:
emotional dynamization.

Example 1 (in *Strike*): the montage of the killing of the workers is actually a cross montage of this carnage with the butchering of a bull in an abattoir. Though the subjects are different, "butchering" is the associative link. This made for a powerful emotional intensification of the scene. As a matter of fact, homogeneity of gesture plays an important part in this case in achieving the effect—both the movement of the dynamic gesture within the frame, and the static gesture dividing the frame graphically.*

This is a principle subsequently used by Pudovkin in *The End of St. Petersburg,* in his powerful sequence intercutting shots of stock exchange and battlefield. His previous film, *Mother,* had a similar sequence: the ice-break on the river, paralleled with the workers' demonstration.

Such a means may decay pathologically if the essential viewpoint—emotional dynamization of the subject—is lost. As soon as the film-maker loses sight of this essence the means ossifies into lifeless literary symbolism and stylistic mannerism. Two examples of such hollow use of this means occur to me:

Example 2 (in *October*): the sugary chants of compromise by the Mensheviki at the Second Congress of Soviets— during the storming of the Winter Palace—are intercut with hands playing harps. This was a purely literary parallelism that by no means dynamized the subject matter. Similarly in Otzep's *Living Corpse,* church spires (in imitation of those in *October*) and lyrical landscapes are intercut with the courtroom speeches of the prosecutor and defense lawyer. This error was the same as in the "harp" sequence.

On the other hand, a majority of *purely dynamic* effects can produce positive results:

Example 3 (in *October*): the dramatic moment of the union of the Motorcycle Battalion with the Congress of Soviets was dynamized by shots of abstractly spinning bicycle wheels, in association with the entrance of the new delegates. In this way the large-scale emotional content of the event was transformed into actual dynamics.

This same principle—giving birth to concepts, to emotions, by juxtaposing two disparate events—led to:

IV. *Liberation of the whole action from the definition of time and space.* My first attempts at this were in *October.*

---

* The montage list of this sequence from *Strike* is given in Appendix 3 of *The Film Sense.*—EDITOR.

Example 1: a trench crowded with soldiers appears to be crushed by an enormous gun-base that comes down inexorably. As an anti-militarist symbol seen from the viewpoint of subject alone, the effect is achieved by an apparent bringing together of an independently existing trench and an overwhelming military product, just as physically independent.

Example 2: in the scene of Kornilov's *putsch*, which puts an end to Kerensky's Bonapartist dreams. Here one of Kornilov's tanks climbs up and crushes a plaster-of-Paris Napoleon standing on Kerensky's desk in the Winter Palace, a juxtaposition of purely symbolic significance.

This method has now been used by Dovzhenko in *Arsenal* to shape whole sequences, as well as by Esther Schub in her use of library footage in *The Russia of Nikolai II and Lev Tolstoy*.

I wish to offer another example of this method, to upset the traditional ways of handling plot—although it has not yet been put into practice.

In 1924-1925 I was mulling over the idea of a filmic portrait of *actual* man. At that time, there prevailed a tendency to show actual man in films only in *long* uncut dramatic scenes. It was believed that cutting (montage) would destroy the idea of actual man. Abram Room established something of a record in this respect when he used in *The Death Ship* uncut dramatic shots as long as 40 meters or 135 feet. I considered (and still do) such a concept to be utterly unfilmic.

Very well—what would be a linguistically accurate characterization of a man?

> His raven-black hair . . .
> The waves of his hair . . .
> His eyes radiating azure beams . . .
> His steely muscles . . .

Even in a less exaggerated description, any verbal account of a person is bound to find itself employing an assortment of waterfalls, lightning-rods, landscapes, birds, etc.

Now why should the cinema follow the forms of theater and painting rather than the methodology of language, which allows wholly new concepts of ideas to arise from the combination of two concrete denotations of two concrete objects? Language is much closer to film than painting is. For example, in painting the form arises from *abstract* elements of line and color, while in cinema the material *concreteness* of the image within the frame presents—as an element—the greatest difficulty in manipulation. So why not rather lean towards the system of language, which is forced to use the same mechanics in inventing words and word-complexes?

On the other hand, why is it that montage cannot be dispensed with in orthodox films?

The differentiation in montage-pieces lies in their lack of existence as single units. Each piece can evoke no more than a certain association. The accumulation of such associations can achieve the same effect as is provided for the spectator by purely physiological means in the plot of a realistically produced play.

For instance, murder on the stage has a purely physiological effect. Photographed in *one* montage-piece, it can function simply as *information*, as a sub-title. *Emotional* effect begins only with the reconstruction of the event in montage fragments, each of which will summon a certain association—the sum of which will be an all-embracing complex of emotional feeling. Traditionally:

1. A hand lifts a knife.
2. The eyes of the victim open suddenly.
3. His hands clutch the table.
4. The knife is jerked up.
5. The eyes blink involuntarily.
6. Blood gushes.
7. A mouth shrieks.
8. Something drips onto a shoe . . .

and similar film clichés. Nevertheless, in regard to the *action as a whole, each fragment-piece* is almost *abstract*. The more differentiated they are the more abstract they become, provoking no more than a certain association.

Quite logically the thought occurs: could not the same thing be accomplished more productively by not following the plot so slavishly, but by materializing the idea, the impression, of *Murder* through a free accumulation of associative matter? For the most important task is still to establish the idea of murder—the feeling of murder, as such. The plot is no more than a device without which one isn't yet capable of telling something to the spectator! In any case, effort in this direction would certainly produce the most interesting variety of forms.

Someone should try, at least! Since this thought occurred to me, I have not had time to make this experiment. And today I am more concerned with quite different problems. But, returning to the main line of our syntax, something there may bring us closer to these tasks.

While, with I, II, and III, tension was calculated for purely physiological effect—from the purely optical to the emotional, we must mention here also the case of the same conflict-tension serving the ends of new concepts—of new attitudes, that is, of purely intellectual aims.

Example 1 (in *October*): Kerensky's rise to power and dictatorship after the July uprising of 1917. A comic effect was gained by sub-titles indicating regular ascending ranks (*"Dictator"—"Generalissimo"—"Minister of Navy—and of Army"*—etc.) climbing higher and higher—cut into five or six shots of Kerensky, climbing the stairs of the Winter Palace, all with exactly the *same* pace. Here a conflict between the flummery of the ascending ranks and the "hero's" trotting up the same unchanging flight of stairs yields an intellectual result: Kerensky's essential nonentity is shown satirically. We have the counterpoint of a literally expressed conventional idea with the *pictured* action of a particular person who is unequal to his swiftly increasing duties. The incongruence of these two factors results in the spectator's purely *intellectual* decision at the expense of this particular person. Intellectual dynamization.

Example 2 (in *October*): Kornilov's march on Petrograd was under the banner of "In the Name of God and Country." Here we attempted to reveal the religious significance of this episode in a rationalistic way. A number of religious images, from a magnificent Baroque Christ to an Eskimo idol, were cut together. The conflict in this case was between the concept and the symbolization of God. While idea and image appear to accord completely in the first statue shown, the two elements move further from each other with each successive image (see Figure 10). Maintaining the denotation of "God," the images increasingly disagree with our concept of God, inevitably leading to individual conclusions about the true nature of all deities. In this case, too, a chain of images attempted to achieve a purely intellectual resolution, resulting from a conflict between a preconception and a *gradual discrediting of it in purposeful steps*.

Step by step, by a process of comparing each new image with the common denotation, power is accumulated behind a process that can be formally identified with that of logical deduction. The decision to release these ideas, as well as the method used, is already *intellectually* conceived.

The conventional *descriptive* form for film leads to the formal possibility of a kind of filmic reasoning. While the conventional film directs the *emotions*, this suggests an opportunity to encourage and direct the whole *thought process*, as well.

These two particular sequences of experiment were very much opposed by the majority of critics. Because they were understood as purely political. I would not attempt to deny that *this form is most suitable for the expression of ideologically pointed theses*, but it is a pity that the critics completely overlooked the purely filmic potentialities of this approach.

In these two experiments we have taken the first embryonic step towards a totally new form of film expression. Towards a purely intellectual film, freed from traditional limitations, achieving direct forms for ideas, systems, and concepts, without any need for transitions and paraphrases. We may yet have a

synthesis of art and science.

This would be the proper name for our new epoch in the field of art. This would be the final justification for Lenin's words, that "the cinema is the most important of all the arts."

Moscow, April 1929

THE FILMIC FOURTH DIMENSION

EXACTLY a year ago, on August 19, 1928, before the montage of *Old and New* had been begun, I wrote, in connection with the visit to Moscow of the Kabuki theater:

In the Kabuki . . . a single monistic sensation of theatrical "provocation" takes place. The Japanese regards each theatrical element, not as an incommensurable unit among the various categories of affect (on the various sense-organs), but as a single unit of *theatre*. . . . Directing himself to the various organs of sensation, he builds his summation [of individual "pieces"] to a grand *total* provocation of the human brain, without taking any notice *which* of these several paths he is following.

My characterization of the Kabuki theater proved prophetic. This method became the basis for the montage of *Old and New*.

Orthodox montage is montage *on the dominant*. I.e., the combination of shots according to their dominating indications. Montage according to tempo. Montage according to the chief tendency within the frame. Montage according to the length (continuance) of the shots, and so on. This is montage according to the foreground.

The dominating indications of two shots side by side produces one or another conflicting interrelation, resulting in one or another expressive effect (I am speaking here of a *purely montage* effect).

This circumstance embraces all intensity levels of montage juxtaposition—all *impulses*:

From a complete opposition of the dominants, i.e., a sharply contrasting construction, to a scarcely noticeable "modulation" from shot to shot; *all* cases of conflict must therefore include cases of a complete *absence* of conflict.

As for the dominant itself, to regard it as something independent, absolute and invariably stable is out of the question. There are technical means of treating the shot so that its dominant may be made more or less specific, but in no case absolute.

The characteristics of the dominant are variable and profoundly relative. A revelation of its characteristics depends on that combination of shots which itself depends on the dominant!

A circle? An equation of two unknown quantities? A dog chasing its tail? No, this is simply an exact definition of a film law. A fact.

If we have even a *sequence* of montage pieces:

A gray old man,
A gray old woman,
A white horse,
A snow-covered roof,

we are still far from certain whether this sequence is working towards a dominating indication of "old age" or of "whiteness."

Such a sequence of shots might proceed for some time before we finally discover that guiding-shot which immediately "christens" the *whole* sequence in one "direction" or another. That is why it is advisable to place this identifying shot as near as possible to the beginning of the sequence (in an "orthodox" construction). Sometimes it even becomes necessary to do this with—a sub-title.

These considerations completely exclude a non-dialectic statement of the question concerning the *single-meaningness* of a frame within itself. The film-frame can never be an inflexible *letter of the alphabet*, but must always remain a multiple-meaning *ideogram*. And it can be read only in juxtaposition, just as an ideogram acquires its specific *significance*, *meaning*, and even *pronunciation* (occasionally in diametric opposition to one another) only when combined with a separately indicated reading or tiny meaning—an indicator for the exact reading—placed alongside the basic hieroglyph.

In distinction from orthodox montage according to *particular dominants, Old and New* was edited differently. In place of an "aristocracy" of individualistic dominants we brought a method of "democratic" equality of rights for all provocations, or stimuli, regarding them as a summary, as a complex.

The point is that the dominant (with all these recognized limitations on its relativity) appears to be, although the most powerful, far from the only stimulus of the shot. For example: the sex appeal of a beautiful American heroine-star is attended by many stimuli: of texture—from the material of her gown; of light—from the balanced and emphatic lighting of her figure; of racial-national (positive for an American audience: "a native American type," or negative: "colonizer-oppressor"—for a Negro or Chinese audience); of social-class, etc. (all brought together in an iron-bound unity of its reflex-physiological essence). In a word, the *central* stimulus (let it be, for instance, sexual as in our example) is attended always by a *whole complex* of secondary stimuli.

What takes place in acoustics, and particularly in the case of instrumental music, fully corresponds with this.

There, along with the vibration of a basic dominant tone, comes a whole series of similar vibrations, which are called *overtones* and *undertones*. Their impacts against each other, their impacts with the basic tone, and so on, envelop the basic tone in a whole host of secondary vibrations. If in acoustics these collateral vibrations become merely "disturbing" elements, these same vibrations in music—in composition, become one of the most significant means for affect by the experimental composers of our century, such as Debussy and Scriabin.

We find the same thing in optics, as well. All sorts of aberrations, distortions, and other defects, which can be remedied by systems of lenses, can also be taken into account compositionally, providing a whole series of definite compositional effects (employing lens-openings from 28 to 310).

In combinations which exploit *these collateral vibrations*—which is nothing less than *the filmed material itself*—we can achieve, completely analogous with music, *the visual overtonal complex of the shot.*

The montage of *Old and New* is constructed with this method. This montage is built, not on *particular* dominants, but takes as its guide the total stimulation through all stimuli. That is the original montage complex within the shot, arising from the collision and combination of the individual stimuli inherent in it.

These stimuli are heterogeneous as regards their "external natures," but their reflex-physiological essence binds them together in an iron unity. Physiological in so far as they are "psychic" in perception, this is merely the physiological process of a *higher nervous activity.*

In this way, behind the general indication of the shot, the physiological summary of its vibrations as a *whole*, as a complex unity of the manifestations of all its stimuli, is present. This is the peculiar *"feeling" of the shot*, produced by the shot as a whole.

This makes the shot as a montage-piece comparable to the separate scenes within the Kabuki method. The basic indication of the shot can be taken as the final summary of its effect on the cortex of the brain as a whole, irrespective of the paths by which the accumulated stimuli have been brought together. Thus the quality of the *totals* can be placed side by side in any conflicting combination, thereby revealing entirely new possibilities of montage solutions.

As we have seen, in the power of the very genetics of these methods, they must be attended by an extraordinary *physiological* quality. As in that music which builds its works on a two-fold use of overtones. Not the *classicism* of Beethoven, but the *physiological quality* of Debussy and Scriabin.

The extraordinary physiological quality in the affect of *Old and New* has been remarked by many of its spectators.

The explanation for this is that *Old and New* is *the first film edited on the principle of the visual overtone*. This method of montage can be interestingly verified.

If in the gleaming classical distances of the cinematography of the future, overtonal montage will certainly be used, simultaneously with montage according to the dominant indication, so as always at first—the new method will assert itself in a question sharpened in principle. Overtonal montage in its first steps has had to take a line in sharp *opposition* to the dominant.

There are many instances, it is true—and in *Old and New*, too—where "synthetic" combinations of tonal and overtonal montage may already be found. For example, in *Old and New*, the climax of the religious procession (to pray for relief from the drought), and the sequence of the grasshopper and the mowing-machine, are edited *visually* according to *sound* associations, with an express development which exists already in their spatial "similarity."

Of particular methodological interest, of course, are constructions that are wholly *a-dominant*. In these the dominant appears in the form of a purely *physiological formulation of the task*. For example, the montage of the beginning of the religious procession is according to "degrees of heat saturation" in the individual shots, or the beginning of the statefarm sequence is according to a line of "carnivorousness." Conditions outside cinematographic discipline provide the most unexpected physiological indications among materials that are logically (both formally and naturally) absolutely neutral in their relations to each other.

There are innumerable cases of montage joinings in this film that make open mockery of orthodox, scholastic montage according to the dominant. The easiest way to demonstrate this is to examine the film on the cutting table. Only then can one see clearly the perfectly "impossible" montage joinings in which *Old and New* abounds. This will also demonstrate the extreme simplicity of its metrics, of its "dimensions."

Entire large sections of certain sequences are made up of

pieces perfectly uniform in length or of absolutely primitively repeated short pieces. The whole intricate, rhythmic, and *sensual* nuance scheme of the combined pieces is conducted almost exclusively according to a line of work on the "psycho-physiological" vibrations of each piece.

It was on the cutting table that I detected the sharply defined scope of the particular montage of *Old and New*. This was when the film had to be condensed and shortened. The "creative ecstasy" attending the assembly and montage—the "creative ecstasy" of "hearing and feeling" the shots—all this was already in the past. Abbreviations and cuts require no inspiration, only technique and skill.

And there, examining the sequence of the religious procession on the table, I could not fit the combination of its pieces into any one of the orthodox categories, within which one can apply one's pure experience. On the table, deprived of motion, the reasons for their choice seem completely incomprehensible. The criteria for their assembly appear to be outside formally normal cinematographic criteria.

And here is observed one further curious parallel between the visual and the musical overtone: It cannot be traced in the static frame, just as it cannot be traced in the musical score. Both emerge as genuine values only in the dynamics of the musical or cinematographic *process*.

Overtonal conflicts, foreseen but unwritten in the score, cannot emerge without the dialectic process of the passage of the film through the projection apparatus, or that of the performance by a symphony orchestra.

The visual overtone is proved to be an actual piece, an actual element of —a fourth dimension!

In three-dimensional space, spatially inexpressible, and only emerging and existing in the fourth dimension (time added to the three dimensions).

The fourth dimension?! Einstein? Or mysticism? Or a joke?

It's time to stop being frightened of this new knowledge of a fourth dimension. Einstein himself assures us:

The non-mathematician is seized by a mysterious shuddering when he hears of "four-dimensional" things, by a feeling not unlike that awakened by thoughts of the occult. And yet there is no more common-place statement than that the world in which we live is a four-dimensional space-time continuum.[1]

Possessing such an excellent instrument of perception as the cinema—even on its primitive level—for the sensation of movement, we should soon learn a concrete orientation in this four-dimensional space-time continuum, and feel as much at home in it as in our own house-slippers. And we'll soon be posing the question of a fifth dimension!

Overtonal montage is revealed as a new category among the other montage processes known up till now. The *applied* significance of this method is immediately immense. And that is why this article appears in a number devoted to the sound film! *

In the article cited at the beginning, pointing to the "unexpected junction"—a similarity between the Kabuki theater and the sound film, I wrote on the contrapuntal method of combining the visual and aural images:

To possess this method one must develop in oneself a new sense: the capacity of reducing visual and aural perceptions to a "common denominator."

And yet we *cannot reduce aural* and *visual* perceptions to a common denominator. They are values of different dimensions. But the visual overtone and the sound overtone are values of a *singly measured* substance. Because, if the frame is a *visual perception,* and the tone is an aural perception, *visual as well as aural overtones are a totally physiological sensation.* And, consequently, they are *of one and the same kind,* outside the sound or aural categories that serve as guides, conductors to its achievement.

* This issue of the newspaper *Kino* for August 27, 1929, was chiefly devoted to the reports and speeches at the All-Union Conference on the Sound Film, held earlier in the month.

For the musical overtone (a throb) it is not strictly fitting to say: "I hear."

Nor for the visual overtone: "I see."

For both, a new uniform formula must enter our vocabulary: "I feel."

The theory and methodology of the overtone have been cultivated and made familiar by, among others, Debussy and Scriabin. *Old and New* introduces a concept of the *visual overtone*. And from the contrapuntal conflict between the visual and aural *overtones* will be born the composition of the Soviet sound film.

[1929]

METHODS OF MONTAGE

> In every art and every discovery, experience
> has always preceded precepts. In the course
> of time, a method has been assigned to the
> practice of the invention.
>
> GOLDONI [1]

IS THE method of overtonal montage unrelated to our previous experience, artificially grafted onto cinematography, or is it simply a quantitative accumulation of one attribute that makes a dialectic leap and begins to function as a new qualitative attribute?

In other words, is overtonal montage a dialectical stage of development within the development of the whole montage system of methods, standing in a successive relation to other forms of montage?

These are the formal categories of montage that we know:

1. Metric Montage

The fundamental criterion for this construction is the *absolute lengths* of the pieces. The pieces are joined together according to their lengths, in a formula-scheme corresponding to a measure of music. Realization is in the repetition of these "measures."

Tension is obtained by the effect of mechanical acceleration by shortening the pieces while preserving the original proportions of the formula. Primitive of the method: three-quarter-time, march-time, waltz-time ($\frac{3}{4}$, $\frac{2}{4}$, $\frac{1}{4}$, etc.), used by Kuleshov; degeneration of the method: metric montage using a measure of complicated irregularity ($\frac{16}{17}$, $\frac{22}{57}$, etc.).

Such a measure ceases to have a physiological effect, for it is contrary to the "law of simple numbers" (relationships).

Simple relationships, giving a clarity of impression, are for this reason necessary for maximum effectiveness. They are therefore found in healthy classics of every field: architecture; the color in a painting; a complex composition by Scriabin (always crystal clear in the relations between its parts); geometrical *mises-en-scène;* precise state planning, etc.

A similar example may be found in Vertov's *Eleventh Year,* where the metric beat is mathematically so complex that it is only "with a ruler" that one can discover the proportional law that governs it. Not by *impression* as perceived, but by *measurement.*

I do not mean to imply that the beat should be recognizable as part of the perceived impression. On the contrary. Though unrecognized, it is nevertheless indispensable for the "organization" of the sensual impression. Its clarity can bring into unison the "pulsing" of the film and the "pulsing" of the audience. Without such a unison (obtainable by many means) there can be no contact between the two.

Over-complexity of the metric beat produces a chaos of impressions, instead of a distinct emotional tension.

A third use of metric montage lies between its two extremes of simplicity and complexity: alternating two varying piecelengths according to two kinds of content within the pieces. Examples: the sequence of the *lezginka* in *October* and the patriotic demonstration in *The End of St. Petersburg.* (The latter example can be considered as classic in the field of *purely metric* montage.)

In this type of metric montage the content within the frame of the piece is subordinated to the absolute length of the piece. Therefore, only the broadly dominant content-character of the piece is regarded; these would be "synonymous" shots.

2. Rhythmic Montage

Here, in determining the lengths of the pieces, the content within the frame is a factor possessing equal rights to consideration.

Abstract determination of the piece-lengths gives way to a flexible relationship of the *actual* lengths.

Here the actual length does not coincide with the mathematically determined length of the piece according to a metric formula. Here its practical length derives from the specifics of the piece, and from its planned length according to the structure of the sequence.

It is quite possible here to find cases of complete metric *identity* of the pieces and their rhythmic measures, obtained through a combination of the pieces according to their content.

Formal tension by acceleration is obtained here by shortening the pieces not only in accordance with the fundamental plan, but also by violating this plan. The most affective violation is by the introduction of material more intense in an easily distinguished tempo.

The "Odessa steps" sequence in *Potemkin* is a clear example of this. In this the rhythmic drum of the soldiers' feet as they descend the steps violates all *metrical* demands. Unsynchronized with the beat of the cutting, this drumming comes in *off-beat* each time, and the shot itself is entirely different in its solution with each of these appearances. The final pull of tension is supplied by the transfer from the rhythm of the descending feet to another rhythm—a new kind of downward movement—the next intensity level of the same activity—the baby-carriage rolling down the steps. The carriage functions as a directly progressing accelerator of the advancing feet. The stepping descent passes into a rolling descent.

Contrast this with the above example from *The End of St. Petersburg*, where intensity is gained by cutting *each and every piece* to its required minimum within the single metric measure.

Such metrical montage is perfectly suitable for similarly simple march-time solutions. But it is inadequate for more complex rhythmic needs.

When it is forcibly applied to such a problem, we find montage failure. This explains such an unsuccessful sequence as that of the religious mask dance in *Storm Over Asia*. Executed on the basis of a complex metrical beat, unadjusted to the specific content of the pieces, this neither reproduces the rhythm of the original ceremony nor organizes a cinematically affective rhythm.

In most cases of this sort, nothing more than perplexity is excited in the specialist, and nothing more than a confused impression is aroused in the lay spectator. (Although an artificial crutch of musical accompaniment may give some support to such a shaky sequence—as it did in the cited example—the basic weakness is still present.)

3. Tonal Montage

This term is employed for the first time. It expresses a stage beyond rhythmic montage.

In rhythmic montage it is movement within the frame that impels the montage movement from frame to frame. Such movements within the frame may be of objects in motion, or of the spectator's eye directed along the lines of some immobile object.

In tonal montage, movement is perceived in a wider sense. The concept of movement embraces *all affects* of the montage piece. Here montage is based on the characteristic *emotional sound* of the piece—of its dominant. The general *tone* of the piece.

I do not mean to say that the emotional sound of the piece is to be measured "impressionistically." The piece's characteristics in this respect can be measured with as much exactitude as in the most elementary case of "by the ruler" measurement in metrical montage. But the units of measurement differ. And the amounts to be measured are different.

For example, the degree of light vibration in a piece cannot only be gauged by a selenium light-element, but every gradation of this vibration is perceptible to the naked eye. If we give the comparative and emotional designation of "more gloomy" to a piece, we can also find for the piece a mathematical co-efficient for its degree of illumination. This is a case of "light tonality." Or, if the piece is described as having a "shrill sound," it is possible to find, behind this description, the many acutely angled elements within the frame, in comparison with other shape-elements. This is a case of "graphic tonality."

Working with combinations of varying degrees of soft-focus or varying degrees of "shrillness" would be a typical use of tonal montage.

As I have said, this would be based on the *dominant* emotional sound of the pieces. An example: the "fog sequence" in *Potemkin* (preceding the mass mourning over the body of Vakulinchuk). Here the montage was based exclusively on the emotional "sound" of the pieces—on rhythmic vibrations that do not affect spatial alterations. In this example it is interesting that, alongside the basic tonal dominant, a secondary, accessory *rhythmic* dominant is also operating. This links the tonal construction of the scene with the tradition of rhythmic montage, the furthest development of which is tonal montage. And, like rhythmic montage, this is also a special variation of metric montage.

This secondary dominant is expressed in barely perceptible changing movements: the agitation of the water; the slight rocking of the anchored vessels and buoys; the slowly ascending vapor; the sea-gulls settling gently onto the water.

Strictly speaking, these too are elements of a *tonal* order. These are movements that move according to tonal rather than to spatial-rhythmic characteristics. Here spatially immeasurable changes are combined according to their emotional sound. But the chief indicator for the assembly of the pieces was according to their basic element—optical light-vibrations (varying degrees of "haze" and "luminosity"). And the organization of these vibrations reveals a complete identity with a minor harmony in music. Moreover, this example furnishes a demonstration of consonance in combining movement as *change* and movement as *light-vibration*.

Increased tension in this level of montage, too, is produced by an intensification of the same "musical" dominant. An especially clear example of such intensification is furnished by the sequence of the delayed harvest in *Old and New*. The construction of this film as a whole, as in this particular sequence, adheres to a basic constructive process. Namely: a conflict between *story* and its *traditional form*.

Emotive structures applied to non-emotional material. The stimulus is transferred from its usual use as situation (for example, as eroticism is usually used in films) to structures paradoxical in tone. When "the pillar of industry" is finally discovered—it is a typewriter. The hero bull and heroine cow are happily wed. It is not the Holy Grail that inspires both doubt and ecstasy—but a cream-separator.*

Therefore, the thematic *minor* of the harvesting is resolved by the thematic *major* of the tempest, of the rain. Yes, and even the stacked harvest, itself—traditional major theme of fecundity basking in the sun—is a resolution of the minor theme, wetted as it is by the rain.

Here the increase of tension proceeds by internal reinforcement of a relentless dominant chord—by the growing feeling within the piece of "oppression before the storm."

As in the preceding example, the tonal dominant—movement as light-vibration—is accompanied by a secondary rhythmic dominant, i.e., movement as change.

Here it is expressed in the growing violence of the wind, embodied in a transfer from currents of air to torrents of rain —a definite analogy with the transfer from the downward steps to the downward rolling carriage.

In general structure the wind-rain element in relation to the dominant can be identified with the bond in the first example (the harbor mists) between its rhythmic rockings and its

* There was even a parallel with the ironic conclusion of *A Woman of Paris* in the original end planned for *Old and New*. This is, by the way, a film unique in the number of references (both in story and in style) to other films: the "pillar of industry" sequence playfully builds its satire on a similar but serious episode in Pudovkin's *End of St. Petersburg;* the tractor's final triumph is an inflated parody of a Wild West film chase, etc. Even Buster Keaton's *Three Ages* was consciously reflected in the original structure of *Old and New*.—EDITOR.

reticular afocality. Actually, the character of the inter-relation is quite different. In contrast with the consonance of the first example, we have here the reverse.

The gathering the skies into a black, threatening mass is contrasted with the intensifying dynamic force of the wind, and the solidification implied in the transition from currents of air to torrents of water is intensified by the dynamically blown petticoats and the scattering sheaves of the harvest.

Here a collision of tendencies—an intensification of the static and an intensification of the dynamic—gives us a clear example of dissonance in tonal montage construction.

From the viewpoint of emotional impression, the harvest sequence exemplifies the tragic (active) minor, in distinction from the lyrical (passive) minor of the harbor fog sequence.

It is interesting that in both examples the montage grows with the increasing change of its basic element—*color:* in the "harbor" from dark gray to misty white (life analogy—the dawn); in the "harvest" from light gray to leaden black (life analogy—the approach of crisis). I.e., along a line of light vibrations increasing in frequency in the one case, and diminishing in frequency in the other.

A construction in simple metrics has been elevated to a new category of movement—a category of higher significance.

This brings us to a category of montage that we may justly name:

4. *Overtonal Montage*

In my opinion, overtonal montage (as described in the preceding essay) is organically the furthest development along the line of tonal montage. As I have indicated, it is distinguishable from tonal montage by the collective calculation of all the piece's appeals.

This characteristic steps up the impression from a melodically emotional coloring to a directly physiological perception. This, too, represents a level related to the preceding levels.

These four categories are *methods* of montage. They become montage *constructions* proper when they enter into relations of conflict with each other—as in the examples cited.

Within a scheme of mutual relations, echoing and conflicting with one another, they move to a more and more strongly defined type of montage, each one organically growing from the other.

Thus the transition from metrics to rhythmics came about in the conflict between the length of the shot and the movement within the frame.

Tonal montage grows out of the conflict between the rhythmic and tonal principles of the piece.

And finally—overtonal montage, from the conflict between the principal tone of the piece (its dominant) and the overtone.

These considerations provide, in the first place, an interesting criterion for the appreciation of montage-construction from a "pictorial" point of view. Pictorialism is here contrasted with "cinematicism," esthetic pictorialism with physiological reality.

To argue about the pictorialism of the film-shot is naive. This is typical of persons possessing a decent esthetic culture that has never been logically applied to films. To this kind of thinking belong, for instance, the remarks on cinema coming from Kasimir Malevich.* The veriest novice in films would not think of analyzing the film-shot from an identical point of view with landscape painting.

The following may be observed as a criterion of the "pictorialism" of the montage-construction in the broadest sense: the conflict must be resolved *within* one or another category of montage, without allowing the conflict to be one of differing categories of montage.

Real cinematography begins only with the collision of various cinematic modifications of movement and vibration. For example, the "pictorial" conflict of figure and horizon (whether this is a conflict in statics or dynamics is unimportant). Or the alternation of differently lit pieces solely from

* The founder of the Suprematist school of painting had delivered some commonplaces about the "photographic" and naturalistic limitations of the cinema.—EDITOR.

the viewpoint of conflicting light-vibrations, or of a conflict between the form of an object and its illumination, etc.

We must also define what characterizes the affect of the various forms of montage on the psycho-physiological complex of the person on the perceiving end.

The first, metric category is characterized by a rude motive force. It is capable of impelling the spectator to reproduce the perceived action, outwardly. For example, the mowing contest in *Old and New* is cut in this way. The different pieces are "synonymous"—containing a single mowing movement from one side of the frame to the other; and I laughed when I saw the more impressionable members of the audience quietly rocking from side to side at an increasing rate of speed as the pieces were accelerated by shortening. The effect was the same as that of a percussion and brass band playing a simple march tune.

I have designated the second category as rhythmic. It might also be called primitive-emotive. Here the movement is more subtly calculated, for though emotion is also a result of movement, it is movement that is not merely primitive external change.

The third category—tonal—might also be called melodic-emotive. Here movement, already ceasing to be simple change in the second case, passes over distinctly into an emotive vibration of a still higher order.

The fourth category—a fresh flood of pure physiologism, as it were—echoes, in the highest degree of intensity, the first category, again acquiring a degree of intensification by direct motive force.

In music this is explained by the fact that, from the moment that overtones can be heard parallel with the basic sound, there also can be sensed vibrations, oscillations that cease to impress as tones, but rather as purely physical displacements of the perceived impression. This particularly refers to strongly pronounced timbre instruments with a great preponderance of the overtone principle. The sensation of physical displacement is sometimes also literally achieved: chimes, organ, very large Turkish drums, etc.

In some sequences *Old and New* succeeds in effecting junctions of the tonal and overtonal lines. Sometimes they even collide with the metric and rhythmic lines, as well. As in the various "tangles" of the religious procession: those who fall on their knees beneath the ikons, the candles that melt, the gasps of ecstasy, etc.

It is interesting to note that, in selecting the pieces for the montage of this sequence, we unconsciously furnished ourselves with proof of an essential equality between rhythm and tone, establishing this gradational unity much as I had previously established a gradational unity between the concepts of shot and montage.

Thus, tone is a level of rhythm.

For the benefit of those who are alarmed by such reductions to a common denominator, and the extension of the properties of one level into another for purposes of investigation and methodology, I recall Lenin's synopsis of the fundamental elements of Hegelian dialectics:

These elements may be presented in a more detailed way thus: . . .

10) an endless process of revealing *new* aspects, relationships, etc.

11) an endless process of deepening human perception of things, appearances, processes and so on, from appearance to essence and from the less profound to the more profound essence.

12) from co-existence to causality and from one form of connection and interdependence to another, deeper, more general.

13) recurrence, on the highest level, of known traits, attributes, etc. of the lowest, and

14) return, so to say, to the old (negation of the negation) . . .²

After this quotation, I wish to define the following category of montage—a still higher category:

5. *Intellectual Montage*

Intellectual montage is montage not of generally physiological overtonal sounds, but of sounds and overtones of an intellectual sort: i.e., conflict-juxtaposition of accompanying intellectual affects.

The gradational quality is here determined by the fact that
there is no difference in principle between the motion of a
man rocking under the influence of elementary metric montage (see above) and the intellectual process within it, for the
intellectual process is the same agitation, but in the dominion
of the higher nerve-centers.

And if, in the cited instance, under the influence of "jazz
montage," one's hands and knees rhythmically tremble, in the
second case such a trembling, under the influence of a different
degree of intellectual appeal, occurs in identically the same
way through the tissues of the higher nerve systems of the
thought apparatus.

Though, judged as "phenomena" (appearances), they seem
in fact different, yet from the point of view of "essence"
(process), they are undoubtedly identical.

Applying the experience of work along lower lines to categories of a higher order, this affords the possibility of carrying
the attack into the very heart of things and phenomena. Thus,
the fifth category is the intellectual overtone.

An example of this can be found in the sequence of the
"gods" in *October*, where all the conditions for their comparison are made dependent on an exclusively class-intellectual
sound of each piece in its relation to God. I say class, for
though the emotional principle is universally human, the intellectual principle is profoundly tinged by class. These pieces
were assembled in accordance with a descending intellectual
scale—pulling back the concept of God to its origins, forcing
the spectator to perceive this "progress" intellectually.*

* A portion of this sequence (omitted from most of the American
prints of *Ten Days That Shook the World*) is reproduced in the section of photographs between pages 52 and 53.

But this, of course, is not yet the intellectual cinema, which I have been announcing for some years! The intellectual cinema will be that which resolves the conflict-juxtaposition of the physiological and intellectual overtones. Building a completely new form of cinematography—the realization of revolution in the general history of culture; building a synthesis of science, art, and class militancy.

In my opinion, the question of the overtone is of vast significance for our film future. All the more attentively should we study its methodology and conduct investigation into it.

Moscow—London, Autumn 1929

A COURSE IN TREATMENT

> *Stephen.* (Looks behind.) So that gesture,
> not music, not odours, would be a universal
> language, the gift of tongues rendering visible
> not the lay sense but the first entelechy, the
> structural rhythm.
>
> JAMES JOYCE [1]

DISCUSSIONS ON "amusement" *vs.* "entertainment" irritate
me. Having spent no small number of man-hours in the matter
of the "enthusiasm" and "involvement" of the audience in a
united and general impulse of absorption, the word "amusement" sounds opposed, alien and inimical to me. Whenever it
is said that a film must "entertain," I hear a voice: "Help yourself."

When the worthy Ivan Ivanovich Pererepenko "treats you
to snuff, he always first licks the lid of his snuff-box with his
tongue, and then taps it with his finger, presenting it to you,
and if you are an acquaintance, says: 'Shall I dare, my dear
sir, to ask you to help yourself?' And if you aren't acquainted
with him, he says: 'Shall I dare, my dear sir, although I have
not the honor of knowing your rank, name and patronymic,
to ask you to help yourself?'" But when Ivan Nikiforovich
Dovgochkhun treats you to snuff, he "puts the snuff-box
straight into your hand, and says only: 'Help yourself.'" [2]

I'm for Ivan Nikiforovich, with his direct "help yourself."

The film's job is to make the audience "help itself," not to
"entertain" it. To grip, not to amuse. To furnish the audience
with cartridges, not to dissipate the energies that it brought
into the theater. "Entertainment" is not really an entirely in-
nocuous term: beneath it is a quite concrete, active process.

But amusement and entertainment must be understood pre-

84

cisely as only a quantitative empowering of the inner thematic material itself, and not in any sense as a qualitative power.

While we had films that "gripped," we did not speak of entertainment. We had no time to be bored. But then this gripping was lost somewhere. The skill of constructing films that gripped was lost. And we began to talk of entertainment.

It is impossible to realize this latter aim, without first mastering the former method.

The slogan in favor of entertainment was regarded by many as countenancing a certain retrogressive element and, in the worst sense, as a perversion of understanding in relation to the ideological premises of our films.

We must once more command a method, a directive guide to embody in stirring works of art. No one can help us in this. We must do it ourselves.

It is on the subject of how to do this,—at least how to get ready to do it, that I wish to speak.

To rehabilitate the ideological premise is not something to be introduced from without "at the pleasure of Repertkom," * but must be thought of as a basic, vivifying, powerful process, fertilizing nothing less than the most thrilling element in the creative work of film direction—the director's "treatment." That is the task of the present essay.

And there is a quite concrete occasion for this—namely, in connection with the formulation of pedagogical work in the third, or graduating, class of the directors' course in the State Cinema Institute where, according to the teaching program, the students must now walk out into creative mastery of directorial work.

The Talmudists of method—the academic high-Marxists—may berate me, but I wish to approach this theme and this teaching simply, as life—as work. For, actually, no one as yet knows concretely how to master this, whether screening oneself behind academic citations or not.

---

* The Repertory Committee is entrusted with the supervision of stage and film repertories.—EDITOR.

For some time, for years, I worried about those certain supernatural powers, transcending common sense and human reason, that seemed indispensable for the comprehension of the "mysteries" of creative film direction.

To dissect the music of creative film direction!

To dissect, but not as a corpse (in Salieri's manner *), the music of creative film direction—that was to be our work with the graduating students of the Institute.

We approach this problem simply, and not from a preconceived position of scholastic methods. And it won't be in the corpses of worn-out film works that we'll examine the processes of producing our own works. The anatomical theater and dissection slab are the least suitable trying grounds for the study of the theater. And the study of cinema must proceed inseparably with the study of theater.

To build cinematography, starting from "the idea of cinematography," and from abstract principles, is barbarous and stupid. Only by a critical comparison with the more basic early forms of the spectacle is it possible to master critically the specific methodology of the cinema.

Criticism must consist in comparing and contrasting a given fact, not with an idea, but with another fact; for this purpose it is only important that both facts, as far as possible, be carefully investigated, and that they both present, in relation to one another, different moments of development.[3]

We shall study this matter in the living creative process. And it will be done by us in this way, primarily.

We must build simultaneously a working process and a method. And we shall proceed not in the Plekhanov manner, from preconceived positions of "method in general" to the concrete particular case, but through given concrete work on particular materials we expect to arrive at a method of cinematographic creation for the director.

For this purpose we must bring out into the open the "inti-

* According to his opening soliloquy in Pushkin's *Mozart and Salieri.*
—EDITOR.

mate" creative process of the director in all its phases and twistings, and stand it before the audience, "in full view."

Many surprises are in store for the youth who is filled with illusions.

In one connection may I, for a moment, list to the side of "entertainment"? Let us cite one of the greatest of all "entertainers"—Alexandre Dumas *père*, for whom his son, Dumas *fils*, apologized: "My father is a great baby of mine—born when I was quite a little child." [4]

Who has not been enchanted by the classic harmony in the labyrinthine structure of *The Count of Monte Cristo!* Who has not been struck by the deadly logic that weaves and interweaves the characters and events of the novel, as if these interrelationships had existed from its very conception. Who has finally not imagined that ecstatic moment when suddenly in the brain of that "fat black" Dumas there flashed the future architecture of the novel in all its details and subtleties, with the title, *Le Comte de Monte Cristo*, blazing across the façade. And this vision has its usual echo, "Oh, how could I ever achieve that!" And how pleasantly bracing it is to recognize by tasting that cooking, how such a remarkable composition was really brought together and given body. How the fabrication of this book came with savage diligence—not in a divine flash.

It is the work of a Negro, but toiling as hard as he would have under the whip of an overseer. Dumas was actually of Negro descent, and he was born in Haiti, as was Toussaint L'Ouverture, the hero of a film I want to make, *The Black Consul.** The nickname of Dumas's grandfather—General Thomas Alexandre—was the "Black Devil." And Dumas himself was called "fat black" by his envious contemporaries and rivals. A certain humbly-named Jacquot, concealed behind the loftier sound of "Eugène de Mirecourt," published an attack entitled *Fabrique de Romans: Maison Alexandre Dumas et Cie*, in which he linked the origins and methods of Dumas:

* An unrealized wish. See "The Work of Eisenstein," in *The Film Sense*.—EDITOR.

Scratch M. Dumas' hide and you will find the savage. . . . He lunches on potatoes taken burning hot from the ashes of the hearth and devours them without removing the skins—a Negro! [As he needs 200,000 francs a year,] he hires intellectual deserters and translators at wages that degrade them to the condition of Negroes working under the lash of a mulatto! [5]

"Your father was black!" someone hurled in his face. "My grandfather was a monkey," he replied. He seems to have been more sensitive to the "factory" charge.

On one day only Dumas was truly grieved. Béranger, whom he really loved, wrote asking him to include an interesting exile "in the number of miners whom he employed to dig out the mineral which he transformed into sterling bullion"; and Dumas replied: "Dear old friend, My only miner is my left hand which holds the book open, while my right works twelve hours a day."
He was exaggerating. He had collaborators, "but as Napoleon had generals." [6]

It is difficult enough to find oneself working with such frenzy. But it is even more difficult to achieve anything adequate without this frenzy.

Miracles of composition—this is merely a question of persistence and the expenditure of time during the "training period" of one's autobiography.

From a viewpoint of productivity this period of romanticism is distinguished for the dizzying speed of its creative tempi: In eight days (from September 17 to September 26, 1829) Victor Hugo wrote 3,000 lines of *Hernani*, which stood the classic theater on its head, *Marion Delorme* in 23 days, *Le Roi s'Amuse* in 20 days, *Lucrèce Borgia* in 11 days, *Angelo* in 19 days, *Marie Tudor* in 19 days, *Ruy Blas* in 34 days. This is echoed quantitatively, as well. The literary heritage of Dumas *père* numbers 1,200 volumes.

The same opportunity of creating such works is equally accessible to all.

Let us examine *The Count of Monte Cristo* in particular. Lucas-Dubreton gives us the history of its composition:

In the course of a Mediterranean cruise, Dumas had passed near a little island, where he had not been able to land because "it was *en contumace.*" It was the island of Monte-Cristo. The name struck him at the time. A few years later, in 1843, he arranged with an editor for the publication of a work to be called *Impressions de Voyage dans Paris*, but he needed a romantic plot. Then one day by good luck he read a story of twenty pages, *Le Diamant et la Vengeance*, which was laid in the period of the second Restoration and was included in Peuchet's volume, *La Police Devoilée*. It caught his fancy. Here was the subject of which he had dreamed: Monte-Cristo should discover his enemies hidden in Paris!

Then Maquet had the idea of telling the story of the love-affair of Monte-Cristo and the fair Mercedes and the treachery of Danglars; and the two friends started off on a new track—*Monte-Cristo*, from being travel impressions in the form of a romance turned into romance pure and simple. The Abbé Faria, a lunatic born at Goa whom Châteaubriand saw vainly trying to kill a canary by hypnotizing it, helped to increase the mystery; and the Château d'If began to appear on the horizon. . . .[7]

This is how things are really put together. And to re-experience this as it takes place, and to participate in it oneself, seems to me a most useful and productive process for a student.

The "method-ists" who preach otherwise and approve other "recipes" are simply wasting our precious time. But "chance" here is far less important than it might appear, and the "regularity" within the creative process is perceived and detected. There is method. But the whole villainy lies in this, that from preconceived methodological positions, nothing grows. And a tempestuous stream of creative energy, unregulated by method, yields even less.

Such analysis of the building of works of art, step by step, will clarify the most severe regularity, governing each support of the super-structure, with which they arise from basic social and ideological premises.

And the gold fever of money-making and self-enrichment of the Louis-Philippe epoch is no less a determining factor for the gilded legend of the fabulous wealth of the former sailor who becomes an omnipotent count, no less determining than Dumas's childhood memories of Scheherazade and the treasures of Ali Baba. And the very fact that a sailor could become a count, meant that "anyone" might.

In the general chase after gold and aristocratic titles, the sailor, Dantès who became the mythically rich Comte de Monte Cristo, served as a splendid "social ideal" for the bourgeoisie who were feverishly enriching themselves. It is not without reason that to this image is ascribed the features of an idealized self-portrait. For Dumas himself, along with the others, bathed in the turbid sea of suspicious gold accumulated through the dubious speculations of the reign of *le roi bourgeois*.

"A million? That's exactly the amount I ordinarily carry for pocket money!"

To an identical degree this remark was the unattainable ideal, both of the "fat black," then the literary sovereign of the newspaper, *feuilleton* and dramatic world of Paris, squandering words and money with equal recklessness, as well as of the vast hordes of greedy sharpers and rogues, overrunning the economic life of Paris.

However, to sense fully how sharply these social, economical and ideological premises determine every slightest twist of form, and how inseparably they are united in their processes, one must independently and conscientiously trace a continuous and complete creative cycle from start to finish.

Of course, what would be most interesting would be to catch another Goethe or Gogol, place him before an audience and set him to writing a third part of *Faust* or to create newly a second volume of *Dead Souls*. But we don't even have a live Alexandre Dumas at our disposal. So we of the Institute's third course transform ourselves into a collective director and film-builder.

The instructor is no more than *primus inter pares*—the first among equals. The collective (and later each member of it individually) works its way through all the difficulties and torments of creative work, through the whole process of creative formation, from the first faint, glimmering hint of the theme, down to a decision on whether the buttons on the leather jacket of the last extra player are suitable for filming purposes.

The instructor's task is only, by a well-timed dexterous shove, to push the collective in the direction of "normal" and "fruitful" difficulties, and to push it in the direction of the collective's correct and distinct presentation (to himself) of exactly those questions, the answers to which lead to *construction* and not to fruitless chatter "around" it.

That is how they teach you to fly in the circus. The trapeze is mercilessly held back, or the pupil finds a fist instead of a helping hand if his timing is false. No great harm if he falls once or twice outside the safety net onto the chairs around the arena. Next time—he won't make that mistake.

But no less carefully, at each stage of the unfolding creative process, must the indicated secondary material and the experience of the "inherited past," at the proper place, be thrust into the hands of the entangled or stuck "warriors." This is not enough, if at hand is not that exhausting synthetic giant of cinema who, at every turn, is more than the "inherited past" and the "living heir," forming in its own field a solid technique.

Within three years a systematic course in special subjects has replaced at the Institute a thin coating of sporadic lectures by all sorts of "prominent" film-workers. These people ran into the Institute as they would into a street-car, strange and unrelated to each other, just like street-car passengers, rushing to the exit as fast as possible, after blurting 45 minutes' worth of something unconnected and episodic. Then they were whirled out of the sight of their dazed proselytes, along the orbit of their private activities.

This "little episode" also had to be re-built in a fundamental way. Within the plan of the general course, specialists are invited in at the proper time, to deal with definite, concrete cases, at a definite stage of the general movement of the unfolding creative process. To deal with that particular question in which he is expert.

All this aims at a properly large project in which the collective or, later, the individual, is responsible to the very end. In getting rid of the "little episodes" in the instructional plan, we have also done away with the pitiable "little episodes" prepared by graduating students. These short "études" of the graduates, miscellaneous and miserable, but self-satisfying, even shorter in intelligence than they are in footage, must be dropped as being wholly inexpedient. After working on a graduate project on the scale, say, of a cathedral, the graduate architect usually finds himself building something accessible to everyone—a privy. But, after designing for graduation one tiny *pisoir*, it is risky to turn to, yes, to what you please! And yet, year after year, we have seen this happen to graduates from the Institute. This has to be fundamentally scrapped.

It is true that in practice a film is broken up into separate episodes. But these episodes all hang from the rod of a single ideological, compositional and stylistic whole.

The art of cinematography is not in selecting a fanciful framing, or in taking something from a surprising camera-angle.

The art is in every fragment of a film being an organic part of an organically conceived whole.

With such organically thought-out and photographed parts of one large significant and general conception, these must be segments of some whole, and by no means with stray, strolling études.

On these filmed segments, on the unfilmed but prepared episodes that are planned to precede or follow these, on the development of montage plans and lists according to the place of these parts in the whole—on such a base creative irresponsibility will be really liquidated among the students.

From beginning to end their work will be examined, simultaneously with responsible demonstrations as to how far they are capable of realizing in practice the firmly planned general concept; although at this stage it is not yet the student's own individual concept, but the collectively worked out concept, but this already teaches the hard lesson of self-discipline.

Self-discipline that will be even more needed at the moment when the concept will be individual and his own.

But before reaching this last stage, this last frontier, already bordering on production away from the school, the students run a long gantlet of living and dead "experts."

At a certain stage this will take the form of a long discussion of the type, image, and character of the characters in his project. The ashes of Balzac, Gogol, Dostoyevsky, and Ben Jonson will be stirred in such discussions. The question will arise as to the personification of such a type, image, or character. Here we'll depend on Kachalov's confession of his work on the rôle of the "Baron" in *The Lower Depths*, Batalov will talk with us, or Max Shtraukh will tell us of the mechanics of creating Rubinchik in Zarkhi's *Joy Street*.

Moving through the forests of story-construction, we'll pull apart with Aksënov the skeletons of the Elizabethans, we'll listen to Dumas *père* and Victor Shklovsky on the outlining of story structures, and on the methods of Weltmann's works. And then, having talked over dramatic situations with the late John Webster, Nathan Zarkhi and Volkenstein, we shall interest ourselves in how these situations are clothed in words.

Alexei Maximovich Gorky will probably not refuse to initiate us in the methods of writing the dialogue for *The Lower Depths* or *Yegor Bulichëv and Others*. Nikolai Erdmann will tell us how it is done in his plays. And Isaac Babel will speak of the specific texture of image and word and of the technique of the extreme laconism of literature's expressive means—Babel who, perhaps, knows in practice better than anyone else, that great secret, that "there is no iron that can enter the human heart with such stupefying effect as a period, placed at the right moment." [8] And he may speak of how, with this laconism, was created so inimitably his wonderful (and far from being sufficiently appreciated) play *Sunset*. This is perhaps the best example of fine dramatic dialogue in recent years.

All this will arise at the corresponding stages of the single progressing creative process of our collective director on his film.

The fusing of the separate stages along independent analytical excursions is not so very strange. Construction of theme and story can sometimes be completely independent of the development in words. Aren't both *Revizor* and *Dead Souls* brilliant examples of the development of stories "set" Gogol from outside? *

The question of a musical accompaniment for the sound medium. The question of material means. Analysis of a number of examples of our "heritage" in other areas as well, and each from the angle of that special need where it, and peculiarly it, can be doubly useful.

James Joyce and Emile Zola.

Honoré Daumier and Edgar Dégas.

Toulouse-Lautrec or Stendhal.

And lengthily and circumstantially will be analyzed by Marxist and Leninist specialists the question of the correct ideological formulation of the problem from the standpoint of approach to the theme and to a social understanding of this thing. In this way we expect to secure those, mobilized with experience and qualified by sustained guidance, who will be capable of creating films.

And the most serious and interesting part of this work—the central part of the director's creative work—is to train students in "treatment" and to work up with them the process of how this proceeds and is carried out.

We work essentially on such a low-experimental triviality of simplified perceived tasks, that we simply do not have occasion to observe works that are original, living, creative, that have an inter-related social treatment and conception, with developed form.

Our works are on such a level of simplification that one recalls the famous cartoon of the automatic sausage factory: from one side enter boxes with handles containing pigs, at the other side the same boxes come out, now containing sausages.

Between the schematic scraped skeleton of *slogan* and the

---

* It was Pushkin who suggested the themes of both these works.—
EDITOR.

empty skin of outer *form* there are no layers of tangible, living flesh and muscle.

There are no organs, acting in relation to each other. And then people are surprised that the skin hangs so formlessly. And through its pitifully thin simplification juts the sharp bones of a mechanical perception of "social" thematics. Not enough flesh and muscle.

That is why Gorky's *Yegor Bulichëv and Others* was greeted with such unanimous joy. Even though the work has not answered a basic problem of ours: the men and women shown in it are not yet ours, and of today. We'll continue to wait for these from the mind of Alexei Maximovich.*

On the other hand, here is flesh. Here is muscle. And this flesh was made today, when all around us on stage and screen are not even the "men in boxes" that Chekhov wrote about, but simply boxes without men. Whereas, tightly packed as they are with vulgar citations, our works resemble the barbed wire of harsh truth, covered with muslin—and we are astonished that blood doesn't circulate through these barbs, and that the muslin doesn't beat an excited pulse.

From the sublime to the ridiculous is one step. From a sublimely premised idea, formulated in a slogan, to a living work of art—is several hundred steps. If we take but one step, we achieve only the ridiculous result of the accommodating trash of the present.

We must begin to learn how to do three-dimensional, rounded works, going from the two-dimensional flat patterns with a "direct wire" from the slogan to the story—without a transfer.

How an ideological concept works, making a serious approach towards a film, we can trace in my own work, although in somewhat unusual social circumstances. This was in Hollywood. In the world of Paramount Pictures, Inc. And the mat-

* *Yegor Bulichëv* was the first of a planned trilogy that was to reach the first post-revolutionary years.[9]

ter concerned the treatment and script of a work of exceptionally high quality.

Even though not beyond ideological defects, *An American Tragedy* by Theodore Dreiser is a work that has every chance of being numbered among the classics of its period and place. That this material contained the collision of two irreconcilable viewpoints—the "front office's" and ours—became clear from the moment of submitting the first rough draft of a script.

"Is Clyde Griffiths guilty or not guilty—in your treatment?" was the first question from the head of Paramount, B. P. Schulberg.

"Not guilty," was our answer.

"But then your script is a monstrous challenge to American society. . . ."

We explained that we consider the crime committed by Griffiths the sum total of those social relations, the influence of which he was subjected to at every stage of his unfolding biography and character, during the course of the film. For us this was, essentially, the whole interest of the work.

"We would prefer a simple, tight whodunit about a murder . . ."

". . . and about the love of a boy and girl," someone added, with a sigh.

The possibility of two such basically opposed treatments of the work's protagonist should not astonish you.

Dreiser's novel is as broad and shoreless as the Hudson; it is as immense as life itself, and allows almost any point of view on itself. Like every "neutral" fact of nature itself, his novel is ninety-nine per cent statement of facts and one per cent attitude towards them. This epic of cosmic veracity and objectivity had to be assembled in a tragedy—and this was unthinkable without a world-attitude of direction and point.

The studio heads were disturbed by the question of guilt or innocence from another point of view: guilty would mean—unattractive. How could we allow a hero to seem unattractive? What would the box-office say?

But if he weren't guilty . . .

Because of the difficulties around "this damned question" *An American Tragedy* lay inactive for five years after its purchase by Paramount. It was approached—but no more than approached—even by the patriarch of films, David Wark Griffith, and Lubitsch, and many others.

With their customary cautious prudence the "heads," in our case too, dodged a decision. They suggested that we complete the script "as you feel it," and then, "we'll see. . . ."

From what I have already said, it must be perfectly evident that in our case, as distinct from previous handlings, the matter of a difference of opinion was not based on a decision as to some particular situation, but was far deeper, touching the question of the social treatment—wholly and fundamentally.

It is now interesting to trace how in this way a taken aim begins to determine the modeling of the separate parts and how this particular aim, with its demands, impregnates all problems of determining situations, of psychological deepening, and of the "purely formal" aspect of the construction as a whole—and how it pushes one toward completely new, "purely formal" methods which, when generalized, can be assembled into a new theoretical realization of the guiding discipline of cinematography as such.

It would be difficult to set forth here the entire situation of the novel: one can't do in five lines what Dreiser required two bulky volumes to do. We shall touch upon only the outer central point of the outer story side of the tragedy—the murder itself, though the tragedy, of course, is not in this, but in that tragic course pursued by Clyde, whom the social structure drives to murder. And fundamental attention is drawn to this in our script.

Clyde Griffiths, having seduced a young factory girl employed in a department managed by him, cannot help her obtain an illegal abortion. He sees himself forced to marry her. Yet this would ruin all his visions of a career, as it would upset his marriage with a wealthy girl who is in love with him.

Clyde's dilemma: he must either relinquish forever a career and social success, or—get rid of the girl.

Clyde's adventures in his collisions with American realities have by this time already molded his psychology, so that after a long internal struggle (not with moral principles, but with his own neurasthenic lack of character), he decides on the latter course.

He elaborately thinks out and prepares her murder—a boat is to be upset, apparently accidentally. All the details are thought out with the over-elaboration of the inexperienced criminal, which subsequently entangles the dilettante in a fatal mesh of incontrovertible evidence.

He sets out with the girl in a boat. In the boat the conflict between pity and aversion for the girl, between his character-less vacillation and his greedy snatching at a brilliant material future, reaches a climax. Half-consciously, half-unconsciously, in a wild inner panic, the boat is overturned. The girl drowns.

Abandoning her, Clyde saves himself as he had planned beforehand, and falls into the very net that he had woven for his extrication.

The boat episode is effected in the way that similar incidents take place: it is neither fully defined nor completely perceived—it is an undifferentiated tangle. Dreiser presents the matter so impartially that the further development of events is left formally, not to the logical course of the story, but to the processes of law.

It was imperative for us to sharpen the *actual* and *formal* innocence of Clyde within the very act of perpetrating the crime.

Only thus could we make sufficiently precise the "monstrous challenge" to a society whose mechanism brings a rather characterless youth to such a predicament and then, invoking morality and justice, seats him in the electric chair.

The sanctity of the *formal* principle in the codes of honor, morality, justice, and religion—is primary and fundamental in America. On this is based the endless game of advocacy in the courts, and the elaborate games among lawyers and parliamentarians. The essence of what is being formally argued is an altogether subsidiary matter.

Therefore the conviction of Clyde, though essentially deserved by his rôle in this affair (which concerns no one), in spite of proof of his *formal* innocence, would be regarded in America as something "monstrous": a judicial murder.

It was therefore imperative to develop the boat scene with indisputable precision as to Clyde's *formal* innocence. Yet without whitewashing Clyde in any way, nor removing any particle of blame.

We chose this treatment: Clyde wants to commit the murder, but he *cannot*. At the moment that requires decisive action, he falters. Simply from weakness of will.

However, before this inner "defeat," he excites in the girl Roberta such a feeling of alarm that, when he leans toward her, already defeated inwardly and ready "to take everything back," she recoils from him in horror. The boat, off-balance, rocks. When, in trying to support her, he accidentally knocks his camera against her face, she finally loses her head and in her terror stumbles, falls, and the boat overturns.

For greater emphasis we show her rising to the surface again. We even show Clyde trying to swim to her. But the machinery of crime has been set in motion and continues to its end, even against Clyde's will: Roberta cries out weakly, tries to retreat from him in her horror, and, not being able to swim, drowns.

Being a good swimmer Clyde reaches the shore and, coming to his senses, continues to act in accordance with the fatal plan he had prepared for the crime—from which he had deviated only for a moment in the boat.

The psychological and tragic deepening of the situation in this form is indubitable. Tragedy is heightened to an almost Grecian level of "blind Moira—fate" that, once conjured into existence, will not relax her hold on the one who summoned her. Heightened to a tragic, racking "causality" that, once it claims its rights, drives on to a logical conclusion whatever has been brought to life through the pitiless course of its processes.

In this crushing of a human being by a "blind" cosmic principle, by the inertia of the progress of laws over which he has no control, we have one of the basic premises of antique tragedy. It mirrors the passive dependence of the man of that day on the forces of nature. It is analogous to what Engels, in connection with another period, wrote of Calvin:

His predestination doctrine was the religious expression of the fact that in the commercial world of competition success or failure does not depend upon a man's activity or cleverness, but upon circumstances uncontrollable by him. It is not of him that willeth or of him that runneth, but of the mercy of unknown superior economic powers. . . .[10]

An ascent to the atavism of primitive cosmic conceptions, seen through an accidental situation of our day, is always a means of racking a dramatic scene to the heights of tragedy. But our treatment was not limited by this. It was pregnant with meaningful sharpnesses along the whole further course of the action.

In Dreiser's book, "for the sake of preserving the honor of the family," Clyde's rich uncle supplies him with the "apparatus" of defense.

The defense lawyers have no essential doubt that a crime was committed. None the less, they invent a "change of heart" experienced by Clyde under the influence of his love and pity for Roberta. Simply invented on the spur of the moment, this is pretty good.

But this is made far more evil when there *really* was such a change. When this change comes from quite different motives. When there really was no crime. When the lawyers are convinced that there was a crime. And with a downright lie, so near the truth and at the same time so far from it, they endeavor in this slanderous way to whitewash and save the accused.

And it becomes still more dramatically evil when, in the adjacent moment, the "ideology" of your treatment disturbs the proportions and, in another place, the epic indifference of Dreiser's narrative.

Almost the whole of the second volume is filled with the

trial of Clyde for the murder of Roberta and with the hunting down of Clyde to a conviction, to the electric chair.

As part of the background of the trial it is indicated that the true aim of the trial and prosecution of Clyde, however, has no relation to him whatsoever. This aim is solely to create the necessary popularity among the farming population of the state (Roberta was a farmer's daughter) for the prosecuting District Attorney Mason, so that he may win the necessary support for his nomination as judge.

The defense take on a case which they know to be hopeless ("at best ten years in the penitentiary") on the same plane of political struggle. Belonging to the opposite political camp, their primary aim is to exert their utmost strength in defeating the ambitious prosecutor. For one side, as for the other, Clyde is merely a means to an end.

Already a toy in the hands of "blind" Moira, fate, "causality" *à la greque*, Clyde also becomes a toy in the hands of the far from blind machinery of bourgeois justice, machinery employed as an instrument of political intrigue.

Thus is tragically expanded and generalized the fortunes of the particular case of Clyde Griffiths into a genuinely "American tragedy in general"—a characteristic story of a young American at the beginning of the twentieth century.

The whole tangle of design within the trial itself was almost entirely eliminated in the script's construction, and was replaced by the pre-election bidding, visible through the manipulated solemnity of the courtroom, being used as nothing more than a drill-ground for a political campaign.

This fundamental treatment of the murder determines the tragic deepening and the strengthened ideological sharpness of yet another part of the film and another figure: the mother.

Clyde's mother runs a mission. Her religion is a purblind fanaticism. She is so convinced of her absurd dogma that her figure inspires one's involuntary respect and grows almost monumental; one detects the glow of a martyr's aureole.

Even in spite of the fact that she is the first embodiment of the guilt of American society in relation to Clyde: her teach-

ings and principles, her aim towards Heaven rather than training her son for work were the initial premises for the ensuing
tragedy.

Dreiser shows her fighting to the last for her son's innocence,
working as a trial-reporter for a newspaper in order to be near
her son, touring America (like the mothers and sisters of the
Scottsboro boys) with lectures, to collect enough money to
appeal the verdict in Clyde's case. She definitely acquires the
self-sacrificial grandeur of a heroine. In Dreiser's work this
grandeur radiates sympathy for her moral and religious doc-
trines.

In our treatment Clyde, in his death-cell, confesses to his
mother (rather than to the Reverend McMillan, as in the novel)
that, though he did not kill Roberta, he had planned to do so.

His mother, for whom the word is the deed, and the thought
of sin equivalent to its execution, is stunned by his confession.
In a way exactly opposite to the grandeur of the mother in
Gorky's novel, this mother also becomes her son's betrayer.
When she goes to the Governor with a petition for her son's
life, she is startled by his direct question: "Do you yourself
believe in your son's innocence?" At this moment that is to
decide the fate of her son—she is silent.

The Christian sophism of an ideal unity (of deed and
thought) and a material unity (*de facto*), a parody of dialectics, leads to the final tragic denouement.

The petition is disregarded, and the dogma and dogmatism
of its bearer are alike discredited. The mother's fatal moment
of silence cannot even be washed away by her tears when she
takes leave forever of the son whom she has, with her own
hands, delivered into the jaws of the Christian Baal. The more
poignant these last scenes become in sadness, the more bitterly
do they lash at the ideology that brought this sadness.

In my opinion our treatment succeeded in ripping some of
the masks—though not all—from the monumental figure of
the mother.

And Dreiser was the first to salute all that had been brought
to his work by our treatment.

In our treatment the tragedy within the framework of the novel was consummated far earlier than in these final scenes. This end—the cell—the electric chair—the brightly polished spittoon (which I saw myself at Sing-Sing) at his feet—all this is no more than an end to one particular embodiment of that tragedy which continues to be enacted every hour and every minute in the United States, far outside the covers of novels.

The choice of such a "dry" and "hackneyed" formula of social treatment affords more than a sharpening of situations and a deepening revelation of images and characters.

Such a treatment profoundly acts also upon purely formal methods. It was thanks particularly to this and out of this that was conclusively formulated the concept of the "inner monologue" in cinema, an idea that I had carried in my mind for six years previously. Before the advent of sound made possible its practical realization.

As we have seen, one needed an extraordinarily differentiated sharpness of exposition of what was taking place within Clyde before that moment of the boat's "accident," and we realized that to develop an outer presentation of this would not solve our problem.

The whole arsenal of knitted brows, rolling eyes, hard breathing, contorted postures, stony faces, or close-ups of convulsively working hands, was inadequate for the expression of those subtleties of the inner struggle in all its nuances.

The camera had to penetrate "inside" Clyde. Aurally and visually must be set down the feverish *race of thoughts*, intermittently with the outer actuality—the boat, the girl sitting opposite him, his own actions. The form of the "inner monologue" was born.

These montage sketches were wonderful.

Even literature is almost powerless in this domain. It is limited either to the primitive rhetoric used by Dreiser to describe Clyde's inner murmurings * or to the worse pseudo-

---

* A sample: "You might save her. But again you might not! For see how she strikes about. She is stunned. She herself is unable to save herself and by her erratic terror, if you draw near her now, may bring

classic tirades of O'Neill's heroes in *Strange Interlude* who tell the audience, in "asides," what they are thinking, to supplement what they say to each other. In this the theater limps more than does orthodox literary prose.

Only the film-element commands a means for an adequate presentation of the whole course of thought through a disturbed mind.

Or, if literature can do it, it is only a literature that breaks through the limits of its orthodox enclosure. Literature's most brilliant achievement in this field has been the immortal "inner monologues" of Leopold Bloom in *Ulysses*. When Joyce and I met in Paris, he was intensely interested in my plans for the inner film-monologue, with a far broader scope than is afforded by literature.

Despite his almost total blindness, Joyce wished to see those parts of *Potemkin* and *October* that, with the expressive means of film culture, move along kindred lines.

The "inner monologue," as a literary method of abolishing the distinction between subject and object in stating the hero's re-experience in a crystallized form, is first observed by research-workers in literary experiment as early as 1887, in the work of Edouard Dujardin, pioneer on the "stream of consciousness," *Les lauriers sont coupés.*[12]

As theme, as world-perception, as "sensation," as description of an object, but not as method, one can find it, of course, even earlier. "Slipping" from the objective into the subjective, and back again, is a characteristic of the writings of the romantics—E. T. A. Hoffmann, Novalis, Gerard de Nerval.[13] But as a method of literary style, rather than as an inter-lacing in the story, or a form of literary description, we first find it used by Dujardin, as a specific method of exposition, as a specific method of construction; its absolute literary perfection is achieved by Joyce and Larbaud, thirty-one years later.

about your own death also. But you desire to live! And her living will make your life not worth while from now on. Rest but a moment— a fraction of a minute! Wait—wait—ignore the pity of that appeal. And then—then— But there! Behold. It is over. She is sinking now. You will never, never see her alive any more—ever."[11]

It finds full expression, however, only in the cinema.

For only the sound-film is capable of reconstructing all phases and all specifics of the course of thought.

What wonderful sketches those montage lists were!

Like thought, they would sometimes proceed with visual images. With sound. Synchronized or non-synchronized. Then as sounds. Formless. Or with sound-images: with objectively representational sounds . . .

Then suddenly, definite intellectually formulated words—as "intellectual" and dispassionate as pronounced words. With a black screen, a rushing imageless visuality.

Then in passionate disconnected speech. Nothing but nouns. Or nothing but verbs. Then interjections. With zigzags of aimless shapes, whirling along with these in synchronization.

Then racing visual images over complete silence.

Then linked with polyphonic sounds. Then polyphonic images. Then both at once.

Then interpolated into the outer course of action, then interpolating elements of the outer action into the inner monologue.

As if presenting inside the characters the inner play, the conflict of doubts, the explosions of passion, the voice of reason, rapidly or in slow-motion, marking the differing rhythms of one and the other and, at the same time, contrasting with the almost complete absence of outer action: a feverish inner debate behind the stony mask of the face.

How fascinating it is to listen to one's own train of thought, particularly in an excited state, in order to catch yourself, looking at and listening to your mind. How you talk "to yourself," as distinct from "out of yourself." The syntax of inner speech as distinct from outer speech. The quivering inner words that correspond with the visual images. Contrasts with outer circumstances. How they work reciprocally. . . .

To listen and to study, in order to understand structural laws and assemble them into an inner monologue construction of the utmost tension of the struggle of tragic re-experience. How fascinating!

And what scope for creative invention and observation. And

how obvious it becomes that the material of the sound-film is not dialogue.

The true material of the sound-film is, of course, the monologue.

And how unexpectedly, in its practical embodiment of an unforeseen, particular, concrete case to be expressed, it calls across to the theoretically long foreseen "last word" on montage form in general. That the montage form, as structure, is a reconstruction of the laws of the thought process.

Here the particularity of treatment, fertilized by a new and not a former formal method, leaves its limits and generalizes in new theoretical scope and in principle the theory of montage form as a whole.

(However, this does not by any means imply that the *thought* process as a *montage form* must necessarily have the process of thought as its *subject!*)

The notes for this 180° advance in sound film culture—languished in a suitcase at the hotel and were eventually buried Pompeii-like, beneath a mass of books, and while they waited for realization . . .

An American Tragedy was given to Josef von Sternberg to film, and he directly, literally, discarded everything on which our treatment had been based, and restored everything that we had discarded.

As for an "inner monologue," it didn't occur to him. . . .

Sternberg confined his attention to the studio's wishes—and filmed a straight detective case.

The old gray lion Dreiser battled for our "distortion" of his work, and brought Paramount, who had filmed a formally and outwardly correct version of his story, into court.

Two years later O'Neill's *Strange Interlude* was "adapted" for the screen, and we were given double and triple explanatory voices around the silent face of the hero, giving additional tonnage to the playwright's cuneiform dramaturgy. A bloody mockery of what might be achieved with correct montage principles—in the inner monologue!

Work of a similar type. Solution by treatment of the work in hand. Estimation by treatment. But of greatest significance, a constructively artistic and formally fruitful rôle for this "boring," "obligatory," "imposed" ideology and ideological restraint.

Not a schematic realization but a living organism of production—this is the fundamental work facing the direction collective of the Third Course at the State Cinema Institute. And with all methods we shall seek the themes for this work in the many-sided thematic ocean all around us.

[1932]

FILM LANGUAGE

> Creation is a concept which we writers use
> all too freely, though we hardly possess the
> right to do so. Creation is a degree of tension
> reached in the work of the memory at which
> the speed of its working draws from the re-
> serves of knowledge and impressions the most
> salient and characteristic facts, pictures, de-
> tails, and renders them into the most precise,
> vivid and intelligible words. Our young litera-
> ture cannot boast of possessing this quality.
> The stock of impressions, the sum of knowl-
> edge of our writers is not large, and there is
> no sign of any special anxiety to extend or
> enrich it.
>
> MAXIM GORKY [1]

GORKY'S SPEECH on the language of literature must be acknowledged—and considering the state of film language, we in films should feel called upon most of all to respond to it.

Film language, to a certain extent, is commonly associated with my works and my commentaries on them. And for this reason I shall take the initiative, by sniping at myself.

I do not propose to talk of the talking film—or, more exactly, of its talking portions. It speaks for itself. It even screams. And its quality, even before cinematically appraising it, contains so much poverty of a purely literary sort that its film claims may be put aside, for the moment.

In any case, it is not of this language I want to speak. (With my reputation as a literary stylist it would be laughable for me to do so.) I want to talk about the lack of culture in fundamentally cinematic diction that we may observe on the screen today.

In this matter of cinematic diction our cinema has accomplished a great deal for the world's film culture. And this accomplishment has been considerably deeper than mere fashion.

It is true that much that is specifically ours in the development of film expressiveness has been entrenched abroad no more deeply than as a passing fashion. Snippets of film, spliced together with nothing more reasonable than film cement, appear on the film-menu as "Russian cutting," "russischen Schnitt," very much in the way that restaurants use the term "Salade russe" for a certain dish of chopped and seasoned vegetables.

Fashion. Fashions pass—culture remains. Occasionally the culture behind the fashion is not noticed. Occasionally a cultural achievement is thrown out with the bath-water of fashion.

Negro sculpture, Polynesian masks, the Soviet manner of editing films have all been, for the West, merely exotica.

Of the extraction of general cultural values—of the mastery of principles—of the use of these accomplishments by the people who, in principle, move culture forward . . . but, of course, conversations on such themes are *so* passé.

What are fashions for? Tomorrow the magnates of mode—Patou, Worth, Mme. Lanvin, from their various yards, launch a new fashion. From somewhere in the Congo some "novelty" is brought—something carved from the ivory tusks of elephants by colonial slaves. Somewhere in the ravines of Mongolia a discovery is made—some patinized bronze sculptures created by the slaves of a long dead chieftain in a long dead epoch. All is well. It's all to the good. It all pays off.

The growth of culture? Who cares about that? It would seem that such relations to culture and to cultural achievements had long since been altered among us here by the October Revolution. One can't force one's way into museums on a free day. A worker with his wife and children stands in line to go through the Tretyakov Galley. One can't squeeze into the reading-rooms—too crowded. Readings, lectures—all overcrowded. Everywhere one finds attention, interest, thrift—an economical mastery of pre-revolutionary achievements.

Only in films is there a purely bourgeois absence of economy. Not only in budget. But thoughtlessness. And not only in schedule. But a total illiteracy and neglect of all that which in the Soviet period, with Soviet hands, on Soviet materials, and by Soviet principles, has been brought into and created in film culture.

Splendid: "We mastered the classics." (Splendid or not—this is a quite different question, and a debatable one, at that!) We are noting assets.

But this does not dismiss my question. Why must we therefore toss into oblivion all the expressive means and potentialities of cinematography, in which these classics have been flashed on the screen?

"We have mastered actors from the theater." (Better than classics.) Splendid!

There's another question, in Krylov's words: "Is auntie holding on to the tail?" Even if this auntie is such a fine actress as Tarasova! * Or is there a danger of film culture not profiting, but being harmed by the excellence of her acting?

As for the shots—"rubbish." And the composition of the shots—"you're just making trouble." And montage is obviously—"jumpy."

With the result, looking at the screen, that you feel a sweetish sensation, as if your eye had been lifted by sugar-tongs and oh-so-gently turned first to the right, then to the left, and finally whirled in a full circle, in order to push it back into a confused orbit. They say: "It's not our fault that you have such eyes." "That's not important to the spectator." "The spectator doesn't notice such things." "I don't hear the spectator screaming." Quite true. Nor does the reader scream. What is needed is not a scream, but a thundering shout. The authoritative shout of Gorky, to make literature notice where it is coming undone, how it is unraveling. The reader will not die of "trouble-making." He doesn't see how "rubbish" can bring him death. And he isn't pushed into his grave by a negligence towards literary language.

* Alla Tarasova, of the Moscow Art Theatre, had appeared in a film version of Ostrovsky's play *Thunderstorm* shortly before this essay was written.—EDITOR.

Nevertheless it has been considered necessary to unite behind literature to defend the reader. In what way does the vision of the reader become worse when he enters a film-theater?

In what way is his ear worse when, united with his eye, it is present at some audio-visual catastrophe, pretending to be audio-visual counterpoint?

Characteristically, films have become known exclusively as "sound-films." Must this mean that what you see while you're listening does not deserve your attention? But this is apparently so.

At this point some viper must be hissing: "Aha! the old devil is going to gallop about montage again."

Yes, montage.

For many film-makers montage and leftist excesses of formalism—are synonymous. Yet montage is not this at all.

For those who are able, montage is the most powerful compositional means of telling a story.

For those who do not know about composition, montage is a syntax for the correct construction of each particle of a film fragment.

And lastly, montage is simply an elementary rule of film-orthography for those who mistakenly put together pieces of a film as one would mix ready-made recipes for medicine, or pickle cucumbers, or preserve plums, or ferment apples and cranberries together.

Not only montage . . . I should like to see the expressive activity of man's hand freed from these lesser portions of his toilette, away from these supporting aggregates.

One encounters in films individually fine shots, but under these circumstances the value of the shot and its independent pictorial quality contradict one another. Out of tune with the montage idea and composition, they become esthetic toys and aims in themselves. The better the shots, the closer the film comes to a disconnected assemblage of lovely phrases, a shop-window full of pretty but unrelated products, or an album of post-card views.

I do not stand, by any means, for the "hegemony" of montage. The time has passed, when with the aims of pedagogy and training, it was necessary to perform tactical and polemical twists, in order to free montage broadly as an expressive means of cinema. But we must face the question of literacy in film-diction. And we must demand that the quality of montage, of film-syntax and film-speech not only never fall back behind the level of previous work, but that these go beyond and surpass their predecessors—this is why we should be deeply concerned in the struggle for a high quality of film culture.

It's easier for literature. In criticizing it, one can stand classics alongside it. Its heritage and achievement have undergone a great deal of investigation and study, down to the most delicate microscopic detail. The analysis of the compositional and imagery structure of Gogol's prose, made by the late Andrei Belyi, stands as a living reproach before any literary flippancy.[2]

And, by the way, Gogol has been brought also into films. Up till now burdened with formless film treatment, he has at last flashed with all the purity of montage form into the sound-film almost as if a Gogol text had been directly transposed into visual material.

Under the splendid visual poem of the Dnieper in the first reel of *Ivan* [1932], Dovzhenko, I believe, could successfully recite Gogol's description of the "wonderful Dnieper," from his *Terrible Revenge*.

The rhythm of the moving camera—floating by the shores. The cutting in of immobile expanses of water. In the alternation and shifting of these is the legerdemain and wizardry of Gogol's imagery and turns of speech. All this "neither stirs nor thunders." All this "you see and you do not know whether its immense breadth is moving or not . . . and it is enchanted, as if it had been poured glass," and so on. Here literature and cinema provide a model of the purest fusion and affinity. And this sequence also recalls—Rabelais. His poetic anticipation of the "imaging" of the theory of relationship is in his description of the isle *"en laquelle les chemins cheminent"*:

. . . and he further informed us that Seleucus [a Roman mathe-matician of the first century] had been of the opinion that the earth really revolved around the poles, rather than the heavens, although the contrary seems to us to be the truth—just as, when we are on the river Loire, the trees along the bank appear to be moving, whereas it is not the trees at all, but ourselves upon the boat, who are in motion.[3] *

We paused on this example, for it seems like the swan-song for the purity of film language on our contemporary screen. For *Ivan*, as well. Its latter reels at no point ascend to the per-fection of this fragment.

I hear someone object, saying that the "wonderful Dnieper" is a poem. The core of the matter is not in this. Based on this it would have to be assumed that the structure of prose, that of Zola for example, must certainly display "naturalistic chaos."

And yet, in the progress of a study being made of his work, I chanced to see pages of *Germinal* broken up into the strophes of an epic poem—they could be recited with no less severity than Homeric hexameters.

These pages contained the episodes, leading up to the sinister scene when, during the uprising before the arrival of the gen-darmes, the women destroy the shop of the usurer and rapist Maigrat. When the infuriated women, under the leadership of La Brûlé and Mouquette, mutilate the corpse of the hated shopkeeper, who had slipped in his escape over the roof and broken his skull on the curbstone. When the bleeding "trophy" is hoisted on a stick and carried at the head of a procession . . .

"What is it they have at the end of that stick?" asked Cécile, who had grown bold enough to look out.

Lucie and Jeanne declared that it must be a rabbit-skin.

* The reader curious to see more of the *haiku* mentioned in a previous essay, will encounter another "anticipation" of Dovzhenko's poetic sequence:

> The sail hoisted,
> The willows on the shore
> Have run away.
>
> JAKUSUI [4]

"No, no," murmured Madame Hennebeau, "they must have been pillaging a pork butcher's, it seems a remnant of a pig."

At this moment she shuddered and was silent. Madame Grégoire had nudged her with her knee. They both remained stupefied. The young ladies, who were very pale, asked no more questions, but with large eyes followed this red vision through the darkness.[5]

This scene, as well as the preceding scene, where this same crowd of women attempts to give a public flogging to Cécile, is a stylized transplanting, obviously, of an episode that struck Zola in the annals of the French Revolution.

The incident of Cécile's encounter with the women reproduces the well-known episode of the attack on Théroigne de Méricourt.

The second scene involuntarily forces a recollection of a less known and less popular episode recorded in the materials gathered by Mercier. When the crowd's hatred of the Princess de Lamballe, Marie Antoinette's closest intimate, burst at the gates of the prison of La Force, and the people's wrath obtained satisfaction from her, one of the participants *"lui coupa la partie virginale et s'en fit des moustaches."* [6]

A pointing finger, indicating the consciously used earlier source for these stylized adaptations, that could not possibly have been accidentally selected, is provided by the title itself, chosen from the calendar of this earlier epoch—*Germinal.* If this appeal for temperament and pathos to a previous pathetic epoch was made largely in the explicitly rhythmic clarity of form of his literary diction, this expanded treatment of little episodes is not amongst his most fortunate passages.

With an analogous image our film *October* also suffered in the sequence of the July uprising. For we had no intention to give, in the authentic incident of the murder of a Bolshevik worker by a brutalized bourgeois, any "note" of the Paris Commune's aftermath. Seen in context, the scene of the lady stabbing the worker with her parasol is completely apart in spirit from the general feeling of the pre-October days.

This is, by the way, an observation that may not be unhelpful. As literary heirs, we frequently make use of the cultural images and language of previous epochs. This naturally determines a large part of our works' color. And it is important to note failures in the use of such decided models.

To return anew to the question of purity of film form, I can easily counter the usual objection that the craft of film diction and film expressiveness is very young as yet, and has no models for a classic tradition. It is even said that I find too much fault with the models of film form at our disposal, and manage with literary analogies alone. Many even consider it dubious that this "half-art" (and you would be surprised to know how many, in and out of films, still refer to the cinema in this way) deserves such a broad frame of reference.

Forgive me. But this is the way things are.

And yet our film language, though lacking its classics, possessed a great severity of form and film diction. On a certain level our cinema has known such a severe responsibility for each shot, admitting it into a montage sequence with as much care as a line of poetry is admitted into a poem, or each musical atom is admitted into the movement of a fugue.

There are plenty of examples that may be brought in from the practice of our silent cinematography. Not having the time to analyze other specimens for this present purpose, I may be allowed to bring here a sample analysis from one of my own works. It is taken from material for the conclusion of my book *Direction* * (Part II—*Mise-en-cadre*) and concerns *Potemkin*. In order to show the compositional dependence between the plastic side of each of the shots, an example has been intentionally chosen not from a climax, but from an almost accidentally hit-upon place: fourteen successive pieces from the scene that precedes the fusillade on the Odessa steps. The scene where the "good people of Odessa" (so the sailors of the

* Left unfinished at the author's death, the completed sections of this definitive work may be prepared for publication by his literary executors. —EDITOR.

Potemkin addressed the population of Odessa) send yawls with provisions to the side of the mutinous battleship.

This sending of greetings is constructed on a distinct cross-cutting of two themes.

1. The yawls speeding towards the battleship.
2. The people of Odessa watching and waving.

At the end the two themes are merged. The composition is basically in two planes: depth and foreground. Alternately, the themes take a dominant position, advancing to the fore-ground, and thrusting each other by turns to the background.

The composition is built (1) on a plastic interaction of both these planes (within the frame) and (2) on a shifting of line and form in each of these planes from frame to frame (by montage). In the second case the compositional play is formed from the interaction of plastic impressions of the preceding shot in collision or interaction with the following shot. (Here the analysis is of the purely spatial and linear directions: the rhythmic and temporal relations will be discussed elsewhere.)

The movement of the composition takes the following course:

I. The yawls in movement. A smooth, even movement, parallel with the horizontals of the frame. The whole field of vision is filled with theme 1. There is a play of small verti-cal sails.

II. An intensified movement of the yawls of theme 1 (the entrance of theme 2 contributes to this). Theme 2 comes to the foreground with the severe rhythm of the vertical motion-less columns. The vertical lines foreshadow the plastic dis-tribution of the coming figures (in IV, V, etc.). Interplay of the horizontal wakes and the vertical lines of both sails and columns. The yawl theme is thrust back in depth. At the bot-tom of the frame appears the plastic theme of the arch.

III. The plastic theme of the arch expands into the entire frame. The play is effected by the shift in the frame's con-tent—from vertical lines to the structure of the arch. The theme of verticals is maintained in the movement of the people—small figures moving away from the camera. The yawl theme is thrust completely into the background.

IV. The plastic theme of the arch finally moves into the foreground. The arc-formation is transposed to a contrary solution: the contours of a group are sketched, forming a circle (the parasol emphasizes the composition). This same transition in a contrary direction also takes place within a vertical construction: the backs of the small figures moving towards the depth are replaced by large standing figures, photographed frontally. The theme of the yawls in movement is maintained by reflection, in the expression of their eyes and in their movement in a horizontal direction.

V. In the foreground is a common compositional variant: an even number of persons is replaced by an uneven number. Two replaced by three. This "golden rule" in shifting the *mise-en-scène* is supported by a tradition that can be traced back to the principles of Chinese painting as well as to the practice of the *Commedia dell'arte*. (The directions of the glances also cross.) The arch motive is again bent, this time in a contrary curve. Repeating and supporting it is a new parallel arch-motif in the background: a balustrade—the yawl theme in movement. The eyes gaze across the whole width of the frame in a horizontal direction.

VI. Pieces I to V give a transition from the yawl theme to the watcher's theme, developed in five montage pieces. The interval from V to VI gives a sharp returning transition from the watchers to the yawls. Strictly following the content, the composition sharply transforms each of the elements in an opposite direction. The line of the balustrade is brought swiftly into the foreground, now as the line of the boat's gunwale. This is doubled by the adjacent line of the water's surface. The basic compositional elements are the same, but counterposed in treatment. V is static; VI is drawn by the dynamics of the boat in motion. The vertical division into "three" is maintained in both frames. The central element is texturally similar (the woman's blouse, and the canvas of the sail). The elements at the sides are in sharp contrast: the dark shapes of the men beside the woman, and the white spaces beside the central sail. The vertical distribution is also contrasted: three figures cut by the bottom horizontal are transformed into a vertical sail, cut by the upper horizontal of the frame. A new theme appears *in the background*—the side of the battleship, cut *at the top* (in preparation for piece VII).

VII. A sharply new thematic turn. A background theme— the battleship—is brought forward into the foreground (the thematic jump from V to VI serves somewhat as an anticipation of the jump from VI to VII). The viewpoint is turned 180°: shooting from the battleship towards the sea—reversing VI. This time the side of the battleship in the *foreground* is also cut—but by the *lower* horizontal of the frame. In the depth is the sail theme, developed in verticals. The verticals of the sailors. The static gun-barrel continues the line of the boat's movement in the preceding shot. The side of the battleship would seem to be an arch, bent into an almost straight line.

VIII. A repetition of IV with heightened intensity. The horizontal play of eyes is transformed into vertically waving hands. The vertical theme has moved from the depth into the foreground, repeating the thematic transfer to the watchers.

IX. Two faces, closer. Speaking generally, this is an unfortunate combination with the preceding shot. It would have been better to have brought between VIII and IX a shot of three faces, to have repeated V with a heightened intensity. This would have produced a 2:3:2 structure. Moreover, the repetition of the familiar groups of IV and V, ending with the new IX, would have sharpened the impression of the last shot. This error is somewhat remedied by the slight change in plane, coming closer to the figures.

X. The two faces change to a single, closer face. The arm is thrown very energetically up and out of the frame. A correct alternation of faces (if the suggested correction were made between VIII and IX)—2:3:2:1. A second pair of shots with a correct enlargement of the dimensions in relation to the first pair (a proper repetition with a qualitative variation). The line of odd numbers differs both in quantity and quality (differing in the dimensions of the faces and differing in their quantities, while retaining the common direction of the odd numbers).

XI. A new sharp thematic turn. A jump, repeating that of V-VI, with new intensity. The vertical *up-throw* of the arm in the preceding shot is echoed by the vertical *sail*. In this the vertical of this sail rushes past in a horizontal line. A repetition of the theme of VI in greater intensity. And a repetition of the composition of II with this difference, that the horizontal theme of the moving yawls and the verticals of the motionless columns are here molded into a single horizontal movement of the *vertical* sail. The composition repeats the *sequence's theme* of an identity between the yawls and the people on the shore (before moving on to the concluding theme of this reel, the fusion of the yawls and the battleship).

XII. The sail of XI is broken up into a multitude of vertical sails, scudding along horizontally (a repetition of piece I with increased intensity). The little sails move in a direction opposite to that of the large single sail.

XIII. Having been broken up into small sails, the large sail is newly re-assembled, but now not as a sail, but as the flag flying over the *Potemkin*. There is a new quality in this shot, for it is both static and mobile,—the mast being vertical and motionless, while the flag flutters in the wind. Formally, piece XIII repeats XI. But the change from sail to banner translates a principle of plastic unification to an ideological-thematic unification. This is no longer a vertical, a plastic union of separate elements of composition,—*this is a revolutionary banner, uniting battleship, yawls and shore.*

XIV. From here we have a natural return from the flag to the battleship. XIV repeats VII, with a lift in intensity. This shot introduces a new compositional group of *interrelationships between the yawls and the battleship*, distinguished from the first group, *yawls and shore*. The first group expressed the theme: "the yawls carry greetings and gifts from the shore to the battleship." This second group will express *the fraternization of yawls and battleship.*

The compositional dividing-point, and simultaneously the ideological uniter of both compositional groups, is the mast with the revolutionary banner.

Piece VII, repeated by the first piece of the second group, XIV, appears as a sort of foreshadowing of the second group and as an element linking the two groups together, as though the latter group had sent out a "patrol" into the territory of the first group. In the second group this rôle will be played by shots of waving figures, cut into scenes of the fraternization between yawls and battleship.

It should not be thought that the filming and montage of these pieces were done according to these calculations, drawn up *a priori*. Of course not. But the assembly and distribution of these pieces on the cutting table was already clearly dictated by the compositional demands of the film form. These demands dictated the selection of these particular pieces from all those available. These demands also established the regularity of the alternation of these pieces. Actually, these pieces, regarded only for their plot and story aspects, could be rearranged in any combination. But the compositional movement through them would hardly prove in that case quite so regular in construction.

One cannot therefore complain of the complexity of this analysis. In comparison with analyses of literary and musical forms my analysis is still quite descriptive and easy.

Setting aside for the present the question of rhythmic examination, in our analysis we have also analyzed the alternations of sound and word combinations.

An analysis of the very lenses employed in filming these shots, and their use along with camera-angles and lighting, all deriving from the demands of the style and the character of the film's content, would serve as an exact analogy to an analysis of the expressiveness of phrases and words and their phonetic indications in a literary work.

Of course the spectator, least of all, is able to verify with calipers the conformity to rule of the successive shot compositions within the montage. But in his perception of a fully realized montage composition the same elements are contributed that stylistically distinguish a page of cultured prose from the pages of "Count Amori," Verbitzkaya or Breshko-Breshkovsky.*

At present Soviet cinematography is historically correct in entering the campaign for the story. Along this path are still many difficulties, many risks of falsely understanding the principles of story-telling. Of these the most terrible is the neglect of those possibilities given us now and again to liberate from the old traditions of the story:

The possibility of principally and newly re-examining the foundations and problems of the film-story.

And to go ahead in a cinematographically progressive movement, not "back to the story," but "to the story ahead of us." There is not yet clear artistic orientation on these ways, although separate positive influences are already becoming visible.

In one way or another we approach the moment when we shall master clearly the realized principles of Soviet story films, and we must meet that moment with all the weapons of faultless purity and culture of film language and speech.

Our great masters of literature from Pushkin and Gogol to Mayakovsky and Gorky are valued by us not only as story-telling masters. We value in them the culture of masters of speech and word.

It is time with all sharpness to pose the problem of the culture of film language. It is important that all the film-workers speak out in this cause. And before all else, in the language of the montage and shots of their own films.

[1934]

* Approximate English and American equivalents for these popular Russian writers of the early twentieth century: Elinor Glyn, Dorothy Dix, Rupert Hughes.—EDITOR.

FILM FORM: NEW PROBLEMS

EVEN THAT old veteran Heraclitus observed that no man can bathe twice in the same river. Similarly no esthetic can flourish on one and the same set of principles at two different stages in its development. Especially when the particular esthetic concerned happens to relate to the most mobile of the arts, and when the division between the epochs is the succession of two Five Year periods in the mightiest and most notable job of construction in the world—the job of building the first Socialist state and society in history. From which it is obvious that our subject is here the esthetic of film, and in particular the esthetic of film in the Soviet land.

During the last few years a great upheaval has taken place in the Soviet cinema. This upheaval is, first and foremost, ideological and thematic. The peak of achievement in the blossoming of the silent cinema was attained under the broadly expansive slogan of mass, the "mass-hero" and methods of cinematographic portrayal directly derivative therefrom, rejecting narrowly dramaturgical conceptions in favor of epos and lyrism, with "type" and episodic protagonists in place of individual heroes and the consequently inevitable principle of montage as the guiding principle of film expressiveness. But during the last few years—the first years, that is, of the Soviet sound-cinema—the guiding principles have changed.

From the former all-pervading mass imagery of movement and experiences of the masses, there begin at this stage to stand out individual hero-characters. Their appearance is accompanied by a structural change in those works where they appear. The former epical quality and its characteristic giant scale begin to contract into constructions closer to dramaturgy in the narrow sense of the word, to a dramaturgy, in fact, of more traditional stamp and much closer to the foreign cinema than those films that once declared war to the death against its very principles and methods. The best films of the most recent period (*Chapayev*, for example) have none the less succeeded in partially preserving the epical quality of the first period of Soviet cinema development, with larger and happier results. But the majority of films have almost completely lost that luggage, comprised of principle and form, which determined in its day the specific and characteristic quality of face of the Soviet cinema, a quality not divorced from the newness and unusualness it bore as reflection of the unusual and never-heretofore-existing land of the Soviets, its strivings, aims, ideals and struggles.

To many it seems that the progressive development of the Soviet cinema has stopped. They speak of retrogression. This is, of course, wrong. And one important circumstance is underestimated by the fervent partisans of the old silent Soviet cinema, who now gaze bewilderedly as there appears Soviet film after film which in so many respects is formally similar to the foreign cinema. If in many cases there must indeed be observed the dulling of that formal brilliance to which the foreign friends of our films had become accustomed, this is the consequence of the fact that our cinematography, in its present stage, is entirely absorbed in another sphere of investigation and deepening. A measure of suspension in the further development of the forms and means of film expressiveness has appeared as an inevitable consequence of the diversion of investigation into another direction, a diversion recently and still obtaining: into the direction of deepening and broadening the thematic and ideological formulation of questions and problems within the content of the film. It is not accidental that precisely at this period, for the first time in our cinematography, there begin to appear the first finished images of personalities, not just of any personalities, but of the finest personalities: the leading figures of leading Communists and Bolsheviks. Just as from the revolutionary movement of the masses emerged the sole revolutionary party, that of the Bolsheviks, which heads the unconscious elements of revolution and leads them towards conscious revolutionary aims, so the film images of the leading men of our times begin during the present period to crystallize out of the general-revolutionary mass-quality of the earlier type of film. And the clarity of the Communist slogan rings more definitely, replacing the general-revolutionary slogan.

The Soviet cinema is now passing through a new phase—a phase of yet more distinct Bolshevization, a phase of yet more pointed ideological and essential militant sharpness. A phase historically logical, natural and rich in fertilizing possibilities for the cinema, as most notable of arts.

This new tendency is no surprise, but a logical stage of growth, rooted in the very core of the preceding stage. Thus one who is perhaps the most devoted partisan of the mass-epical style in cinema, one whose name has always been linked to the "mass"-cinema—the author of these lines—is subject to precisely this same process in his penultimate film—*Old and New*, where Marfa Lapkina appears already as an exceptional individual protagonist of the action.

The task, however, is to make this new stage sufficiently synthetic. To ensure that in its march towards new conquests of ideological depths, it not only does not lose the perfection of the achievements already attained, but advances them ever forward toward new and as yet unrealized qualities and means of expression. To raise form once more to the level of ideological content.

Being engaged at the moment on the practical solution of these problems in the new film *Bezhin Meadow*, only just begun, I should like to set out here a series of cursory observations on the question of the problem of form in general.

The problem of form, equally with the problem of content at the present stage, is undergoing a period of most serious deepening of principle. The lines which follow must serve to show the direction in which this problem is moving and the extent to which the new trend of thought in this sphere is closely linked in evolution to the extreme discoveries on this path made during the peak period of our silent cinema.

Let us start at the last points reached by the theoretical researches of the stage of Soviet cinema above referred to (1924-1929).

It is clear and undoubted that the *ne plus ultra* of those paths was the theory of the "intellectual cinema."

This theory set before it the task of "restoring emotional fullness to the intellectual process." This theory engrossed itself as follows, in transmuting to screen form the abstract concept, the course and halt of concepts and ideas—without intermediary. Without recourse to story, or invented plot, in fact directly—by means of the image-composed elements as filmed. This theory was a broad, perhaps even a too broad, generalization of a series of possibilities of expression placed at our disposal by the methods of montage and its combinations. The theory of intellectual cinema represented, as it were, a limit, the *reductio ad paradox* of that hypertrophy of the montage concept with which film esthetics were permeated during the emergence of Soviet silent cinematography as a whole and my own work in particular.

Recalling the "establishment of the abstracted concept" as a framework for the possible products of the intellectual cinema, as the basic foundation of its film canvasses; and acknowledging that the movement forward of the Soviet cinema is now following other aims, namely, the demonstration of such conceptual postulates by agency of concrete actions and living persons as we have noted above, let us see what can and must be the further fate of the ideas expressed at that time.

Is it then necessary to jettison all the colossal theoretical and creative material, in the turmoil of which was born the conception of the intellectual cinema? Has it proved only a curious and exciting paradox, a *fata morgana* of unrealized compositional possibilities? Or has its paradoxicality proved to lie not in its essence, but in the sphere of its application, so that now, after examining some of its principles, it may emerge that, in new guise, with new usage and new application, the postulates then expressed have played and may still continue to play a highly positive part in the theoretical grasping and understanding and mastering of the mysteries of the cinema?

The reader, doubtless, has already guessed that this is precisely how we incline to consider the situation, and all that follows will serve to demonstrate, perhaps only in broad outline, exactly what we understand by it, and use now as a working basis, and which, as a working hypothesis in questions of the culture of film form and composition, is fortified more and more into a complete logical conception of everyday practice.

I should like to begin with the following consideration:

It is exceedingly curious that certain theories and points of view which in a given historical epoch represent an expression of scientific knowledge, in a succeeding epoch decline as science, but continue to exist as possible and admissible not in the line of science but in the line of art and imagery.

If we take mythology, we find that at a given stage mythology is nothing else than a complex of current knowledge about phenomena, chiefly related in imagery and poetic language. All these mythological figures, which at the best we now regard as the materials of allegory, at some stage represented an image-compilation of knowledge of the cosmos. Later, science moved on from imagery narratives to concepts, and the store of former personified-mythological nature-symbols continued to survive as a series of pictorial images, a series of literary, lyrical and other metaphors. At last they become exhausted even in this capacity and vanish into the archives. Consider even contemporary poetry, and compare it with the poetry of the eighteenth century.

Another example: take such a postulate as the a-priority of the idea, spoken of by Hegel in relation to the creation of the world. At a certain stage this was the summit of philosophical knowledge. Later, the summit was overthrown. Marx turns this postulate head over heels in the question of the understanding of real actuality. However, if we consider our works of art, we do in fact have a condition that almost looks like the Hegelian formula, because the idea-satiation of the author, his subjection to prejudice by the idea, must determine actually the whole course of the art-work, and if every element of the art-work does not represent an embodiment of the initial idea, we shall never have as result an art-work realized to its utmost fullness. It is of course understood that the artist's idea itself is in no way spontaneous or self-engendered, but is a socially reflected mirror-image, a reflection of social reality. But from the moment of formation within him of the view-point and idea, that idea appears as determining all the actual and material structure of his creation, the whole "world" of his creation.

Suppose we take another field, Lavater's "Physiognomy." This in its day was regarded as an objective scientific system. But physiognomy is now no science. Lavater was already laughed at by Hegel, though Goethe, for example, still collaborated with Lavater, if anonymously. (To Goethe must be assigned the authorship of, for example, a physiognomical study devoted to the head of Brutus.) We do not attribute to physiognomy any objective scientific value whatsoever, but the moment we require, in course of the all-sided representation of character denoting some type, the external characterization of a countenance, we immediately start using faces in exactly the same way as Lavater did. We do so because in such a case it is important to us to create first and foremost an impression, the subjective impression of an observer, not the objective co-ordination of sign and essence actually composing character. In other words, the viewpoint that Lavater thought scientific is being "exhausted" by us in the arts, where it is needed in the line of imagery.

What is the purpose of examining all this? Analogous situations occur sometimes among the methods of the arts, and sometimes it occurs that the characteristics which represent logic in the matter of construction of form are mistaken for elements of content. Logic of this kind is, as a method, as a principle of construction, fully permissible, but it becomes a nightmare if this same method, this logic of construction, is regarded simultaneously as an exhaustive content.

You will perceive already whither the matter is tending, but I wish to cite one more example, from literature. The question relates now to one of the most popular of all literary genres—the detective story.

What the detective story represents, of which social formations and tendencies it is the expression, this we all know. On this subject Gorky recently spoke sufficiently at the Congress of Writers. But of interest is the origin of some of the characteristics of the genre, the sources from which derives the material that has gone towards creation of the ideal vessel of the detective story form in embodying certain aspects of bourgeois ideology.

It appears that the detective novel counts among its forerunners, aiding it to reach full bloom at the beginning of the nineteenth century, James Fenimore Cooper—the novelist of the North American Indians. From the ideological point of view, this type of novel, exalting the deeds of the colonizers, follows entirely the same current as the detective novel in serving as one of the most pointed forms of expression of private-property ideology. To this testified Balzac, Hugo, Eugène Sue, who produced a good deal in this literary-composition model from which later was elaborated the regular detective novel.

Recounting in their letters and diaries the inspirational images which guided them in their story constructions of flight and chase (*Les Miserables, Vautrin, Le Juif errant*), they all write that the prototype that attracted them was the dark forest background of James Fenimore Cooper, and that they had wished to transplant this dark forest and the action within it from the virgin backwoods of America to the labyrinth of the alleys and byways of Paris. The accumulation of clues derives from the methods of the "Pathfinders" whom Cooper portrayed in his works.

Thus the image "dark forest" and the technique of the "pathfinder" from Cooper's works serve the great novelists such as Balzac and Hugo as a sort of initial metaphor for their intrigue of detection and adventure constructions within the maze of Paris. They contribute also to formalizing as a genre those ideological tendencies which lay at the base of the detective novel. Thus is created a whole independent type of story construction. But, parallel with this use of the "heritage" of Cooper, we see yet another sort: the type of literal transplantation. Then we have indeed nonsense and nightmare. Paul Féval has written a novel in which redskins do their stuff in Paris and a scene occurs where three Indians scalp a victim in a cab!

I cite this example in order to return once more to the intellectual cinema. The specific quality of the intellectual cinema was proclaimed to be the content of the film. The trend of thoughts and the movement of thoughts were represented as the exhaustive basis of everything that transpired in the film, i.e., a substitute for the story. Along this line—exhaustive replacement of content—it does not justify itself. And in sequel perhaps to the realization of this, the intellectual cinema has speedily grown a new conception of a theoretical kind: the intellectual cinema has acquired a little successor in the theory of the "inner monologue."

The theory of the inner monologue warmed to some extent the ascetic abstraction of the flow of concepts, by transposing the problem into the more story-ish line of portraying the hero's emotions. During the discussions on the subject of the inner monologue, there was made none the less a tiny reservation, to the effect that this inner monologue could be used to construct things and not only for picturing an inner monologue.* Just a tiny hook hanging there in parentheses, but on it hung the crux of the whole affair. These parentheses must be opened immediately. And herein lies the principal matter with which I wish to deal.

* See "A Course in Treatment," page 106.

Which is—the syntax of inner speech as opposed to that of uttered speech. Inner speech, the flow and sequence of thinking unformulated into the logical constructions in which uttered, formulated thoughts are expressed, has a special structure of its own. This structure is based on a quite distinct series of laws. What is remarkable therein, and why I am discussing it, is that the laws of construction of inner speech turn out to be precisely those *laws which lie at the foundation of the whole variety of laws governing the construction of the form and composition of art-works.* And there is not one formal method that does not prove the spit and image of one or another law governing the construction of inner speech, as distinct from the logic of uttered speech. It could not be otherwise.

We know that at the basis of the creation of form lie sensual and imagist thought processes.* Inner speech is precisely at the stage of image-sensual structure, not yet having attained that logical formulation with which speech clothes itself before stepping out into the open. It is noteworthy that, just as logic obeys a whole series of laws in its constructions, so, equally, this inner speech, this sensual thinking, is subject to no less clear-cut laws and structural peculiarities. These are known and, in the light of the considerations here set out, represent an inexhaustible storehouse, as it were, of laws for the construction of form, the study and analysis of which have immense importance in the task of mastering the "mysteries" of the technique of form.

For the first time we are placed in possession of a firm storehouse of postulates, bearing on what happens to the initial thesis of the theme when it is translated into a chain of sensory images. The field for study in this direction is colossal. The

---

* This thesis is not offered as either new or original. Hegel and Plekhanov gave equal attention to sensual thought processes. What appears to be new here is a constructive distinction of the laws of this sensual thinking, for these classics do not particularize on this aspect, while no operative application of this thesis can be made to artistic practice and craft training without this distinction. The following development of these considerations, materials, and analyses, has set itself this particular operative aim of practical use.

point is that the forms of sensual, pre-logical thinking, which are preserved in the shape of inner speech among the peoples who have reached an adequate level of social and cultural development, at the same time also represent in mankind at the dawn of cultural development norms of conduct in general, i.e., the laws according to which flow the processes of sensual thought are equivalent for them to a "habit logic" of the future. In accordance with these laws they construct norms of behavior, ceremonials, customs, speech, expressions, etc., and, if we turn to the immeasurable treasury of folklore, of out-lived and still living norms and forms of behavior preserved by societies still at the dawn of their development, we find that, what for them has been or still is a norm of behavior and custom-wisdom, turns out to be at the same time precisely what we employ as "artistic methods" and "technique of embodiment" in our art-works. I have no space to discuss in detail the question of the early forms of thought process. I have no opportunity here to picture for you its basic specific characteristics, which are a reflection of the exact form of the early social organization of the communal structures. This is no time to pursue the manner in which, from these general postulates, are worked out the separate characteristic marks and forms of the construction of representations. I will limit myself to quoting two or three instances exemplifying this principle, that one or other given moment in the practice of form-creation is at the same time a moment of custom-practice from the stage of development at which representations are still constructed in accordance with the laws of sensual thinking. I emphasize here, however, that such construction is not of course in any sense exclusive. On the contrary, from the very earliest period there obtains simultaneously a flow of practical and logical experiences, deriving from practical labor processes; a flow that gradually increases on the basis of them, discarding these earlier forms of thinking and embracing gradually all the spheres not only of labor, but also of other intellectual activities, abandoning the earlier forms to the sphere of sensual manifestations.

Consider, for example, that most popular of artistic methods, the so-called *pars pro toto*. The power of its effectiveness is known to everyone. The pince-nez of the surgeon in *Potemkin* are firmly embedded in the memory of anyone who saw the film. The method consisted in substituting the whole (the surgeon) by a part (the pince-nez), which played his rôle, and, it so happened, played it much more sensual-intensively than it could have been played even by the re-appearance of the surgeon. It so happens that this method is the most typical example of a thinking form from the arsenal of early thought processes. At that stage we were still without the unity of the whole and the part as we now understand it. At that stage of non-differentiated thinking the part *is* at one and the same time also the whole. There is no unity of part and whole, but instead obtains an objective identity in representation of whole and part. It is immaterial whether it be part or whole—it plays invariably the rôle of aggregate and whole. This takes place not only in the simplest practical fields and actions, but immediately appears as soon as you emerge from the limits of the simplest "objective" practice. Thus, for example, if you receive an ornament made of a bear's tooth, it signifies that the whole bear has been given to you, or, what in these conditions signifies the same thing,* the strength of the bear as a whole. In the conditions of modern practice such a proceeding would be absurd. No one, having received a button off a suit, would imagine himself to be dressed in the complete suit. But as soon even as we move over into the sphere in which sensual and image constructions play the decisive rôle, into the sphere of artistic constructions, the same *pars pro toto* begins immediately to play a tremendous part for us as well. The pince-nez, taking the place of a whole surgeon, not only completely fills his rôle and place, but does so with a huge sensual-emotional increase in the intensity of the impression, to an extent considerably greater than could have been obtained by the re-appearance of the surgeon-character himself.

* A differentiated concept of "strength" outside the concrete specific bearer of that strength equally does not exist at this stage.

As you perceive, for the purposes of a sensual artistic impression, we have used, as a compositional method, one of those laws of early thinking which, at appropriate stages, appear as the norms and practice of everyday behavior. We made use of a construction of a sensual thinking type, and as a result, instead of a "logico-informative" effect, we receive from the construction actually an emotional sensual effect. We do not register the fact that the surgeon has drowned, we emotionally react to the fact through a definite compositional presentation of this fact.

It is important to note here that what we have analyzed in respect to the use of the close-up, in our example of the surgeon's pince-nez, is not a method characteristic solely of the cinema alone and specific to it. It equally has a methodological place and is employed in, for example, literature. "*Pars pro toto*" in the field of literary forms is what is known to us under the term synecdoche.

Let us indeed recall the definition of the two kinds of synecdoche. The first kind: this kind consists in that one receives *a presentation of the part instead of the whole*. This in turn has a series of sorts:

1. Singular instead of plural. ("The Son of Albion reaching for freedom" instead of "The sons of, etc.")

2. Collective instead of composition of the clan. ("Mexico enslaved by Spain" instead of "The Mexicans enslaved.")

3. Part instead of whole. ("Under the master's eye.")

4. Definite instead of indefinite. ("A hundred times we've said . . .")

5. Species instead of genus.

The second series of synecdoches consists in *the whole instead of the part*. But, as you perceive, both series and all their several subdivisions are subject to one and the same basic condition. Which condition is: the identity of the part and the whole and hence the "equivalence," the equal significance in replacing one by the other.

No less striking examples of the same occur in paintings

and drawings, where two color spots and a flowing curve give a complete sensual replacement of the whole object.

What is of interest here is not this list itself, but the fact that is confirmed by the list. Namely, that we are dealing here not with specific methods, peculiar to this or that art-medium, but first and foremost with a specific course and condition of embodied thinking—with sensual thinking, for which a given structure is a law. In this special, synecdochic, use of the "close-up," in the color-spot and curve, we have but particular instances of the operation of this law of *pars pro toto*, characteristic of sensual thinking, dependent upon whatever art-medium in which it happens to be functioning for its purpose of embodiment of the basic creative scheme.

Another example. We are well aware that every embodiment must be in strict artistic accord with the story situation being embodied. We know that this concerns costume, setting, accompanying music, light, color. We know that this accord concerns not only the demands made by naturalistic conviction, but also, and perhaps to a greater degree, the demands of sustaining the emotional expression. If a dramatist's scene "sounds" a certain key, then all elements of its embodiment must sound the same key. There is an unsurpassed classical example of this in *King Lear*, whose inner tempest echoes the tempest on the moor, raging round him on the stage. We can also find examples of a reverse construction—for purposes of contrast: say that a maximum raging of passion is to be resolved by an intentional static and immobile quality. Here, too, all elements of the embodiment would be realized with just as strict a sustaining and accord with the theme, though in this case with opposite indications, as well.

Such a demand also spreads over into the shot and the montage, whose means must likewise compositionally echo and respond to the basic compositional key for the treatment of the entire work and of each scene in it.*

---

* The considerable skill achieved in this field by our silent cinema fell perceptibly from the moment of transition to sound-film—for evidence, see most of our sound-films.

It appears that this element, sufficiently recognized and universal in art, can be found on a certain level of development in similar inevitable and obligatory modes of behavior in life. Here is an example from Polynesian practice—a practice that is preserved in customs today with little change. When any Polynesian woman is in confinement, there is a peremptory rule that all gates in the settlement must be opened, all doors thrown open, that everyone (including men, as well) is to remove any sashes, aprons, headbands, that all tied knots are to be untied, and so forth; that is, all circumstances, all concomitant details, must be arranged in a character exactly corresponding to the basic theme of what is occurring: everything must be opened, untied, to give maximum ease to the appearance in the world of the new child!

Let us now turn to another medium. Let us take a case where the material of the form-creation turns out to be the artist himself. This also confirms the truth of our thesis. Even more: in this instance the structure of the finished composition not only reproduces, as it were, a reprint of the structure of the laws along which flow sensual thought-processes. In this instance the circumstance itself, here united with the object-subject of creation, as a whole duplicates a picture of the psychic state and representation corresponding to the early forms of thought. Let us look once more at two examples. All investigators and travelers are invariably somewhat astonished at one characteristic of early forms of thought quite incomprehensible to a human being accustomed to think in the categories of current logic. It is the characteristic involving the conception that a human being, while being himself and conscious of himself as such, yet simultaneously considers himself to be also some other person or thing, and, further, to be so, just as definitely and just as concretely, materially. In the specialized literature on this subject there is the particularly popular example of one of the Indian tribes of Northern Brazil.

The Indians of this tribe—the Bororo—maintain that, while human beings, they are none the less at the same time also a special kind of red parakeet common in Brazil. Note that by this they do not in any way mean that they will become these birds after death, or that their ancestors were such in the remote past. Not at all. They directly maintain that they are in reality these actual birds. It is not here a matter of identity of names or relationship; they mean a complete simultaneous identity of both.

However strange and unusual this may sound to us, it is nevertheless possible to quote from artistic practice quantities of instances which would sound almost word for word like the Bororo idea concerning simultaneous double existence of two completely different and separate and, none the less, real images. It is enough only to touch on the question of the self-feeling of the actor during his creation or performance of a rôle. Here, immediately, arises the problem of "I" and "him." Where "I" is the individuality of the performer, and "he" the individuality of the performed image of the rôle. This problem of the simultaneity of "I" and "not I" in the creation and performance of a rôle is one of the central "mysteries" of acting creation. The solution of it wavers between complete subordination of "him" to "I"—and "he" (complete trans-substantiation). While the contemporary attitude to this problem in its formulation approaches the clear enough dialectic formula of the "unity of inter-penetrating opposites," the "I" of the actor and the "he" of the image, the leading opposite being the image, nevertheless in concrete self-feeling the matter is by a long way not always so clear and definite for the actor. In one way or another, "I" and "he," "their" inter-relationship, "their" connections, "their" interactions inevitably figure at every stage in the working out of the rôle. Let us quote at least one example from the most recent and popular opinions on the subject.

The actress Serafima Birman (an advocate of the second extreme) offers this:

I read of a professor who celebrated neither his children's birthdays nor their name-days. He made an anniversary of the day on which a child ceased to speak of himself in the third person: "Lyalya wants go walk," and said: "I want go walk." The same kind of anniversary for the actor is that day and even minute of that day on which he ceases to speak of the image as "he," and says "I." Where indeed this new "I" is not the personal "I" of the actor or actress but the "I" of his or her image. . . .[1]

No less revealing are descriptions in the memoirs of a whole series of actors of their behavior at the moment of putting on make-up or their costume, which they accompany by a complete "magic" operation of "transformation" with whisperings, such as "I am already not me," "I am already so-and-so," "See, I'm beginning to be him," and so on.

In one way or another, more or less controlled, simultaneous actuality in the playing of the rôle is bound to be present in the creative process of even, albeit, the most inveterate supporter of complete "trans-substantiation." There are, in fact, too few cases known in the history of the theater of an actor leaning on the "fourth [non-existent] wall!"

It is characteristic that a similarly fluctuating dual apprehension of stage action as both a reality of theater and a reality of representation exists also with the spectator. Here too, correct apprehension is a united duality, on the one hand preventing the spectator from killing the villain, in that he remembers the latter is not a reality, while on the other giving him the occasion for laughter or tears, in that he forgets that he is witnessing a representation, a play-acting.

Let us note another example. In his *Völkerpsychologie* Wilhelm Wundt quotes certain early speech constructions. (We are not concerned here with Wundt's own views, but only with a properly authenticated documentary specimen cited by him.) The meaning:

"The Bushman was at first received kindly by the white man in order that he might be brought to herd his sheep; then the white man maltreated the Bushman; the latter ran away, whereupon the white man took another Bushman, who suffered the same experience."

This simple concept (describing a situation simple and casual in colonial manners) is approximately expressed in the language of the Bushman in this way:

"Bushman-there-go, here-run-to-white man, white man-give-to-bacco, Bushman-go-smoke, go-fill-tobacco-pouch, white man-give-meat-Bushman, Bushman-go-eat-meat, stand-up-go-home, go happily, go-sit-down, herd-sheep-white man, white man-go-strike Bushman, Bushman-cry-loud-pain, Bushman-go-run-away-white man, white man-run-after-Bushman, Bushman-then-another, this one-herd-sheep, Bushman-all-gone." [2]

We are astonished by this long series of descriptive single images, almost an asyntactic series. But suppose we take it into our heads to portray in action on the stage or screen those two lines of the situation implicit in the initial concept, we shall see to our surprise that we have begun to construct something very close to that which has been given as an example of Bushman construction. And this something, just as asyntactic, but supplied only with . . . a sequence of numbers, turns out to be something familiar to every one of us—a shooting script, an instrument to transpose a fact, abstracted into a concept, back into a chain of concrete single actions, which also happens to be the process of translating stage directions into action. "Ran away [from him]"—in Bushman language this appears as an orthodox editing description for two shots: "Bushman-go-run-away-white man," and "white man-run-after-Bushman"—the embryo for the montage of an American "chase sequence."

The abstract "received kindly" is expressed by most valuable concrete items, by means of which the representation of a kindly reception takes shape: a lighting of pipes, a filled tobacco pouch, cooked meat, etc. Again we have an example to show how, the moment we have to pass from informative to realistic expressiveness, we inevitably pass over to structural laws corresponding to sensual thinking, which plays the dominant rôle in representations characteristic of early development.

In this connection there is another illuminating example. It is known that still at this stage of development there are not yet generalizations and generalized "spinal" concepts. Lévy-Bruhl shows a factual instance of this in the Klamath language.[3] Their language contains no concept of "walking"; instead they employ an infinite series of terms for each particular form of walking. Rapid walking. Waddling. Tired walking. Stealthy walking, and so on. Each type of walking, no matter how delicate its nuances, is given its own term. This may seem strange to us—but only until we are called upon to open the parenthetical direction, "He approaches . . . ," in any play, and reveal it as a chain of approaching steps by one actor to another. The most splendidly conscious comprehension of the term "walking" fails one utterly. And if in the actor (and the director) this comprehension of "walking" does not at once flash "backwards" to a whole accumulation of possible and known particular cases of possible approaches, from which he can choose the most appropriate variant for his situation . . . then his performance can be expected to be a most sad and even tragic fiasco! *

How clear this is, even in details, can be seen by comparing different versions of a writer's manuscripts. Between the earlier drafts and the final version "the polish of style" in many works, particularly of poetry, very often takes the form of what seem insignificant transpositions of words, but this transposition is conditioned by exactly the same kind of laws. Indeed very often it is found that all that is involved in such transpositions is the mere shifting of a verb and noun. A business-like and prosaic statement, "An old woman lived there and then . . ." in its poetic variant inevitably runs, "There was an old woman who lived in a shoe." Preceding the introduction of the old

* The differences of both examples here will be that details of walking and selected movements, however refined they may be, in a genuine master would always be, at the same time, also a "conductor" of the generalized content which he produces in a particularized embodiment. Especially if his task is to transform the simple "approach" to an intricate reconstruction of an interplay of psychological states. Without this neither type nor realism is possible.

woman there appears a verbal form of an indefinite kind. And yet, thereby, the phrase at once assumes no longer the conversational character of everyday life, but one connected in some way with poetic-compositional representation.

This kind of effect has been pointed out by Herbert Spencer.[4] He recognizes such a transposition as more artistic. However, he gives no explanation of it. At best, he refers only to the "economy of the mental energies and sensibilities" of the second type of construction, which in itself most certainly requires a better explanation.

Meanwhile the secret lies hidden precisely in that fact which we persist in pointing to. The cause of it resides, once again, in the fact that this transposition corresponds to a thought process of earlier times. A characterization of this process may be found in Engels:

> When we consider and reflect upon nature at large, or the history of mankind, or our own intellectual activity, at first we see the picture of an endless entanglement of relations and reactions, permutations and combinations, in which nothing remains what, where, and as it was, but everything moves, changes, comes into being and passes away. We see, therefore, at first the picture as a whole, with its individual parts still more or less kept in the background; we observe the movements, transitions, connections, rather than the things that move, combine, and are connected.[5]

It follows that a word-order in which the term describing movement or action (the verb) precedes the person or thing moving or acting (the noun) corresponds more nearly to that form of construction that is more primal. This is true moreover outside the limits of our own language—Russian—as of course it should be inasmuch as it is linked, primarily, with the specific structure of thinking. In German *Die Gänse flogen* (the geese flew) sounds dry and informative, whereas even merely such a turn of speech as *Es flogen die Gänse* already contains an element of verse or balladry.

The indications of Engels and the characteristics of the phenomena just described, as phenomena of approach and return to forms characteristic for earlier levels, can be well illustrated with cases in which we ourselves are faced by graphic and attested pictures of psychic regression. For example, such phenomena of regression can be observed in certain brain operations. In the Moscow Neuro-Surgical Clinic, specializing in brain surgery, I have had the opportunity of witnessing the most interesting case of this sort. One of the patients, immediately after the operation, in proportion to his psychic regression, showed his verbal definition of an object going gradually and clearly through the phases outlined above: in this instance objects previously *named* were then identified by the *specific verbs indicating an act performed with the aid of the object.*

In the course of my exposition I have repeatedly had occasion to make use of the phrase "early forms of thought-process" and to illustrate my reflections by representational images current with peoples still at the dawn of culture. It has already become a traditional practice with us to be on our guard in all instances involving these fields of investigation. And not without reason: These fields are thoroughly contaminated by every kind of representative of "race theory," or even less concealed apologists for the colonial politics of imperialism. It would not be bad, therefore, to emphasize sharply that the considerations here expressed follow a sharply different line.

Usually the construction of so-called early thought-processes is treated as a form of thinking fixed in itself once and for all, characteristic of the so-called "primitive" peoples, racially inseparable from them and not susceptible to any modification whatsoever. In this guise it serves as scientific apologia for the methods of enslavement to which such peoples are subjected by white colonizers, inasmuch as, by inference, such peoples are "after all hopeless" for culture and cultural reciprocity.

In many ways even the celebrated Lévy-Bruhl is not exempt from this conception, although he does not pursue such an aim consciously. Along this line we quite justly attack him, since we know that forms of thinking are a reflection in consciousness of the social formations through which, at the given historical moment, this or that community collectively is passing. But in many ways, also, the opponents of Lévy-Bruhl fall into the opposite extreme, trying carefully to avoid the specificity of this independent individuality of early thought-forms. Among these, for instance, is Olivier Leroy, who, on the basis of analyzing-out a high degree of logic in the productive and technical inventiveness of the so-called "primitive" peoples, completely denies any difference between their system of thought-process and the postulates of our generally accepted logic. This is just as incorrect, and conceals beneath it an equal measure of denial of the dependence of a given system of thought from the specifics of the production relations and social premises from which it derives.

The basic error, in addition to this, is rooted in both camps in that they appreciate insufficiently the quality of gradation subsisting between the apparently incompatible systems of thought process, and completely disregard the qualitative nature of the transition from one to the other. Insufficient regard for this very circumstance frequently scares even us whenever discussion centers round the question of early thought-processes. This is the more strange in that in the Engels work cited there are actually three whole pages comprising an exhaustive examination of all the three stages of construction of thinking through which mankind passes in development. From the early diffuse-complex, part of the remarks about which we quoted above, through the formal-logical stage that negates it. And, at last, to the dialectical, absorbing "in photographic degree" the two preceding. Such a dynamic perception of phenomena does not of course exist for the positivistic approach of Lévy-Bruhl.

But of principal interest in all this matter is the fact that not only does the process of development itself not proceed in a straight line (just like any development process), but that it marches by continual shifts backwards and forwards, independently of whether it be progressively (the movement of backward peoples towards the higher achievements of culture under a socialist regime), or retrogressively (the regress of spiritual super-structures under the heel of national-socialism).

This continual sliding from level to level, forwards and backwards, now to the higher forms of an intellectual order, now to the earlier forms of sensual thinking, occurs also at each point once reached and temporarily stable as a phase in development. Not only the content of thinking, but even its construction itself, are deeply qualitatively different for the human being of any given, socially determined type of thinking, according to whatever state he may be in. The margin between the types is mobile and it suffices a not even extraordinarily sharp affective impulse to cause an extremely, it may be, logically deliberate person suddenly to react in obedience to the never dormant inner armory of sensual thinking and the norms of behavior deriving thence.

When a girl to whom you have been unfaithful, tears your photo into fragments "in anger," thus destroying the "wicked betrayer," for a moment she re-enacts the magical operation of destroying a man by the destruction of his image (based on the early identification of image and object).* By her momentary regression the girl returns herself, in a temporary aberration, to that stage of development in which such an action appeared fully normal and productive of real consequences. Relatively not so very long ago, on the verge of an epoch that already knew minds such as Leonardo and Galileo, so brilliant a politician as Catherine de' Medici, aided by her court magician, wished ill to her foes by sticking pins into their miniature wax images.

In addition to this we know also not just momentary, but (temporarily!) irrevocable manifestations of precisely this same psychological retrogression, when a whole social system is in regress. Then the phenomenon is termed reaction, and the most brilliant light on the question is thrown by the flames

* Even to the present day Mexicans in some of the remoter regions of the country, in times of drought, drag out from their temples the statue of the particular Catholic saint that has taken the place of the former god responsible for rains and, on the edge of the fields, whip him for his non-activity, imagining that thereby they cause pain to him whom the statue portrays.

of the national-fascist *auto-da-fé* of books and portraits of un-wanted authors in the squares of Berlin!

One way or another, the study of this or that thinking con-struction locked within itself is profoundly incorrect. The quality of sliding from one type of thinking to another, from category to category, and more—the simultaneous co-presence in varying proportions of the different types and stages and the taking into account of this circumstance, are equally as im-portant, explanatory and revealing in this as in any other sphere:

An exact representation of the universe, of its evolution, of the development of mankind, and of the reflection of this evolution in the minds of men, can therefore only be obtained by the methods of dialectics, with its constant regard to the innumerable actions and reactions of life and death, of progressive or retrogres-sive changes.[6]

The latter in our case has direct relation to those transitions in the forms of sensual thinking which appear sporadically in states of aberrations or similar conditions, and the images constantly present in the elements of form and composition based on the laws of sensual thinking, as we have tried to demonstrate and illustrate above.

After examining the immense material of similar phenomena, I naturally found myself confronted with a question which may excite the reader, too. This is, that art is nothing else but an artificial retrogression in the field of psychology towards the forms of earlier thought-processes, i.e., a phenomenon identical with any given form of drug, alcohol, shamanism, religion, etc.! The answer to this is simple and extremely in-teresting.

The dialectic of works of art is built upon a most curious "dual-unity." The affectiveness of a work of art is built upon the fact that there takes place in it a dual process: an impetu-ous progressive rise along the lines of the highest explicit steps of consciousness and a simultaneous penetration by means of the structure of the form into the layers of profoundest sensual thinking. The polar separation of these two lines of flow creates that remarkable tension of unity of form and content characteristic of true art-works. Apart from this there are no true art-works.

In this remarkable fact and attribute concerning a work of art lies its infinite distinction in principle from all adjacent, similar, analogous, and "reminiscent" areas, where phenomena attached to "early forms of thought" also have a place. In an inseparable unity of these elements—of sensual thinking with an explicitly conscious striving and soaring—art is unique and inimitable in those fields where a comparative deciphering is depended upon for correlative analysis. That is why, with this basic thesis in mind, we need not be afraid of an analytical deciphering of the most basic laws of sensual thinking, by firmly keeping in mind the necessity for unity and harmony in both elements, which produce a fully worthy work only in this unity.

By allowing one or the other element to predominate the art-work remains unfulfilled. A drive towards the thematic-logical side renders the work dry, logical, didactic. But over-stress on the side of the sensual forms of thinking with insufficient account taken of thematic-logical tendency—this is equally fatal for the work: the work becomes condemned to sensual chaos, elementalness, raving. Only in the "dually united" interpenetration of these tendencies resides the true tension-laden unity of form and content. Herein resides the root principle difference between the highest artistic creative activity of man and, in contradistinction therefrom, all other fields wherein also occur sensual thinking or its earlier forms (infantilism, schizophrenia, religious ecstasy, hypnosis, etc.).

And if we are now on the verge of considerable successes in the field of comprehension of the universe in the first line (to which the latest film productions bear witness), then, from the viewpoint of the technique of our craftsmanship, it stands necessary for us in every way to delve more deeply now also into the questions of the second component. These, however fleeting, notes that I have been able to set forth here serve this task. Work here is not only not finished, it has barely begun. But work here is in the extremest degree indispensable for us. The study of the corpus of material on these questions is highly important to us.

By study and absorption of this material we shall learn a very great deal about the system of laws of formal constructions and the inner laws of composition. And along the line of knowledge in the field of the system of laws of formal constructions, cinematography and indeed the arts generally are still very poor. Even at the moment we are merely probing in these fields a few bases of the systems of laws, the derivative roots of which lie in the nature itself of sensual thinking.

In comparison with music or literature, we find little, but by analyzing along this line a whole series of problems and phenomena, we shall store up in the field of form a great corpus of exact knowledge, without which we shall never attain that general ideal of simplicity which we all have in mind. To attain this ideal and to realize this line, it is very important to guard ourselves against another line which might also begin to crop up: the line of simplificationism. This tendency is to some extent already present in the cinema, which a few already wish to expound in this way, that things should be shot "straight" and, in the last resort, it does not matter how. This is terrible, for we all know that the crux is not in shooting ornately and prettily (photography becomes ornate and pretty-pretty when the author knows neither what he wants to take nor how he must take what he wants).

The essence is in shooting expressively. We must travel toward *the ultimate-expressive and ultimate-affective form and use the limit of simple and economic form that expresses what we need*. These questions, however, can successfully be approached only by means of very serious analytical work and by means of very serious knowledge of the inward nature of artistic form. Hence we must proceed not by the path of mechanical simplification of the task, but by the path of planned analytical ascertaining of the secret of the very nature of affective form.

I have sought here to show the direction in which I am now working on these problems, and I think this is the right road of investigation. If we now look back at the intellectual cinema, we shall see that the intellectual cinema did one service, in spite of its self-*reductio ad absurdum* when it laid claim to exhaustive style and exhaustive content.

This theory fell into the error of letting us have not a unity of form and content, but a coincidental identity of them, because in unity it is complicated to follow exactly how an affective embodiment for ideas is built. But when these things become "telescoped" into "one," *then was discovered the march of inner thinking as the basic law of construction of form and composition.* Now we can use the laws thus discovered already not along the line of "intellectual constructions," but along the line of completely manifold constructions, both from story and image viewpoints, since we already know some "secrets," and fundamental laws of construction of form and affective structure generally.

From what I have elucidated along the lines of the past and along the lines on which I am now working, one more qualitative difference appears:

It is this, that when in our various "schools" we proclaimed the paramount importance of montage, or of the intellectual cinema, or of documentalism or some such other fighting program, it bore primarily the character of a tendency. What I am now trying briefly to expound about what I am now working on has an entirely different character. It bears a character not specifically tendentious (as futurism, expressionism or any other "program")—but delves into the question of the nature of things and here questions are already not concerned with the line of some given stylization, but with the line of search for a general method and mode for the problem of form, equally essential and fit for any genre of construction within our embracing style of *socialist realism.* Questions of tendentious interests begin to spread over into a deepened interest in the whole culture itself of the medium in which we work, i.e., the tendentious line here takes a turn towards the research-academic line. I have experienced this not merely creatively, but also biographically: at the moment at which I began to interest myself in these basic problems of the culture of form and the culture of cinema, I found myself in life not in film production, but engaged in creation of an academy of cinematography, the road to which has been laid down by my three years' work in the All-Union State Cinema Institute, in Moscow, and which is only now developing. Moreover, it is of interest that the phenomenon noted above is not at all isolated, this quality is not at all exclusively characteristic of our cinematography. We can perceive a whole series of theoretical and tendentious routes ceasing to exist as original "currents," and beginning by way of transmutation and gradual change to be included in questions of methodology and science.

It is possible to point to such an example in the teaching of Marr, and the fact that his teaching, which was formerly a "japhetic" tendency in the science of languages, has now been revised from the viewpoint of Marxism and entered practice no longer as a tendency but as a generalized method in the study of languages and thinking. It is not by chance that on almost all fronts around us there are now being born academies; it is not by chance that disputes in the line of architecture are no longer a matter of rival tendencies (Le Corbusier or Zheltovski); discussion proceeds no longer about this question, but controversy is about a synthesis of "the three arts," the deepening of research, the nature itself of the phenomenon of architecture.

I think that in our cinematography something very similar is now occurring. For, at the present stage, we craftsmen have no differences of principle and disputes about a whole series of program postulates such as we had in the past. There are, of course, individual shades of opinion within the comprehensive conception of the single style: Socialist Realism.

And this is in no way a sign of moribundity, as might appear to some—"unless they fight, they're stiffs"—quite the contrary. Precisely here, and precisely in this, I find the greatest and most interesting sign of the times.

I think that now, with the approach of the sixteenth year of our cinematography, we are entering a special period. These signs, to be traced today also in the parallel arts as well as being found in the cinema, are harbingers of the news that Soviet cinematography, after many periods of divergence of opinion and argument, is entering into its classical period, because the characteristics of its interests, the particular approach to its series of problems, this thirst for synthesis, this postulation of and demand for complete harmony of all the elements from the subject matter to composition within the frame, this demand for fullness of quality and all the features on which our cinematography has set its heart—these are the signs of highest flowering of an art.

I consider that we are now on the threshold of the most remarkable period of classicism in our cinematography, the best period in the highest sense of the word. Not to participate creatively in such a period is no longer possible. And if for the last three years I have been completely engrossed in scientific-investigatory and pedagogical work (a side of which is very briefly related above), then now I undertake simultaneously once again to embark upon production,* in order to strive for a classicism that will contain some part of the huge endowment left us.

[1935]

* In the spring of 1935 Eisenstein did return to active production, with *Bezhin Meadow* from a scenario by Alexander Rzheshevsky. The film was left unfinished in 1937; see *The Film Sense,* appendices 1 (page 226) and 8 (page 274).

THE STRUCTURE OF THE FILM

> This is an Art
> Which does mend Nature: change it rather, but
> The Art itselfe, is Nature.
>
> SHAKESPEARE, *The Winter's Tale*

> All is in man—all is for man.
>
> GORKY [1]

LET US say that grief is to be represented on the screen. There is no such thing as grief "in general." Grief is concrete; it is always attached to something; it has conveyors, when your film's characters grieve; it has consumers, when your portrayal of grief makes the spectators sorrow, too.

This latter result is not always obligatory for your portrayal of grief: the grief of an enemy, after his defeat, arouses joy in the spectator, who identifies his feelings with those of the conqueror on the screen.

Such considerations are obvious enough, yet beneath them lies one of the most difficult problems in constructing works of art, touching the most exciting part of our work: *the problem of portraying an attitude toward the thing portrayed.*

One of the most active means of portraying this attitude is in composition. Though this attitude can never be shown by composition alone. Nor is it the sole task of composition.

I wish to take up in this essay this particular question: how far the embodiment of this attitude can be achieved within narrowly compositional means. We have long since realized that an attitude to a portrayed fact can be embodied in the *way* the fact is presented. Even such a master of "attitude" as Franz Kafka recognized physical viewpoint as critical:

The diversity of ideas which one can have, say, of an apple: the apple as it appears to the child who must stretch his neck so as barely to see it on the table, and the apple as it appears to the master of the house who picks it up and lordily hands it to his guest.[2]

At once the question arises: with what methods and means must the filmically portrayed fact be handled so that it simultaneously shows not only *what* the fact is, and the character's attitude towards it, but also *how* the author relates to it, and how the author wishes the spectator to receive, sense, and react to the portrayed fact.

Let us look at this from the viewpoint of composition alone, and there examine an instance where this task, of embodying the author's relation to a thing, is served primarily by composition, here understood as a law for the construction of a portrayal. This is extremely important for us, for though little enough has been written on the rôle of composition in cinema, the features of composition that we speak of here have been left unmentioned in film literature.

The object of imagery and the law of structure, by which it is represented, can coincide. This would be the simplest of cases, and the compositional problem in such an aspect more or less takes care of itself. This is the simplest type of structure: "sorrowful sorrow," "joyful joy," "a marching march," etc. In other words: the hero sorrows, and in unison with him sorrows nature, and lighting, sometimes the composition of the shot, and (more rarely) the rhythm of the montage—but most often of all, we just add sad music to it. The same thing happens when we handle "joyful joy," and other similar simplicities.

Even in these simplest cases it is perfectly evident what nourishes composition and from where it derives its experience and material: *composition takes the structural elements of the portrayed phenomena* and from these composes its *canon for building the containing work.*

In doing this composition actually takes such elements, first of all, from the structure of the *emotional behavior of man,* joined with the *experienced content* of this or that portrayed phenomenon.

It is for this reason that real composition is invariably *profoundly human*—be it the "leaping" rhythmic structure of gay episodes, the "drawn-out monotonal" montage of a sad scene, or the "joyful sparkling" tone of a shot.

Diderot deduced the theory that compositional *principles* in vocal, and later in instrumental, music derived from the basic intonations of living emotional speech (as well as from sound phenomena perceived by our ancestors in surrounding nature).

And Bach—master of the most intricate compositional forms —maintained a similarly *human approach* to the fundamentals of composition as a direct pedagogical premise. In describing Bach's teaching methods, Forkel writes:

He considered his voices as if they were persons who conversed together like a select company. If there were three, each could sometimes be silent and listen to the others till it again had something to the purpose to say.[3]

It is exactly thus, on a base of interplaying human emotions, on a base of human experience, that the cinema must also build its structural approaches and its most difficult compositional constructions.

Take, for example, one of the most successful scenes in *Alexander Nevsky*—the attack by the German wedge on the Russian army at the beginning of the Battle on the Ice.

This episode passes through all the shades of an experience of increasing terror, where approaching danger makes the heart contract and the breathing irregular. The structure of this "leaping wedge" in *Alexander Nevsky* is, with variations, exactly modeled on the inner process of such an experience. This dictated all the rhythms of the sequence—cumulative, disjunctive, the speeding up and slowing down of the movement. The boiling pulsing of an excited heart dictated the rhythm of the leaping hoofs: pictorially—the *leap* of the galloping knights; compositionally—the *beat* to the bursting point of an excited heart.

To produce the success of this sequence, both the pictorial

and compositional structures are fused in the welded unity of a terrifying image—the beginning of a battle that is to be a fight to the finish.

And the event, as it is unfolded on the screen according to a timetable of the running of this or that passion, thrown back from the screen, involves the emotions of the spectator according to the same timetable, arousing in him the same tangle of passions which originally designed the compositional scheme of the work.

This is the secret of the genuinely emotional affect of real composition. Employing for source *the structure of human emotion, it unmistakably appeals to emotion,* unmistakably arouses the complex of those feelings that gave birth to the composition.

In all the media of art—and in film art most of all, no matter how neglected by this medium—it is by such means, primarily, that is achieved what Lev Tolstoy said of music:

Music carries me immediately and directly into that mental condition in which the man was who composed it.[4]

That—from the simplest to the most complicated cases—is *one* of the possible *types* of construction to be considered.

But there is also another case, when, instead of a resolution of the "joyful joy" type, the author is forced to find the compositional vessel for, say, the theme of "life-affirming death."

What would happen here?

Apparently, the law of constructing works of art in such a case cannot be nourished *exclusively* by elements issuing directly from the natural and habitual emotions, conditions, and sensations of man, attendant on such a phenomenon.

Yet the law of composition remains unchanged in such a case.

Such schemes of composition will have to be sought not so much among the emotions attached to the portrayed thing, but primarily among the emotions attached to the author's *relationship to the thing portrayed.*

Strictly speaking, this also is a factor in the above example

of the "wedge" in *Alexander Nevsky*, only with this peculiarity, that there the emotion of the portrayed thing *coincides*
with the emotion of the author's relationship to the portrayed
thing.

But such a case is rather rare and is by no means obligatory
for all cases. In such cases there commonly arises a quite curious
and often unexpected picture of a transferred phenomenon,
constructed in a way unusual in "normal" circumstances. Literature abounds in such examples of all degrees, often touching
the primary elements of compositional development, such as
an imagist structure, resolved possibly through a system of
similes.

The pages of literature offer us models of completely unexpected compositional structures, in which are presented phenomena that "in themselves" are quite ordinary. These structures are not in the least determined, nourished, or brought into
being by formalist excesses or extravagant researches.[*]

The examples I have in mind come from realistic classics—
and they are classical because with these means the examples
embody with maximum clarity a maximum clear *judgment* of
a phenomenon, a maximum clear *relation* to the phenomenon.

How often in literature do we encounter descriptions of
"adultery"! No matter how varied the situations, circumstances,
and imagist comparisons in which this has been portrayed—
there is hardly a more impressive picture than the one where
"the sinful embrace of the lovers" is imagistically compared
with—murder.

She felt so guilty, so much to blame, that it only remained for
her to humble herself and ask to be forgiven; but she had no one
in the world now except him, so that even her prayer for for-
giveness was addressed to him. Looking at him, she felt her hu-
miliation physically, and could say nothing more. He felt what a
murderer must feel when looking at the body he has deprived of
life. The body he had deprived of life was their love, the first
period of their love. There was something frightful and revolting
in the recollection of what had been paid for with this terrible

* Two phrases commonly employed by Eisenstein's critics.—EDITOR.

price of shame. The shame she felt at her spiritual nakedness communicated itself to him. But in spite of the murderer's horror of the body of his victim, that body must be cut in pieces and hidden away, and he must make use of what he has obtained by the murder.

Then, as the murderer desperately throws himself on the body, as though with passion, and drags it and hacks it, so Vronsky covered her face and shoulders with kisses.

She held his hand and did not move. Yes! These kisses were what had been bought by that shame! "Yes, and this hand, which will always be mine, is the hand of my accomplice." [5]

In this passage from *Anna Karenina* the imagist structure of its simile throughout the whole magnificently ferocious scene is resolved from the most profound relation of its author to the phenomenon, rather than from the feelings and emotions of its participants (as is this same theme, for example, in infinite variations, solved by Zola throughout the *Rougon-Macquart* cycle).

On *Anna Karenina* Tolstoy placed an epigraph from the Epistle to the Romans: "*Vengeance is mine; I will repay, saith the Lord.*" In a letter to Veresayev (23 May 1907) Mikhail Sukhotin quoted what Tolstoy meant by this epigraph, which had moved Veresayev:

. . . I must repeat, that I chose this epigraph to express the idea that whatever is evil, whatever man does, brings bitter consequences, not from people, but from God and from what Anna Karenina experiences herself.[6]

It is in the second part of the novel, from which our passage is taken, that Tolstoy assumes the particular task of demonstrating "whatever is evil, whatever man does."

The temperament of the writer forces him to feel in the forms of the highest level of evil—in crime. The temperament of the moralist forces him to appraise this evil on the highest level of crime against a person—murder. And finally, the temperament of the artist forces this estimate of the behavior of his character to be presented with the help of all expressive means available to him.

Crime—murder—is established as *the basic expressive rela-tion of the author* to the phenomenon, and is simultaneously established as *the determinant of all basic elements for the com-positional treatment of the scene.*

It dictates the images and the similes:

He felt what a murderer must feel when looking at the body he has deprived of life. The body he had deprived of life was their love. . . .

as well as the images of the characters' behavior, prescribing the fulfillment of actions, peculiar to love, in forms peculiar to murder:

. . . as the murderer desperately throws himself on the body, as though with passion, and drags it and hacks it, so Vronsky cov-ered her face and shoulders with kisses.

These absolutely exact "directives," defining the shading of behavior, were chosen from thousands of possibilities for the reason that they correspond identically with the relation of the author himself to the phenomenon.

The idea of evil, compositionally expressed through the image of crime—murder—as resolved in the cited scene, can be encountered elsewhere in Tolstoy's art. For him, this is a beloved image.

This is his compositional-imagist structure, not only for "adultery," but also for the "swinish connexion" within the bonds of marriage.

We again find this theme in *The Kreutzer Sonata.* Two frag-ments from Pozdnyshev's narrative show it clearly. The sec-ond of these (regarding the children) expands the frame of reference, providing a renewed unexpectedness of outer com-positional construction, issuing as a whole, however, from Tol-stoy's inner relation to the theme:

"I wondered what embittered us against one another, yet it was perfectly simple: that animosity was nothing but the protest of our human nature against the animal nature that overpowered it.

"I was surprised at our enmity to one another; yet it could not have been otherwise. That hatred was nothing but the mutual hatred of accomplices in a crime—both for the incitement to the crime and for the part taken in it. What was it but a crime, when she, poor thing, became pregnant in the first month, and our *swinish* connexion continued? You think I am straying from my subject? Not at all! I am telling you *how* I killed my wife. They asked me at the trial with what, and how, I killed her. Fools! They thought I killed her with a knife, on the 5th of October. It was not then I killed her, but much earlier. Just as they are all now killing, all, all. . . ." [7]

"So the presence of children not only failed to improve our life, but poisoned it. Besides, the children were a new cause of dissension. As soon as we had children they became the means and the object of our discord, and more often the older they grew. They were not only the object of discord, but the weapons of our strife. We used our children, as it were, to fight one another with. Each of us had a favorite weapon among them for our strife. I used to fight her chiefly through Vasya, the eldest boy, and she me through Lisa. . . . They, poor things, suffered terribly from this, but we, with our incessant warfare, had no time to think of that. . . ." [8]

As we can see, no matter what example we take, the method of composition remains the same. In all cases, its basic determinant remains primarily *the relation of the author*. In all cases, it is the *deed* of man and the *structure* of human deeds that prefigures the composition.

The decisive factors of the compositional structure are taken by the author from the basis of his relation to phenomena. This dictates structure and characteristics, through which the portrayal itself is unfolded. Losing none of its reality, the portrayal emerges from this, immeasurably enriched in both intellectual and emotional qualities.

Another example may be offered here. Its interest lies in the delineation of two characters by an imagery that is customary and even routine, perfectly natural in both structure and characteristics, but the structural means is consciously produced by . . . *an exchange of structures!*

These personages are a German officer and a French prostitute.

The imagist structure of a "noble officer" is employed for the prostitute. In the same way the most repellent elements in the imagist structure of a prostitute serve as skeletal outline for the German officer.

This ingenious "contra-dance" idea was Maupassant's—used in "Mademoiselle Fifi."

The image of the Frenchwoman is woven from all the traits of nobility, linked with a middle-class attitude towards army officers. Consistent with this method, the *substance* of the German officer is revealed in its prostitute nature. From this "nature" Maupassant seized only one trait—its destructiveness of the "moral principles" of bourgeois society. Further interest for us is lent to this aspect in that Maupassant took this over from a similar scheme that in a finished form was well-known and fresh in the public's memory—perhaps so that his readers could not possibly miss his point! The portrait structure of his German officer is cut from a pattern designed by Zola.

The Baron Wilhelm von Eyrick, nicknamed "Mademoiselle Fifi," is, of course, "Nana."

Not the whole figure of Nana, but Nana in that part of the novel where Zola raises this image to immense destructive powers that are directed against well-ordered families, symbolically climaxed by Nana's destructive caprice in smashing the family heirlooms brought to her by her admirers. The generalized presentation of the courtesan's destructive powers for family and society is further "materialized" by the particular breaking of the bonbonnière of Dresden china and her "general massacre" of the heap of other valuable gifts that serve as a symbol of the "high society" which is mockingly broken by Nana's caprices.

The structure of the officer's behavior is absolutely identical with the structure of Nana's behavior in this scene. Even within the surface similarity of the names of "Nana" and "Fifi" there is a further clue to this identity: the Baron's nickname was given him for his habit of expressing his contempt for everyone and everything around him—"*fi, fi, donc!*"

And in the story as a whole we have a fine model of the compositional re-channeling of a customary naturalistic imagery into a structural framework suitable to the author's requirements.

We have examined cases that are quite descriptive, palpable, and easily apparent. The very same principles, however, lie in the deepest elements of compositional structure, in those strata that can be uncovered only by the scalpel of the most pedantic and probing analysis.

And everywhere we see as basic the same *humanity* and *human psychology, nourishing and shaping the most intricate compositional elements of form exactly as it feeds and defines the content of the work.*

I wish to illustrate this with two complex and seemingly abstract examples, in regard to the composition of *Potemkin.* These will serve as examples of structure and composition in the broadest sense of the terms, corroborating what has been said above.

When *Potemkin* is discussed two of its features are commonly remarked: The organic construction of its composition as a whole. And the pathos * of the film. Sacrificing grace to precision, we can refer to these two qualities as:

ORGANIC-NESS and PATHOS

Taking these two most noticed features of *Potemkin*, let us attempt to uncover the means by which they were achieved, primarily in the field of composition. We shall observe the first feature in the composition as a whole. For the second, we shall take the episode of the Odessa steps, where the pathos of the film achieves its greatest dramatic tension.

We are here concerned with how the organic-ness and pathos of the theme are resolved by specifically compositional

---

* This is a much abused term, used here in its original sense.

means. In the same way we could take apart these qualities to see how they are resolved by other factors; we could examine the contribution to organic-ness and pathos made by the actors' performances, by the treatment of the story, by the light and color scale of the photography, by the mass-scenes, by the natural backgrounds, etc.

That is, we take up this matter from one narrow, particular question of structure, and by no means pretend to a thorough analysis of all the film's aspects.

However, in an organic work of art, elements that nourish the work as a whole pervade all the features composing this work. A unified canon pierces not only the whole and each of its parts, but also each area that is called to participate in the work of composition. One and the same principle will feed any area, advancing in each its own qualitative signs of distinction. And only in such a case may one speak of the organic-ness of a work, for an organism is here understood as defined by Engels in *Dialectics of Nature*: ". . . *the organism is certainly a higher unity* . . ."

These considerations bring us at once to our first matter—to the question of the "organic" structure of *Potemkin*.

We shall attempt to approach this question, proceeding from the premise established at the opening of this essay. The organic-ness of a work, as well as the sensation of organic-ness that is received from the work, must rise in that case where the law of building the work answers *the law of structure in natural organic phenomena*.

It must be quite evident that we are speaking here of the sensation of compositional organic-ness in the whole. This can break down the resistance even of that spectator whose class allegiance is in sharp opposition to the direction taken by the subject and the theme of the work, i.e., those spectators for whom neither theme nor subject is "organic." This partially explains the reception given *Potemkin* outside the Soviet Union.

Let us be more precise: What do we mean by the organic-ness of building the work? I should say that we have two kinds of organic-ness.

The first is characteristic of any work that possesses whole-ness and inner laws. In this case organic-ness can be defined by the fact that the work as a whole is governed by a certain law of structure and that all its parts are subordinated to this canon. The German estheticians would label this: organic-ness of a general order. It is apparent that in our instance of this principle we have a pattern of the principle on which natural phenomena are built and about which Lenin said:

The particular does not exist outside that relationship which leads to the general. The general exists only in the particular, through the particular. . . .[9]

But the *law* itself by which these natural phenomena are constructed, as yet in this first case by no means certainly coin-cides with that canon on which one or another work of art is constructed.

The second kind of organic-ness of a work is present to-gether with not only the very *principle of organic-ness*, but also the *canon itself*, according to which natural phenomena are built. This may be termed organic-ness of a *particular* or *exceptional kind*. And it is this that is of especial interest for us.

We have before us a case where a work of art—*an art-ificial work*—is built on those same laws by which *non*-artistic phe-nomena—the "organic" phenomena of nature—are constructed.

There is in this case, not only a truthful realistic subject, but also, in its forms of compositional embodiment, a truthful and full reflection of a canon peculiar to actuality.

Evidently, whatever may be the kind of organic-ness in it, the work has a completely individual affect on its perceivers, not only because it is raised to the level of natural phenomena, but also because the laws of its construction are simultaneously the laws governing those who perceive the work, inasmuch as this audience is also part of organic nature. Each spectator feels himself organically related, fused, united with a work of such a type, just as he senses himself united and fused with organic nature around him.

To a greater or lesser degree each of us inevitably experiences this sensation, and the secret lies in the fact that in this case *we and the work* are governed *by one and the same canon.* We can observe nature operating within this canon in both the examples chosen, though they would appear to touch two different and independent questions. These do, however, meet each other finally.

The first example is devoted to an analysis of this canon in static conditions; the second analyzes the dynamic operation of this canon.

Our first example will raise questions of parts and *proportions* in the structure of the work. Our second—the *movement* of the structure of the work.

This means that the solution of the first question of the organic structure of *Potemkin* must begin with the deciphering of that which is subordinate to the first structural condition—*organic-ness of a general kind.*

Potemkin looks like a chronicle (or newsreel) of an event, but it functions as a drama.

The secret of this lies in the fact that the chronicle pace of the event is fitted to a severely tragic composition. And furthermore, to tragic composition in its most canonic form—the five-act tragedy. Events, regarded almost as naked facts, are broken into five tragic acts, the facts being selected and arranged in sequence so that they answer the demands set by classical tragedy: a third act quite distinct from the second, a fifth distinct from the first, and so on.

The utility in the choice of a five-act structure in particular for this tragedy was, of course, by no means accidental, but was the result of prolonged natural selection—but we need not go into this history here. Enough that for the basis of our drama we took a structure that had been particularly tested by the centuries. This was further emphasized by the individual titling of each "act." * Here, in condensation, are the contents of the five acts:

Part I—"Men and Maggots." Exposition of the action. Milieu of the battleship. Maggoty meat. Discontent ferments among the sailors.

Part II—"Drama on the Quarterdeck." "All hands on deck!" Refusal of the wormy soup. Scene with the tarpaulin. "Brothers!" Refusal to fire. Mutiny. Revenge on the officers.

Part III—"Appeal from the Dead." Mist. The body of Vakulinchuk is brought into Odessa port. Mourning over the body. Indignation. Demonstration. Raising the red flag.

Part IV—"The Odessa Steps." Fraternization of shore and battleship. Yawls with provisions. Shooting on the Odessa steps. The battleship fires on the "generals' staff."

Part V—"Meeting the Squadron." Night of expectation. Meeting the squadron. Engines. "Brothers!" The squadron refuses to fire. The battleship passes victoriously through the squadron.

In the action of its episodes each part of the drama is totally unlike the others, but piercing and, as it were, cementing them, there is a repeat.

In "Drama on the Quarterdeck," a tiny group of rebelling sailors (a small particle of the battleship) cries "Brothers!" as they face the guns of the firing squad. And the guns are lowered. The whole organism of the battleship joins them.

In "Meeting the Squadron," the whole rebellious battleship (a small particle of the fleet) throws the same cry of "Brothers!" towards the guns of the flagship, pointed towards the *Potemkin.* And the guns are lowered: the whole organism of the fleet has joined them.

From a tiny cellular organism of the battleship to the organism of the entire battleship; from a tiny cellular organism

* When *Potemkin* was exhibited outside the Soviet Union, these part-titles were invariably removed by the various adaptors; the only foreign prints of *Potemkin* restored to its original form are those circulated by the Museum of Modern Art Film Library.—EDITOR.

of the fleet to the organism of the whole fleet—thus flies through the theme the revolutionary feeling of brotherhood. And this is repeated in the structure of the work containing this theme—brotherhood and revolution.

Over the heads of the battleship's commanders, over the heads of the admirals of the tzar's fleet, and finally over the heads of the foreign censors, rushes the whole film with its fraternal "Hurrah!" just as within the film the feeling of brotherhood flies from the rebellious battleship over the sea to the shore. The organic-ness of the film, born in the cell within the film, not only moves and expands throughout the film as a whole, but appears far beyond its physical limits—in the public and historical fate of the same film.

Thematically and emotionally this would, perhaps, be sufficient in speaking of organic-ness, but let us be formally more severe.

Look intently into the structure of the work.

In its five acts, tied with the general thematic line of revolutionary brotherhood, there is otherwise little that is similar externally. But in one respect they are absolutely *alike:* each part is distinctly broken into two almost equal halves. This can be seen with particular clarity from the second act on:

II. Scene with the tarpaulin   → mutiny
III. Mourning for Vakulinchuk → angry demonstration
IV. Lyrical fraternization   → shooting
 V. Anxiously awaiting the fleet → triumph

Moreover, at the "transition" point of each part, the halt has its own peculiar kind of *caesura.*

In one part (III), this is a few shots of clenched fists, through which the theme of mourning the dead leaps into the theme of fury.

In another part (IV), this is a sub-title—*"SUDDENLY"*—cutting off the scene of fraternization, and projecting it into the scene of the shooting.

The motionless muzzles of the rifles (in Part II). The gaping mouths of the guns (in Part V). And the cry of "Brothers," upsetting the awful pause of waiting, in an explosion of brotherly feeling—in both moments.

And it should be further noted that the transition within each part is not merely a transition to a merely *different* mood, to a merely *different* rhythm, to a merely *different* event, but each time the transition is to a sharply opposite quality. Not merely contrasting, but *opposite*, for each time it *images exactly that theme from the opposite point of view*, along with the theme that *inevitably grows from it*.

The explosion of mutiny after the breaking point of oppression has been reached, under the pointed rifles (Part II).

Or the explosion of wrath, organically breaking from the theme of mass mourning for the murdered (Part III).

The shooting on the steps as an organic "deduction" of the reaction to the fraternal embrace between the *Potemkin's* rebels and the people of Odessa (Part IV), and so on.

The unity of such a canon, recurring in *each act* of the drama, is already self-evident.

But when we look at the work as a whole, we shall see that such is the whole structure of *Potemkin*.

Actually, near the middle, the film as a whole is cut by the dead halt of a *caesura;* the stormy action of the beginning is completely halted in order to take a fresh start for the second half of the film. This similar *caesura*, within the film as a whole, is made by the episode of the dead Vakulinchuk and the harbor mists.

For the entire film this episode is a halt before the same sort of transfer that occurs in those moments cited above within the separate parts. And with this moment the theme, breaking the ring forged by the sides of one rebellious battleship, bursts into the embrace of a whole city which is topographically *opposed to the ship*, but is in feeling fused into a unity with it; a unity that is, however, broken away from it by the soldiers' boots descending the steps at that moment when the theme once more returns to the drama at sea.

We see how organic is the progressive development of the theme, and at the same time we also see how the structure of

Potemkin, as a whole, flows from this movement of the theme, which operates *for the whole* exactly as it does *for its fractional members.*

We need not seek in nature for what appears to be pathos *per se.* We shall confine ourselves to an analysis in a work of pathos from the viewpoint of its receiver or, more exactly, in regard to the theatrical media, from the viewpoint of its affect on the spectator. Moving from these basic features of affect we shall attempt to define those basic features of construction which a composition of pathos must possess. And then we can verify these features with the particular example that concerns us. Nor will I deny myself the satisfaction of concluding with a few general considerations.

For our purpose let us first sketch in a few words the affect of pathos. We'll deliberately do this with the most trivial and banal symptoms possible. Out of this the most prominent and characteristic features will bring themselves to our attention.

For the most primitive illustration let us take a simple description of the superficial signs of external behavior in a spectator gripped by pathos.

But these signs are so symptomatic that they at once bring us to the core of the question. Pathos shows its affect—when the spectator is compelled to jump from his seat. When he is compelled to collapse where he stands. When he is compelled to applaud, to cry out. When his eyes are compelled to shine with delight, before gushing tears of delight. . . . In brief—when the spectator is forced "to go out of himself."

To use a prettier term, we might say that the affect of a work of pathos consists in whatever "sends" the spectator into ecstasy. Actually there is nothing to be added to such a formulation, for the symptoms above say exactly this: *ex-stasis*—literally, "standing out of oneself," which is to say, "going out of himself," or "departing from his ordinary condition."

All our symptoms follow this formula to the letter. Seated—

he stands. Standing—he collapses. Motionless—he moves. Silent—
he cries out. Dull—he shines. Dry—he is moistened by tears.
In each instance occurs a "departure from a condition," a
"going out of himself."

But this is not all: "to go out of oneself" is not to go into
nothing. To go out of oneself inevitably implies a transition
to something else, to something different in quality, to something opposite to what was (immobility—into movement;
silence—into noise; etc.).

Even in such a superficial description of ecstatic affect, produced by a structure of pathos, it is self-evident what basic
indications structure must possess in a composition of pathos.
By all its indications such a structure must maintain the condition of "going out of oneself" and incessant transition to differing qualities.

To leave oneself, to remove oneself from one's customary
equilibrium and condition, and to pass over into a new condition—all this of course penetrates the affective conditions of
every art that is capable of gripping a perceiver. And the
media of art tend to group themselves according to their ca-
pability in achieving this affect. Ranged in this way, the possession of this general quality shows its fundamental vitality
to the highest degree. Apparently, structures of pathos are the
culminating points along this single road.

And, apparently, all other varieties of composition in artistic works may be examined, and they will be found to be
diminished derivatives of *maximum instances* (producing "de-
partures from oneself" to a maximum degree), employing a
pathetic type of structure.

No one should be alarmed by the fact that in speaking of
pathos, I have not yet once touched the question of theme
and content. We are not discussing here pathetic content in
general, but rather of the meaning of pathos as realized in composition. The same fact may enter a work of art in any aspect
of treatment: from the cold protocol form of a précis to a
hymn of genuine pathos. And it is these particular artistic

means, lifting the "recording" of an event to the heights of pathos, that interest us here.

Unquestionably this primarily depends on the author's relation to the content. But composition in this meaning, as we comprehend it here, *is also a construction which, in the first place, serves to embody the author's relation to the content,* at the same time compelling the spectator to relate himself to the content in the same way.

In this essay we are therefore less interested in the question of the "nature" of pathos in one or another phenomenon; this is always socially relative. We shall also not pause on the character of the author's pathetic *relation* to this or to that phenomenon, just as obviously socially relative. We are interested (by the *a priori* presence of both) in the narrowly posed problem of how this "relation" to "natural phenomena" is realized by composition within the conditions of a pathetic structure.

And so, in following that thesis, already once justified in the question of organic-ness, we can affirm that, in wishing to gain a maximum "departure from oneself" in the spectator, we are obliged in the work to suggest to him a corresponding "guide." Following this guide he will enter into the desired condition.

The simplest "prototype" of such imitative behavior will be, of course, that of a person ecstatically following, on the screen, a personage gripped by pathos, a personage who in one way or another, "goes out of himself."

Here structure will coincide with imagery. And the object of the imagery—the *behavior* of such a man—will *itself* flow according to the conditions of "ecstatic" structure. This may even be shown in speech indications. The *unorganized* customary flow of speech, made pathetic, immediately invents the pattern of clearly behavioristic *rhythm;* prose that is also *prosaic* in its forms, begins to scintillate at once with forms and turns of speech that are *poetic* in nature (unexpected metaphors, the appearance of expressive images, etc.). There is no indication of speech or other human manifestation that would not show, at such a moment, this transfer *from one quality into a new quality.*

On this ladder the first rung is a line of compositional possibilities. A case will become more complicated and more affective when this basic condition does not stop with man, but goes itself "beyond the limits" of man, radiating out into the surroundings and environment of a personage, that is, when his very surroundings also are presented in, say, his condition of "frenzy." Shakespeare has given us a classical example of this in the "frenzy" of Lear, a frenzy that goes beyond the boundaries of the personage, into the "frenzy" of nature itself—into a tempest.

For the same resolutions of material in any customary means, examples may be found in the richest abundance among the naturalists of the Zola school and, in the first place, in Zola himself. In Zola the very description of the surroundings, fusing its details with the separate phases of an event in each scene, is always selected and presented in a *realistic* and *physical* way, but always as required *by the structure* of the condition.* This holds true for any of his compositional structures, but is particularly graphic in those cases where Zola raises to pathos an event that is by no means obliged to be pathetic.

Not in the rhythm of prose, nor in a system of images and similes, nor in the scenic structure—nor in any purely compositional elements of episodes does a structural canon seem absolutely necessary to Zola for his scenes; he is almost solely guided by his formula in portraying phenomena and the portrayed people act according to the author's laws.

This is so typical for Zola's manner that it would be possible to take this as a specific process characteristic of the methods

---

* Though Zola prided himself on his "scientific documentation," he was a master in selecting and arranging raw material for his own undeniably artistic purposes. Even in his "documentary" notes for *L'Assommoir* one sees the compositional imagination at work in the naked "lists" describing, for example, his central tenement, or the opening violence in the washing-house, or the bitterly fantastic details of Coupeau's alcoholic death.[10] The works of Frank Norris reveal similar environmental compositions.

used by the naturalists of this school. In this way primary
value is given to *an arrangement of phenomena, which themselves flow ecstatically*, in themselves "going out of themselves," for it is at exactly such moments of their existence that
they are seized for description.

And this method is also accompanied by a second, already
rudimentary compositional method: the representation of
phenomena as distributed in such a way *among themselves,
that each of them in relation to each other seems a transition
from one intensity to another, from one "dimension" to another.*

And it is only in the third and last place that this school
rarely employs conditions pointing towards such purely compositional elements as movements within the changing rhythms
of prose, within the nature of the language, or general structure in the movement of episodes and links between episodes.

This part of work falls historically to the share of the school
that replaced that of "naturalism," the school which in its
enthusiasm for this side of the matter often achieves this to
the detriment of a good "Rubens-esque" materiality of imagery, so characteristic for Zola.

With this in mind let us return to the principal object of
our inspection—to the "Odessa steps." Look how this event
there is presented and arranged.

In the first place, noticing the *frenzied condition of the
people and masses that are portrayed*, let us go on to find
what we are looking for in structural and compositional indications.

Let us concentrate on the line of *movement*.

There is, before all else, a chaotic *close-up* rush of figures.
And then, as chaotic a rush of figures in *long-shot*.

Then the *chaos* of movement changes to a design: the
rhythmic descending feet of the soldiers.

Tempo increases. Rhythm accelerates.

In this acceleration of *downward* rushing movement there
is a suddenly upsetting opposite movement—*upward:* the
break-neck movement of the *mass* downward leaps over into a

slowly solemn movement upward of the mother's *lone* figure, carrying her dead son.

Mass. Break-neck speed. Downward.

And then suddenly: A lone figure. Slow solemnity. Upward.

But—this is only for an instant. Once more we experience a returning leap to the downward movement.

Rhythm accelerates. Tempo increases.

Suddenly the tempo of the *running crowd* leaps over into the next category of speed—into a *rolling baby-carriage*. It propels the idea of rushing downward into the next dimension—*from rolling, as understood "figuratively," into the physical fact of rolling*. This is not merely a change in levels of *tempo*. This is furthermore as well a *leap in display method* from the figurative to the physical, taking place within the representation of rolling.

Close-ups leap over into long-shots.

Chaotic movement (of a mass)—into *rhythmic* movement (of the soldiers).

One aspect of moving speed (rushing people)—into the next stage of the same theme of moving speed (rolling baby-carriage).

Movement *downward*—into movement *upward*.

Many volleys of *many* rifles—into *one* shot from *one* of the battleship's guns.

Stride by stride—a leap from dimension to dimension. A leap from quality to quality. So that in the final accounting, rather than in a separate episode (the baby-carriage), *the whole method of exposing* the entire event likewise accomplishes its leap: a *narrative* type of exposition is replaced (in the montage rousing of the stone lion) and transferred to the concentrated structure of *imagery*. Visually rhythmic prose leaps over into visually poetic speech.

In a compositional structure identical with human behavior in the grip of pathos, as remarked above, the sequence of the Odessa steps is carried along with such transfers to opposites: chaos is replaced by rhythm, prose—by poetic treatment, etc. Down each step gallops the action, propelled downward by an *ascending* leap from quality to quality, to deeper intensity, to broader dimension.

And we see the theme of pathos, rushed down the steps by the pathos of the shooting, piercing as well to the depths of the basic structure, which gives a plastic and rhythmic accompaniment to the event.*

Is this episode on the steps unique? Does it fall away from, in this feature, from the general type of construction? Not in the least. In it these features, characteristic for the method, are only a pointed culmination, as pointed as the episode itself, which is a culmination in the tragic quality of the film as a whole.

I have mentioned the *caesurae* in the action, "leaping over" or "transferring" to a new quality that was, in each case, the *maximum of all availables*, and was, each time, a leap *into opposition*. All determining compositional elements encountered anywhere appear in such a way, showing us a fundamental ecstatic formula: the leap "out of oneself" invariably becomes a leap to a new quality, and most often of all achieves the diapason of a leap into opposition.

Here is another organic secret: a leaping imagist movement from quality to quality is *not a mere formula of growth*, but is more, *a formula of development*—a development that involves us in its canon, not only as *a single "vegetative" unit, subordinate to the evolutionary laws of nature*, but makes us, instead, *a collective and social unit, consciously participating in its development*. For we know that this very leap, in the interpretation of social phenomena, is present in those revolutions to which social development and the movement of society are directed.

For the third time the organic-ness of *Potemkin* appears before us, *for that leap which characterizes the structure of each compositional link and the composition of the film as a whole, is an infusion into the compositional structure of the most de-*

---

* I have pointed out previously that this analysis is of solely compositional "main-lines." The fabric of *Potemkin* holds up, however, just as well under more microscopic examination, as in the analysis of fourteen shots, on pages 115-120.

termining element of the content's very theme—the revolutionary explosion, as one of the leaps which function as inseparable bonds of the conducting consciousness of social development.

But:

A leap. A transition from quantity to quality. A transition to opposition.

All these are elements of a dialectical movement of development, elements which enter into the comprehension of materialist dialectics. And from this—for the structure of the work we are analyzing as well as for the structure of any construction of pathos—we can say that a pathetic structure is one that compels us, echoing its movement, *to re-live the moments of culmination and substantiation* that are in the canon of all dialectical processes.

We understand a *moment* of culmination to mean those points in a process, those *instants* in which water becomes a new substance—steam, or ice—water, or pig-iron—steel. Here we see the same going out of oneself, moving from one condition, and passing from quality to quality, *ecstasis*. And if we could register psychologically the perceptions of water, steam, ice, and steel at these critical *moments*—moments of *culmination* in the leap, this would tell us something of pathos, of ecstasy!

Born from the pathos of the theme, the compositional structure echoes that basic and unique canon, by which is achieved the organic, social, or any other process given substance by the universe and through participation in this canon (the reflection of which is our consciousness, and its area of application—all our existence) cannot but fill us to the highest point with emotional sensation—pathos.

A question remains—How is the artist to achieve practically these formulae of composition? By a druggist's prescription? By some slide-rule? By specimens of penmanship? With a skeleton key?

These compositional formulae are to be found in any fully pathetic work. But they are not to be achieved by any single *a priori* compositional computation. Skill alone, craftsmanship alone, mastery alone, is not enough.

To achieve the heights of genuine organic-ness, of genuine pathos, in its highest form, all this is absolutely necessary, but this alone is too little.

Only when the work becomes organic, only when it can enter the conditions of a higher organic-ness—into the field of pathos as we understand it, when the theme and content and idea of the work become an organically continuous unity with the ideas, the feelings, with the very breath of the author.

Only when organic-ness itself takes on the strictest forms of constructing a work, only when the artistry of a master's perceptions reach the last gleam of formal perfection.

Then and then only will occur a genuine organic-ness of a work, which enters the circle of natural and social phenomena as a fellow member with equal rights, as an independent phenomenon.

1 January 1939

Post Scriptum:

This may be the most appropriate place for an answer to a question in regard to the connection between the eccentricism that was characteristic of my theater work, and the pathos that distinguishes my film work. This is an apparent paradox that was pointed out, many years ago, by Victor Shklovsky:

> For the creation of his heroic style Eisenstein had to come to it through the montage of eccentric attractions.[11]

Let us go back to those tendencies in the field of expressiveness that led to eccentricism in my theater work of 1920-23.

I dreamed then of a theater "of such emotional saturation that the wrath of a man would be expressed in a backward somersault from a trapeze."

And this dream was connected with the dramatic or, more exactly, the melodramatic—the *serious*—theater!

Of course, this was not without the intertwining of the most varied influences, but in this initial formula there was already the inference of two basic theses, altogether individual and characteristic for my future program of activity as well as for the methods of its execution.

The first was *a maximum degree of passion as a point of departure*. And, second—*a breaking of the customary dimension as a method of its embodiment*.

From this point of view, our program doesn't sound so "crazy."

In those first days, however, these theses were used not as *principles*, but were carried out *directly* and *literally*. And therefore they found their way, not into drama, but were made familiar through the buffonade, eccentricism, and the montage of attractions.

This dream was realized in its purest form in the circus treatment given Ostrovsky's *Enough Simplicity in Every Sage*. In one scene Maxim Shtraukh, playing Mamayev, and growing angry with his nephew for a caricature he had made of him, threw himself at him head first, breaking through the paper of the portrait in a flying somersault beyond the frame.

This moment can be thought of as symbolic of the whole production both in form and in execution: intensity of action everywhere "flew" beyond the limits of the accepted norm of representation, forcing the action with an unusual degree of tension to jump beyond the limits of the accepted measure and the accepted dimension.

In another part of the play we needed a "tense" scene. Glumov's diary is stolen by Golutvin and handed over to Mamayeva.

"Tension" was taken beyond the frame of a tense performance of the dialogue: we introduced a *new measure* of tension into the scene—a tight-rope. Golutvin, balancing and running along it, spoke his lines. The tension of such an "act on wire" extends the *conventional* tension of acting and transfers it into a new level of *real* physical tension.

Throughout the production there was a continuity of theatrical playing, but at the slightest "rise in temperature," this theatrical "play" leaped over into circus "work": a running jump from quality to quality.

A gesture turns into gymnastics, rage is expressed through a somersault, exaltation through a salto-mortale, lyricism on "the mast of death." The grotesque of this style permitted leaps from one type of expression to another. . . .*

The method worked in comedy, for the leap—a *dynamic* characteristic in a successive process—always proceeds from inside a *static* condition—of a forced external observance of *simultaneity* (i.e., of the same dimension).

The "new quality" was treated as if it were the old—the "preceding" quality. This is in itself one of the means of achieving comic effects. How amusing it is, for example, when the latest stage of conveyance is forced to be dependent on the conveyance of an earlier epoch—when an automobile is harnessed to . . . oxen (as in *Little Red Devils*) or to mules (as in *Le dernier milliardaire*).

It is important that the author himself, in this case, while accomplishing the leap from theater to cinema, also accomplished an inner leap in understanding the method: in practice he understood that the method of the leap, comical under conditions of static appearance, works pathetically under conditions of a dynamic process. But this is something to be discussed in more detail on another occasion.

It is sufficient in the present essay to say that the connection between my eccentric theater work and my pathetic cinema work is more sequential and organic than one might have supposed at first glance!

A NOTE:

Sometimes it seems strange that in matters of practice in the sound-film, that I should resemble the last to arrive at the wedding! Youngest of our directors at the time of its inaugura-

* See "Through Theater to Cinema," above, page 7.

tion, and last to take part in its work. But on closer examination this is not quite so.

My first work in the sound-film was . . . in 1926. And in connection with (again!) *Potemkin*.

Potemkin—at least in its foreign circulation—had a special score written for it. The composer was Edmund Meisel, who wrote music for other silent films, both before and after his work on *Potemkin*. But there was nothing particularly extraordinary in this fact—for the history of silent films is sprinkled with such special scores. Music had even been used within the *filming* of certain films—for example, Ludwig Berger had filmed *Ein Walzertraum* to the music of Strauss.

Less usual, perhaps, was the way the *Potemkin* score was composed. It was written very much as we work today on a sound-track. Or rather, as we *should always work*, with creative friendship and friendly creative collaboration between composer and director.

With Meisel this took place in spite of the short time for composition that he was given, and the brevity of my visit to Berlin in 1926 for this purpose. He agreed at once to forego the purely illustrative function common to musical accompaniments at that time (and not only at that time!) and stress certain "effects," particularly in the "music of machines" in the last reel.

This was my only categorical demand: not only to reject customary melodiousness for this sequence of "Meeting the Squadron," relying entirely on a rhythmic beating of percussion, but also to give substance to this demand by establishing in the music as well as in the film at the decisive place a "throwing over" into a "new quality" in the *sound structure*.

So it was *Potemkin* at this point that stylistically broke away from the limits of the "silent film with musical illustrations" into a new sphere—into *sound-film*, where true models of this art-form live in a unity of fused musical and visual images,*

---

* As we see, our "Statement," appearing two years later [see page 257], posing in this way the question of the audio-visual image, was based on a few proved experiments.

composing the work with a united audio-visual image. It is exactly owing to these elements, *anticipating the potentialities of an inner substance for composition in the sound-film,* that the sequence of "Meeting the Squadron" (which along with the "Odessa steps" had such "crushing" effect abroad) deserves a leading place in the anthology of cinema.

It is especially interesting for me that the general construction of *Potemkin* (a leap into a new quality) maintained in the music everything that pierced the pathetic construction—the condition of a qualitative leap which we have seen in *Potemkin* was inseparable from the organism of the theme.

Here the "silent" *Potemkin* teaches the sound-film a lesson, emphasizing again and again the position that for an organic work a single law of construction must penetrate it decisively in all its "significances," and in order to be not "off-stage," but stand as an organic part of the film, the music must also be governed, not only by the same images and themes, but as well by the same basic laws and principles of construction that govern the work as a whole.

To a considerable degree I was able to accomplish this in the sound-film proper—in my first sound-film, *Alexander Nevsky.* It was possible to accomplish this, thanks to the collaboration with such a wonderful and brilliant artist as Sergei Prokofiev.[12]

ACHIEVEMENT

NEW INTELLECTUAL content, new forms for the embodiment of this content, new methods of theoretical comprehension—these are what startled foreign audiences of the Soviet cinema.

Though not always complete in their thematic solutions, nor perfected in their formal embodiment, and far from conclusive in theoretical knowledge and comprehension (all of which was critically perceived by ourselves), our films came as a revelation in the capitalist countries.

What an unexpected intellectual shock came to America and Europe with the appearance of films in which social problems were suddenly presented with all the dots on all the "i's"—to audiences that had heretofore seen only the rarest and vaguest hints of even an undotted "i" on their screens.

But that in itself was not enough. In this first formally imperfect period, our films, though novel in theme, aroused little more than curiosity.

I recall a half-ironical, half-fastidious appraisal (in, I believe, *Filmkurier*) at the time *Palace and Fortress*, one of our first exported films, was shown in Berlin:

This eye-scratching imperfection of harsh lighting, plus the crudeness of the whole treatment, does have a certain appeal and even piquancy for our jaded vision. . . .

And how deeply the emotions of the foreign spectator were scratched when, after *Potemkin*, our films charged down on him!

Born of new intellectual demands, and of the desire to live up to these demands and to be adequate to them, the formal singularities of our films astonished these audiences no less than had their themes and ideas.

Often preceding official, diplomatic recognition of our country, our films successfully forced their way across frontiers, despite the obstacles of censorship, and with their art enlisted friends even among those who could not immediately realize the scope of our ideals.

So it was our cinema—youngest in years, but the most vigorous, vital and rich in emotion and depth of idea—that very soon took the lead of its older sister arts on the other side of the barriers around us.

And its influence abroad was immense.

If in our beginnings we were more than a little indebted to American film-makers, it may also be said that this debt has been repaid with interest.

When I arrived in New York in 1930 I was literally swamped with clippings referring to Milestone's film version of *All Quiet on the Western Front*, which had just appeared. There was not one review that did not mention our influence on the making of this film!

If Raisman had happened to arrive simultaneously with the appearance of King Vidor's *Our Daily Bread*, he would doubtless have seen similar references to *The Soil Is Thirsty*.

Sternberg's *Shanghai Express* was called to life by Ilya Trauberg's *China Express*, and the obligation of *Wild Boys of the Road* to *Road to Life* is generally admitted.

The German film industry considered *Unser Emden* a direct reply to *Potemkin*, while it may be said that *Viva Villa* reflected the influence of all Soviet film-makers, including *October*—not to mention our unfinished Mexican film, *Que Viva Mexico!* Mamoulian's first film, *Applause*, was completely enslaved by "symbolism of objects," so typical of our films of the 1920's.

This influence of the Soviet cinema is many-sided—with countless indirect instances for each of the cited direct examples. It is sometimes revealed in attempts to deal with broader themes than the eternal triangle—or in a bolder portrayal of reality, a characteristic of our films' search for fidelity—or in the mere wish to make use of those formal methods that are the fruit of our cinema's new intellectual content.

As for a theoretical comprehension of the cinema, there are still few individual efforts in this field outside our country, for only here is there any intensive or systematic attempt by film-makers themselves to work on research and analysis of this most amazing of the arts.

As a genuinely major *art* the cinema is unique in that it is, in the full sense of the term, a child of socialism. The other arts have centuries of tradition behind them. The *years* covered by the *entire* history of cinematography are fewer than the *centuries* in which the other arts have developed.

Yet what is most essential is that *cinema as an art* in general, and, further, as an art not only equal to, but in many respects superior to, its fellow-arts, began to be spoken of seriously only with the beginning of Socialist cinematography.

Though it was a matter of years before the full realization of our cinema, that some of the greatest minds pointed in our country to the cinema as the most important of the arts and the one of greatest mass-potency, it required the appearance of a brilliant constellation of Soviet films before people across the frontier began to speak of the cinema as an art deserving as serious attention as is ordinarily given the theater, literature, or painting.

It was only then that the cinema rose above the level of the music-hall, the amusement park, the zoo, and the chamber of horrors, to take its place within the family of great arts.

The cinema would seem to be the highest stage of embodiment for the potentialities and aspirations of each of the arts.

Moreover, the cinema is that genuine and ultimate synthesis of all artistic manifestations that fell to pieces after the peak of Greek culture, which Diderot sought vainly in opera, Wagner in music-drama, Scriabin in his color-concerti, and so on and on.

For sculpture—cinema is a chain of changing plastic forms, bursting, at long last, ages of immobility.

For painting—cinema is not only a solution for the problem of movement in pictorial images, but is also the achievement of a new and unprecedented form of graphic art, an art that is a free stream of changing, transforming, commingling forms, pictures, and compositions, hitherto possible only in music.

Music has always possessed this possibility, but with the advent of cinema, the melodious and rhythmic flow of music acquired new potentialities of imagery—visual, palpable, concrete (true, our practice of the new art knows as yet but few cases of any complete fusion of aural and visual images).

For literature—cinema is an expansion of the strict diction achieved by poetry and prose into a new realm where the desired image is directly materialized in audio-visual perceptions.

And finally, it is only in cinema that are fused into a real unity all those separate elements of the spectacle once inseparable in the dawn of culture, and which the theater for centuries has vainly striven to amalgamate anew.

Here is real unity:

Of mass and individual, in which the mass is genuine, and not a handful of participants in a "crowd scene," hurrying around back-stage in order to reappear from the opposite wings to give a "bigger" impression.

Here is a unity of man and space. How many inventive minds have striven unsuccessfully to solve this problem on the stage! Gordon Craig, Adolphe Appia, and how many others! And how easily this problem is solved in cinema.

The screen need not adapt itself to the abstractions of Craig in order to make man and his environment commensurate. Not satisfied with the mere reality of the setting, the screen compels reality itself to participate in the action. "Our woods and hills will dance"—this is no longer merely an amusing line from a Krylov fable, but the orchestral part played by the landscape, which plays as much of a part in the film as does everything else. In a single cinematographic act, the film fuses people and a single individual, town and country. It fuses them with dizzying change and transfer. With an all-embracing compass of whole countries or of any single character. With its ability to follow watchfully not only the clouds gathering in the hills, but also the swelling of a tear from beneath an eyelash.

The diapason of the dramatist's creative potentialities widens beyond all limits. And the keyboard of the sound mixer, who long ago ceased to be a mere composer, stretches for miles to the right and to the left, embracing not only all the sounds of nature, but also any that the author may invent.

We sometimes forget that we have in our hands—a genuine miracle, a miracle of technical and artistic potentialities, only a fraction of which we have as yet learned to utilize.

We who have learned that there are neither limits nor insurmountable barriers to creative activity shall do well to recall this.

Again and again and again will all the advantages of the cinema flash out if we can picture the arts arranged according to the degree in which they are adapted to their chief task— the reflection of reality and the master of this reality—man.

How narrow is the diapason of sculpture which in most cases is obliged to tear man from his inseparable environment and society in order to hint—by his features and posture—at his inner world which is a mirror of the world around him. A diapason bereft of word, color, movement, the changing phases of drama, the progressive unfolding of events.

How frustrated have been those efforts by composers—Richard Strauss, in particular—to burden music with the task of conveying specific images.

How bound is literature, capable of penetrating into the most subtle coils of a man's consciousness, as well as into the movement of events and epochs, with speculative methods and melodic-rhythmic means, but can only hint at that amplitude of the senses, called for by every line and every page.

How imperfect and limited, too, is the theater in this respect! Only by external "*physical action*" *and behavior* is it able to convey to the spectator the inner content, the inner movement of consciousness and feelings, the inner world in which live the characters and the author himself. But this is not the material of representation alone.

Rejecting incidentals as well as the "imitative limitations" of the arts as defined by Lessing, and basing ourselves on the most important factors, we might describe the method of each of the arts:

The method of sculpture—patterned on the human body's structure.

The method of painting—patterned on the positions of bodies and their relations with nature.

The method of literature—patterned on the interrelations of reality and man.

The method of theater—patterned on the behavior and activity of people roused by outer and inner motives.

The method of music—patterned on the laws of the inner harmonies of emotionally apprehended phenomena.

In one way or another, all of these—from the most external and lapidary, but more material and less ephemeral, to the most subtle and plastic, but less concrete and tragically ephemeral—with all the means at their disposal, strain towards a single aim.

And that is, through their structures and methods—to reconstruct, to reflect reality, and above all the consciousness and feelings of man. None of the "previous" arts has been able to achieve this purpose to the full.

For the ceiling of one is—the body of man.

The ceiling of another—his acts and behavior.

The ceiling of a third—is the elusive emotional harmony that attends these.

The full embrace of the whole inner world of man, of a whole reproduction of the outer world, cannot be achieved by any one of them.

When any of these arts strives to accomplish this end, by venturing outside its own frame, the very base that holds the art together is inevitably broken.

The most heroic attempt to achieve this in literature was made by James Joyce in *Ulysses* and in *Finnegans Wake*.

Here was reached the limit in reconstructing the reflection and refraction of reality in the consciousness and feelings of man.

Joyce's originality is expressed in his attempt to solve this task with a special dual-level method of writing: unfolding the display of events simultaneously with the particular manner in which these events pass through the consciousness and feelings, the associations and emotions of one of his chief characters. Here literature, as nowhere else, achieves an almost physiological palpability. To the whole arsenal of literary methods of influence has been added a compositional structure that I would call "ultra-lyrical." For while the lyric, equally with the imagery, reconstructs the most intimate passage of the inner logic of feeling, Joyce patterns it on the physiological organization of the emotions, as well as on the embryology of the formation of thought.

The effect at times is astounding, but the price paid is the entire dissolution of the very foundation of literary diction, the entire decomposition of literary method itself; for the lay reader the text has been turned into abracadabra.

In this Joyce shared the sad fate of all the so-called "left" tendencies in art that reached full flower with the entry of capitalism into its imperialist stage.

And if we examine these "leftist" arts from the viewpoint of the tendency as described, we find an extremely curious explanation of this phenomenon.

On the one hand, there is a firm belief in the permanency of the existing order, and hence—a conviction of the limitations of man.

On the other hand, the arts feel a need to step beyond their limitations.

This frequently produces an explosion, but an explosion directed not outwards, towards the widening of the art's frame, which is only to be achieved by extending its content in an anti-imperialist and revolutionary direction, but inwards, towards *means*, not towards *content*. The explosion is not creative and progressive, but destructive.

The arts themselves can escape the fetters of bourgeois limitations only in a revolutionary ideology and in revolutionary themes.

As for their expressive means, escape here lies in a transition to a more perfected stage of all their potentialities—to cinema.

For only the cinema can take, as the esthetic basis of its

dramaturgy, not only the statics of the human body and the dynamics of its action and behavior, but an infinitely broader diapason, reflecting the manifold movement and changing feelings and thoughts of man. This is not merely material for the depiction of man's action and behavior on the screen, but is also the compositional framework over which is distributed a conscious and sensed reflection of the world and reality.

How easily the cinema is able to spread out in an equal graphic of sound and sight the richness of actuality and the richness of its controlling forces, compelling the theme more and more to be born through the process of cinematographic narrative, written from a position of emotion indivisible from the feeling and thinking man.

This is not a task for the theater. This is a level above the "ceiling" of its possibilities. And when it wishes to leap over the limits of these possibilities it also, no less than literature, has to pay the price of its life-like and realistic qualities. It has to retire into the immateriality of a Maeterlinck, as we have seen in his works, and whose "*program*" dreamed for the theater found this ideal as elusive as his own blue-bird!

What debris of anti-realism does the theater inevitably land in the moment it sets itself "synthetic" aims! We need only point to two illustrations of this truth: the *Théâtre d'Art* and the *Théâtre des Arts*—both opening in Paris, in 1890 and 1910 respectively.

The maxim of the first of these theaters, founded by the symbolist poet Paul Fort, was: *La parole crée le décor comme le reste.*[1]

In practice, this led to the productions such as of Pierre Quillard's *La Fille aux mains coupées* (1891). This play,

... in the form of a dialogue poem, was staged in this way: a narrator, standing at the side of the proscenium, read the prose passages indicating scene-changes and plot-exposition, while on the stage, veiled by a gauze curtain, the actors moved and declaimed the verses against the background of a golden panel representing primitive ikon-like figures of angels in prayer, painted by Paul Séruzier. This stylized scenery was ... to serve as a means for "disclosing the lyricism imprisoned in the verses." [2]

The critic Pierre Véber wrote:

Preference is given the lyrical word. The theater seems to vanish, to make way for dialogue declamation, itself a sort of poetic scenery.

Pierre Quillard demanded that "the scenery be a purely ornamental figment, serving to supplement the illusion by analogies, in color and line, with the drama." [3]

Seeking new methods of "inductive contagion" of the spectators, Paul Fort's theater sought to give the substance of practice to the theory of correspondences between the different senses, a popular idea among the poets and theoreticians of symbolism. . . .[4]

These new directions in the theater, by no means reprehensible in themselves, led to the most absurd and superficial excesses.

[Paul Fort] presented Le Cantique des Cantiques by J.-Napoléon Roinard "in eight mystical emblems and three paraphrases," with an accompaniment of music and of perfumes "composed in a tonality corresponding to the various verses." For the author, inspired by Rimbaud's Voyelles, by René Ghil's theory of instrumentation and by the Livre d'orchestration des Parfums by Chardin Hardancourt, sought to establish a harmony of musical tone, of poem and of setting, and of the odors of perfumes.[5]

I believe that it was an imperfection of correspondence found among the other elements that led to this absurdity.

The program of the latter theater (founded by the wealthy dilettante, Jacques Rouché) contained many items of a similar nature, such as, "the designers Dethomas, Drésa, and Piot excelled in the invention of conventionalized scenery, attempting to compose 'a symphony of colors supplementing the symphony of sounds.'" [6]

All such attempts at synthesis inevitably wreck themselves and lead only to anti-realism.

Yet when these same aims are set for cinema, they not only do not lead it away from realism, but actually increase the power of its realistic affect.

The unexpected "informing" narrator, for example, who is patterned after the narrator in the Kabuki theater, was perfectly and organically interwoven in the form of sub-titles into the texture of the film even in its silent period.

Today the sub-title still unobtrusively narrates "prose passages indicating scene-changes and plot-exposition," while leaving the lyrical experience of the characters to the pictorial element of the film.

Even in the silent film we made attempts to move further in this direction by weaving the sub-titles into the very thick of the action, dramatizing them with montage and varying proportions within the frame. Recall the titles within the opening sequence of *Old and New*, which were brought directly into the emotional rhythm and the atmosphere of the film.

100

not 10,

not 20,

but precisely

one hundred

billion   and so on.[7]

In the sound-film the sub-title, maintaining its place among the expressive means (try to remove the titles from *Minin and Pozharsky* * and see what is left!), and its counterpart, the actual voice of the narrator (a "convention" nearly identical with that of the theaters we have been describing), are successfully employed. The latter means is a voice whose dramatically weaving potentialities have scarcely been touched by the cinema.

The late Pirandello used to dream aloud of what could be done with this voice, when we met in Berlin in 1929.

How close is such a voice, intervening in the action from outside the action, to Pirandello's whole concept! Its employment for ironical purposes was quite successfully demonstrated by René Clair in *Le dernier milliardaire*, and even more cleverly by Kuleshov in his O. Henry film, *The Great Consoler*.

In Soviet films the only dramatic and even tragic design has been given this voice by Esther Schub and the author of her commentary, Vsevold Vishnevsky, in *Spain*, though its effect was obscured by insufficiently considered composition of the narration and by poor recording. However, the original for this and many other similar uses in the documentary film can be found in Ernest Hemingway's text, written and spoken for Ivens's *The Spanish Earth*.

The "mystery" of the gauze stretched across the stage of the *Théâtre d'Art* apparently lies in a desire to "unify" the diversity of the materially real environment of painted scenery, three-dimensional people, and real textures (such as gilded surfaces).

This is the most difficult of problems for the theater (a solution for it has been sought in hundreds of variations, almost always leading to some degree of meaninglessness), but the cinema is able to solve the problem with the greatest of ease, operating as it does with photographically captured images equally as real in appearance as the objects themselves. In the

---

* Written by Victor Shklovsky and directed by Pudovkin, this is the least known of Pudovkin's films in the United States, receiving here in 1940 only a limited circulation without superimposed English titles. —EDITOR.

mysteries of fanciful, active, and not merely naturalistically passive sound-recording, lies the similar secret potentiality of harmonizing sounds, which in their direct, life-like substance, may not be capable of combination and orchestration.

Lastly, the cinema achieves its greatest success in a field from which the theater has had to retire, defeated. This is not only in that "symphony of colors supplementing the symphony of sounds," where the cinema has enjoyed an especially happy victory.*

No, this is in a victory within reach of the cinema alone.

This is a genuine and complete "disclosure of the lyricism imprisoned in the verses,"—that lyricism which inevitably possesses the author of a film in its particularly emotional passages.

We have remarked the frustrating results of this attempt in both the "left" theater and in "left" literature.

The solution of this problem has been left entirely to the cinema.

Only here can real events, preserving all the richness of material and sensual fullness, be *simultaneously*—

epic, in the revelation of their content,

dramatic, in the treatment of their subject, and

lyrical to that degree of perfection from which is echoed the most delicate nuance of the author's experience of the theme— possible only in such an exquisite model of form as the system of audio-visual images of the cinema.

When a film-work or any part of one achieves this triple dramatic synthesis, its impressive power is particularly great.

The three sequences which I consider most successful in my own work have this character: they are epic, dramatic, and at the same time, most lyrical, if lyricism is understood as those nuances of multiple individual experience which determine the resulting forms.

These sequences are the "Odessa steps" and "meeting the

---

* I do not mean only in the use of processes, such as Technicolor, Agfacolor, etc., but in the sensitive use of the rich range from black to white, within the sound film.

squadron" in *Potemkin*, and the "attack of the knights" in *Alexander Nevsky*. I have written in detail * of the first and third of these sequences, saying of the steps sequence that in its compositional progress "it behaves like a human being in a state of ecstasy," and that the advancing gallop of the knights is "in subject—the beat of hoofs; in structure—the beat of an excited heart. . . ."

The same may be said of the *Potemkin*'s meeting with the fleet, where the pounding machinery was meant to embody the excited collective heart of the battleship, while the rhythm and cadences of this beating were meant to reproduce the lyrical experience of the author as he imagined himself in the position of the rebellious ship.

Cinema solves such problems with the utmost ease.

But the point is not the ease with which it does so, nor that it can do so at all. What matters is the concreteness, materiality, and absolute compatibility of all these achievements with the demands of realism, that categorical condition for vital, worthy, and fruitful art—for Socialist art.

Thus, in respect to all these features the cinema is a step ahead of all related fields, while remaining a contemporary of theater, painting, sculpture, and music. There was a time when, with youthful presumption, I considered that it was time for all the other arts to retire, now that an art had appeared more advanced than any of them in their own potentialities and functions. Fifteen years ago, when I was just "contemplating" film work, I called theater and cinema "the two skulls of Alexander the Great." [8] Recalling the anecdote of the museum show-booth, among whose displays were the skull of Alexander at the age of twenty-five and, alongside it, his skull at the age of forty, I held that the existence of the theater alongside the cinema was equally absurd, for the cinema was actually the grown-up age of the theater. . . .

Of course, this was rather a fact from my own biography, for it was I that was growing up, out of the theater into cin-

* In the preceding essay.

ema. It cannot be denied that the theater has staunchly with-
stood my attacks, and is still consorting peaceably with its
more advanced form, which is cinema.

Perhaps this advance is not quite obvious to somebody? Is
there any need to pile instance on instance to prove this self-
evident fact over and over again?

Let us confine the case at this time to one theatrical element, to the most theatrical element in the theater—the actor.
Has not the cinema made demands on the actor that surpass
in refinement all that he needs for survival on the stage?

Look at the film work of even the best actors, especially in
their first steps in this medium. Isn't it true that what seemed
the height of truth and emotional fidelity on the stage howls
from the screen as the most extraordinary overacting and epi-
leptic grimaces?

How much effort had to be made by even the finest masters
of the stage before they were able to rebuild a craft developed
in the wide frame of the theater—in the "narrow gate" of the
screen! How much more exquisite and subtle their acting becomes from scene to scene, and even from film to film! Under
the very eyes of the spectator "theatricality" is transformed
into genuine vitality on the screen. How astonishing and illuminating in this respect was the development of the late Boris
Shchukin not only from rôle to rôle, but from film to film,
playing the same rôle! Watch him in *Lenin in October*, and
then in *Lenin in 1918!*

Self-control exerted to the millimeter of movement. A degree of fidelity of feeling that permits no refuge in theatrical
conventions abolished by cinema. Super-concentration and instantaneous assumption of rôle, both incomparably more difficult in films than in the theater where the actor does not have
to burn under the lights of the studio or create his rôle in the
midst of a city street, or in the ocean surf, or in the cockpit
of a supposedly looping plane—or to first play death and then
two months later, to play the cold that led to it!

As we can see, the indices are the same, but the demands have
grown enormously, and a retrospective enrichment of previous

stages of development, proceeding alongside, is obvious and undeniable.

And conversely.

To discriminate and, having discriminated, to develop one or another element of cinema is possible only through a thorough study of the basic phenomena of cinema. And the origin of each of these elements lies in other arts.

No one, without learning all the secrets of *mise-en-scène* completely, can learn montage.

An actor who has not mastered the entire arsenal of theater craft can never fully develop his screen potentialities.

Only after mastering the whole culture of the graphic arts can a cameraman realize the compositional basis of the shot.

And only on a foundation of the entire experience of dramaturgy, epos, and lyricism, can a writer create a finished work in that unprecedented literary phenomenon—film-writing, which includes in itself just such a synthesis of literary forms as the cinema as a whole comprises a synthesis of all forms of art.

The inexhaustible potential of all art, having achieved its highest level of development in the form of cinema, is offered not only to masters, artists, craftsmen. Just as priceless is what this furthest development of art as a whole offers to those who meditate on the general laws of artistic creation—and to those who endeavor theoretically to grasp the phenomena of art generally as a social phenomenon with its original and inimitable methods of reflecting the world and actuality.

For this purpose our cinema is an inexhaustible quarry for the definition of general laws and conditions of art as one of the most characteristic reflections of man's spiritual activity.

Having at our disposal so perfect a stage of development of all the arts, fused into one—in cinematography, we may already make infinite deductions from it as to the entire system and method of art, exhaustive for all arts, yet peculiar and individual for each of them.

For here—in cinema—for the first time we have achieved *a genuinely synthetic art—an art of organic synthesis in its very*

*essence, not a "concert" of co-existent, contiguous, "linked,"
but actually independent arts.*

At last we have had placed in our hands a means of learning
the fundamental laws of art—laws which hitherto we could
snatch at only piecemeal, here a bit from the experience of
painting, there a bit from theater practice, somewhere else
from musical theory. So, the *method of cinema, when fully
comprehended, will enable us to reveal an understanding of the
method of art in general.*

We indeed have something to be proud of on this twentieth
anniversary of our cinema. Within our country. And beyond
its borders. Within the art of cinema itself—and far beyond its
borders, throughout the whole system of art.

Yes, we have something to be proud of—and to work
towards.

[1939]

DICKENS, GRIFFITH,
AND THE FILM TODAY

> People talked as if there had been no dra-
> matic or descriptive music before Wagner; no
> impressionist painting before Whistler; whilst
> as to myself, I was finding that the surest way
> to produce an effect of daring innovation and
> originality was to revive the ancient attraction
> of long rhetorical speeches; to stick closely
> to the methods of Molière; and to lift char-
> acters bodily out of the pages of Charles
> Dickens.
>
> GEORGE BERNARD SHAW [1]

"THE KETTLE began it. . . ."

Thus Dickens opens his *Cricket on the Hearth.*

"The kettle began it. . . ."

What could be further from films! Trains, cowboys, chases
. . . And *The Cricket on the Hearth?* "The kettle began it!"
But, strange as it may seem, movies also were boiling in that
kettle. From here, from Dickens, from the Victorian novel,
stem the first shoots of American film esthetic, forever linked
with the name of David Wark Griffith.

Although at first glance this may not seem surprising, it
does appear incompatible with our traditional concepts of cinematography, in particular with those associated in our minds
with the American cinema. Factually, however, this relationship is organic, and the "genetic" line of descent is quite consistent.

Let us first look at that land where, although not perhaps its
birthplace, the cinema certainly found the soil in which to
grow to unprecedented and unimagined dimensions.

We know from whence the cinema appeared first as a world-wide phenomenon. We know the inseparable link between the cinema and the industrial development of America. We know how production, art and literature reflect the capitalist breadth and construction of the United States of America. And we also know that American capitalism finds its sharpest and most expressive reflection in the American cinema.

But what possible identity is there between this Moloch of modern industry, with its dizzy tempo of cities and subways, its roar of competition, its hurricane of stock market transactions on the one hand, and . . . the peaceful, patriarchal Victorian London of Dickens's novels on the other?

Let's begin with this "dizzy tempo," this "hurricane," and this "roar." These are terms used to describe the United States by persons who know that country solely through books— books limited in quantity, and not too carefully selected.

Visitors to New York City soon recover from their astonishment at this sea of lights (which is actually immense), this maelstrom of the stock market (actually its like is not to be found anywhere), and all this roar (almost enough to deafen one).

As far as the speed of the traffic is concerned, one can't be overwhelmed by this in the streets of the metropolis for the simple reason that speed can't exist there. This puzzling contradiction lies in the fact that the high-powered automobiles are so jammed together that they can't move much faster than snails creeping from block to block, halting at every crossing not only for pedestrian crowds but for the counter-creeping of the cross-traffic.

As you make your merely minute progress amidst a tightly packed glacier of other humans, sitting in similarly high-powered and imperceptibly moving machines, you have plenty of time to ponder the duality behind the dynamic face of America, and the profound interdependence of this duality in everybody and everything American. As your 90-horsepower motor pulls you jerkily from block to block along the steep-cliffed streets, your eyes wander over the smooth surfaces of the skyscrapers. Notions lazily crawl through your brain: "Why don't they seem high?" "Why should they, with all that height, still seem cozy, domestic, small-town?"

You suddenly realize what "trick" the skyscrapers play on you: although they have many floors, each floor is quite low. Immediately the soaring skyscraper appears to be built of a number of small-town buildings, piled on top of each other. One merely needs to go beyond the city-limits or, in a few cities, merely beyond the center of the city, in order to see the same buildings, piled, not by the dozens, and fifties, and hundreds, on top of each other, but laid out in endless rows of one- and two-storied stores and cottages along Main Streets, or along half-rural side-streets.

Here (between the "speed traps") you can fly along as fast as you wish; here the streets are almost empty, traffic is light—the exact opposite of the metropolitan congestion that you just left—no trace of that frantic activity choked in the stone vises of the city.

You often come across regiments of skyscrapers that have moved deep into the countryside, twisting their dense nets of railroads around them; but at the same rate small-town agrarian America appears to have overflowed into all but the very centers of the cities; now and then one turns a skyscraper corner, only to run head on into some home of colonial architecture, apparently whisked from some distant savannah of Louisiana or Alabama to this very heart of the business city.

But there where this provincial wave has swept in more than a cottage here or a church there (gnawing off a corner of that monumental modern Babylon, "Radio City"), or a cemetery, unexpectedly left behind in the very center of the financial district, or the hanging wash of the Italian district, flapping just around the corner, off Wall Street—this good old provincialism has turned inward to apartments, nestling in clusters around fireplaces, furnished with soft grandfather-chairs and the lace doilies that shroud the wonders of modern technique: refrigerators, washing-machines, radios.

And in the editorial columns of popular newspapers, in the aphorisms of broadcast sermon and transcribed advertisement, there is a firmly entrenched attitude that is usually defined as "way down East"—an attitude that may be found beneath many a waistcoat or bowler where one would ordinarily expect to find a heart or a brain. Mostly one is amazed by the abundance of small-town and patriarchal elements in American life and manners, morals and philosophy, the ideological horizon and rules of behavior in the middle strata of American culture.

In order to understand Griffith, one must visualize an America made up of more than visions of speeding automobiles, streamlined trains, racing ticker tape, inexorable conveyor-belts. One is obliged to comprehend this second side of America as well—America, the traditional, the patriarchal, the provincial. And then you will be considerably less astonished by this link between Griffith and Dickens.

The threads of both these Americas are interwoven in the style and personality of Griffith—as in the most fantastic of his own parallel montage sequences.

What is most curious is that Dickens appears to have guided *both* lines of Griffith's style, reflecting both faces of America: Small-Town America, and Super-Dynamic America.

This can be detected at once in the "intimate" Griffith of contemporary or past American life, where Griffith is profound, in those films about which Griffith told me, that "they were made for myself and were invariably rejected by the exhibitors."

But we are a little astonished when we see that the construction of the "official," sumptuous Griffith, the Griffith of tempestuous tempi, of dizzying action, of breathtaking chases—has also been guided by the same Dickens! But we shall see how true this is.

First the "intimate" Griffith, and the "intimate" Dickens. *The kettle began it. . . .*

As soon as we recognize this kettle as a typical close-up, we exclaim: "Why didn't we notice it before! Of course this is the purest Griffith. How often we've seen such a close-up at the beginning of an episode, a sequence, or a whole film by him!" (By the way, we shouldn't overlook the fact that one of Griffith's earliest films was based on *The Cricket on the Hearth!* *)

Certainly, this kettle is a typical Griffith-esque close-up. A close-up saturated, we now become aware, with typically Dickens-esque "atmosphere," with which Griffith, with equal mastery, can envelop the severe face of life in *Way Down East,* and the icy cold moral face of his characters, who push the guilty Anna (Lillian Gish) onto the shifting surface of a swirling ice-break.

Isn't this the same implacable atmosphere of cold that is given by Dickens, for example, in *Dombey and Son?* The image of Mr. Dombey is revealed through cold and prudery. And the print of cold lies on everyone and everything—everywhere. And "atmosphere"—always and everywhere—is one of the most expressive means of revealing the inner world and ethical countenance of the characters themselves.

We can recognize this particular method of Dickens in Griffith's inimitable bit-characters who seem to have run straight from life onto the screen. I can't recall who speaks with whom in one of the street scenes of the modern story of *Intolerance.* But I shall never forget the mask of the passer-by with nose pointed forward between spectacles and straggly beard, walking with hands behind his back as if he were manacled. As he passes he interrupts the most pathetic moment in the conversation of the suffering boy and girl. I can remember next to nothing of the couple, but this passer-by, who is visible in the shot only for a flashing glimpse, stands alive before me now—and I haven't seen the film for twenty years!

Occasionally these unforgettable figures actually walked into Griffith's films almost directly from the street: a bit-player, developed in Griffith's hands to stardom; the passer-by who may never again have been filmed; and that mathematics

* Released on May 27, 1909, with Herbert Pryor, Linda Arvidson Griffith, Violet Mersereau, Owen Moore, this film followed the dramatic adaptation of the *Cricket* made by Albert Smith with Dickens's approval.

teacher who was invited to play a terrifying butcher in *America*—the late Louis Wolheim—who ended the film career thus begun with his incomparable performance as "Kat" in *All Quiet on the Western Front*.

These striking figures of sympathetic old men are also quite in the Dickens tradition; and these noble and slightly one-dimensional figures of sorrow and fragile maidens; and these rural gossips and sundry odd characters. They are especially convincing in Dickens when he uses them briefly, in episodes.

The only other thing to be noticed about [Pecksniff] is that here, as almost everywhere else in the novels, the best figures are at their best when they have least to do. Dickens's characters are perfect as long as he can keep them out of his stories. Bumble is divine until a dark and practical secret is entrusted to him. . . . Micawber is noble when he is doing nothing; but he is quite unconvincing when he is spying on Uriah Heep. . . . Similarly, while Pecksniff is the best thing in the story, the story is the worst thing in Pecksniff. . . .[2]

Free of this limitation, and with the same believability, Griffith's characters grow from episodic figures into those fascinating and finished images of living people, in which his screen is so rich.

Instead of going into detail about this, let us rather return to that more obvious fact—the growth of that second side of Griffith's creative craftsmanship—as a magician of tempo and montage; a side for which it is rather surprising to find the same Victorian source.

When Griffith proposed to his employers the novelty of a parallel "cut-back" for his first version of *Enoch Arden* (*After Many Years*, 1908), this is the discussion that took place, as recorded by Linda Arvidson Griffith in her reminiscences of Biograph days:

When Mr. Griffith suggested a scene showing Annie Lee waiting for her husband's return to be followed by a scene of Enoch cast away on a desert island, it was altogether too distracting. "How can you tell a story jumping about like that? The people won't know what it's about."

"Well," said Mr. Griffith, "doesn't Dickens write that way?"

"Yes, but that's Dickens; that's novel writing; that's different."

"Oh, not so much, these are picture stories; not so different." [3]

But, to speak quite frankly, all astonishment on this subject and the apparent unexpectedness of such statements can be ascribed only to our—ignorance of Dickens.

All of us read him in childhood, gulped him down greedily, without realizing that much of his irresistibility lay not only in his capture of detail in the childhoods of his heroes, but also in that spontaneous, childlike skill for story-telling, equally typical for Dickens and for the American cinema, which so surely and delicately plays upon the infantile traits in its audience. We were even less concerned with the technique of Dickens's composition: for us this was non-existent—but captivated by the effects of this technique, we feverishly followed his characters from page to page, watching his characters now being rubbed from view at the most critical moment, then seeing them return afresh between the separate links of the parallel secondary plot.

As children, we paid no attention to the mechanics of this. As adults, we rarely re-read his novels. And becoming film-workers, we never found time to glance beneath the covers of these novels in order to figure out what exactly had captivated us in these novels and with what means these incredibly many-paged volumes had chained our attention so irresistibly.

Apparently Griffith was more perceptive . . .

But before disclosing what the steady gaze of the American film-maker may have caught sight of on Dickens's pages, I wish to recall what David Wark Griffith himself represented to us, the young Soviet film-makers of the 'twenties.

To say it simply and without equivocation: a revelation.

Try to remember our early days, in those first years of the October socialist revolution. The fires *At the Hearthsides* of our native film-producers had burnt out, the *Nava's Charms* *

---

* *Nava's Charms* (by Sologub) and *At the Hearthside*, two pre-Revolutionary Russian films, as is also *Forget the Hearth*. The names that follow are of the male and female film stars of this period.—EDITOR.

of their productions had lost their power over us and, whispering through pale lips, "Forget the hearth," Khudoleyev and Runich, Polonsky and Maximov had departed to oblivion; Vera Kholodnaya to the grave; Mozhukhin and Lisenko to expatriation.

The young Soviet cinema was gathering the experience of revolutionary reality, of first experiments (Vertov), of first systematic ventures (Kuleshov), in preparation for that unprecedented explosion in the second half of the 'twenties, when it was to become an independent, mature, original art, immediately gaining world recognition.

In those early days a tangle of the widest variety of films was projected on our screens. From out of this weird hash of old Russian films and new ones that attempted to maintain "traditions," and new films that could not yet be called Soviet, and foreign films that had been imported promiscuously, or brought down off dusty shelves—two main streams began to emerge.

On the one side there was the cinema of our neighbor, postwar Germany. Mysticism, decadence, dismal fantasy followed in the wake of the unsuccessful revolution of 1923, and the screen was quick to reflect this mood. *Nosferatu the Vampire*, *The Street*, the mysterious *Warning Shadows*, the mystic criminal *Dr. Mabuse the Gambler*,* reaching out towards us from our screens, achieved the limits of horror, showing us a future as an unrelieved night crowded with sinister shadows and crimes. . . .

The chaos of multiple exposures, of over-fluid dissolves, of split screens, was more characteristic of the later 'twenties (as in *Looping the Loop* or *Secrets of a Soul* †), but earlier German films contained more than a hint of this tendency. In the

---

* *Nosferatu* (1922), directed by F. W. Murnau; *Die Strasse* (1923), directed by Karl Grune; *Schatten* (1923), directed by Arthur Robison; *Dr. Mabuse, der Spieler* (1922), directed by Fritz Lang.

† *Looping the Loop* (1928), directed by Arthur Robison; *Geheimnisse einer Seele* (1926), directed by G. W. Pabst.

over-use of these devices was also reflected the confusion and chaos of post-war Germany.

All these tendencies of mood and method had been fore-shadowed in one of the earliest and most famous of these films, *The Cabinet of Dr. Caligari* (1920), this barbaric carnival of the destruction of the healthy human infancy of our art, this common grave for normal cinema origins, this combination of silent hysteria, particolored canvases, daubed flats, painted faces, and the unnatural broken gestures and actions of monstrous chimaeras.

Expressionism left barely a trace on our cinema. This painted, hypnotic "St. Sebastian of Cinema" was too alien to the young, robust spirit and body of the rising class.

It is interesting that during those years inadequacies in the field of film technique played a positive rôle. They helped to restrain from a false step those whose enthusiasm might have pulled them in this dubious direction. Neither the dimensions of our studios, nor our lighting equipment, nor the materials available to us for make-up, costumes, or setting, gave us the possibility to heap onto the screen similar phantasmagoria. But it was chiefly another thing that held us back: our spirit urged us towards life—amidst the people, into the surging actuality of a regenerating country. Expressionism passed into the formative history of our cinema as a powerful factor—of repulsion.

There was the rôle of another film-factor that appeared, dashing along in such films as *The Gray Shadow, The House of Hate, The Mark of Zorro.** There was in these films a world, stirring and incomprehensible, but neither repulsive nor alien. On the contrary—it was captivating and attractive, in its own way engaging the attention of young and future film-makers, exactly as the young and future engineers of the time were attracted by the specimens of engineering techniques unknown

---

* *The House of Hate* (1918), a serial directed by George Seitz, with Pearl White; *The Mark of Zorro* (1921), directed by Fred Niblo, with Douglas Fairbanks. The American film released in Russia as *The Gray Shadow* has not been identified.—EDITOR.

to us, sent from that same unknown, distant land across the ocean.

What enthralled us was not only these films, it was also their possibilities. Just as it was the possibilities in a tractor to make collective cultivation of the fields a reality, it was the boundless temperament and tempo of these amazing (and amazingly useless!) works from an unknown country that led us to muse on the possibilities of a profound, intelligent, class-directed use of this wonderful tool.

The most thrilling figure against this background was Griffith, for it was in his works that the cinema made itself felt as more than an entertainment or pastime. The brilliant new methods of the American cinema were united in him with a profound emotion of story, with human acting, with laughter and tears, and all this was done with an astonishing ability to preserve all that gleam of a filmically dynamic holiday, which had been captured in *The Gray Shadow* and *The Mark of Zorro* and *The House of Hate*. That the cinema could be incomparably greater, and that this was to be the basic task of the budding Soviet cinema—these were sketched for us in Griffith's creative work, and found ever new confirmation in his films.

Our heightened curiosity of those years in *construction and method* swiftly discerned wherein lay the most powerful affective factors in this great American's films. This was in a hitherto unfamiliar province, bearing a name that was familiar to us, not in the field of art, but in that of engineering and electrical apparatus, first touching art in its most advanced section—in cinematography. This province, this method, this principle of building and construction was *montage*.

This was the montage whose foundations had been laid by American film-culture, but whose full, completed, conscious use and world recognition was established by our films. Montage, the rise of which will be forever linked with the name of Griffith. Montage, which played a most vital rôle in the creative work of Griffith and brought him his most glorious successes.

Griffith arrived at it through the method of parallel action. And, essentially, it was on this that he came to a standstill. But we mustn't run ahead. Let us examine the question of how montage came to Griffith or—how Griffith came to montage.

Griffith arrived at montage through the method of parallel action, and he was led to the idea of parallel action by—Dickens!

To this fact Griffith himself has testified, according to A. B. Walkley, in *The Times* of London, for April 26, 1922, on the occasion of a visit by the director to London. Writes Mr. Walkley:

He [Griffith] is a pioneer, by his own admission, rather than an inventor. That is to say, he has opened up new paths in Film Land, under the guidance of ideas supplied to him from outside. His best ideas, it appears, have come to him from Dickens, who has always been his favorite author. . . . Dickens inspired Mr. Griffith with an idea, and his employers (mere "business" men) were horrified at it; but, says Mr. Griffith, "I went home, re-read one of Dickens's novels, and came back next day to tell them they could either make use of my idea or dismiss me."

Mr. Griffith found the idea to which he clung thus heroically in Dickens. That was as luck would have it, for he might have found the same idea almost anywhere. Newton deduced the law of gravitation from the fall of an apple; but a pear or a plum would have done just as well. The idea is merely that of a "break" in the narrative, a shifting of the story from one group of characters to another group. People who write the long and crowded novels that Dickens did, especially when they are published in parts, find this practice a convenience. You will meet with it in Thackeray, George Eliot, Trollope, Meredith, Hardy, and, I suppose, every other Victorian novelist. . . . Mr. Griffith might have found the same practice not only in Dumas *père*, who cared precious little about form, but also in great artists like Tolstoy, Turgeniev, and Balzac. But, as a matter of fact, it was not in any of these others, but in Dickens that he found it; and it is significant of the predominant influence of Dickens that he should be quoted as an authority for a device which is really common to fiction at large.

Even a superficial acquaintance with the work of the great English novelist is enough to persuade one that Dickens may have given and did give to cinematography far more guidance than that which led to the montage of parallel action alone.

Dickens's nearness to the characteristics of cinema in method, style, and especially in viewpoint and exposition, is indeed amazing. And it may be that in the nature of exactly these characteristics, in their community both for Dickens and for cinema, there lies a portion of the secret of that mass success which they both, apart from themes and plots, brought and still bring to the particular quality of such exposition and such writing.

What were the novels of Dickens for his contemporaries, for his readers? There is one answer: they bore the same relation to them that the film bears to the same strata in our time. They compelled the reader to live with the same passions. They appealed to the same good and sentimental elements as does the film (at least on the surface); they alike shudder before vice,* they alike mill the extraordinary, the unusual, the fantastic, from boring, prosaic and everyday existence. And they clothe this common and prosaic existence in their special vision.

Illumined by this light, refracted from the land of fiction back to life, this commonness took on a romantic air, and bored people were grateful to the author for giving them the countenances of potentially romantic figures.

This partially accounts for the close attachment to the novels of Dickens and, similarly, to films. It was from this that the universal success of his novels derived. In an essay on Dickens, Stefan Zweig opens with this description of his popularity:

* As late as April 17, 1944, Griffith still considered this the chief social function of film-making. An interviewer from the Los Angeles *Times* asked him, "What is a good picture?" Griffith replied, "One that makes the public forget its troubles. Also, a good picture tends to make folks think a little, without letting them suspect that they are being inspired to think. In one respect, nearly all pictures are good in that they show the triumph of good over evil." This is what Osbert Sitwell, in reference to Dickens, called the "Virtue *v.* Vice Cup-Tie Final."

The love Dickens's contemporaries lavished upon the creator of Pickwick is not to be assessed by accounts given in books and biographies. Love lives and breathes only in the spoken word. To get an adequate idea of the intensity of this love, one must catch (as I once caught) an Englishman old enough to have youthful memories of the days when Dickens was still alive. Preferably it should be someone who finds it hard even now to speak of him as Charles Dickens, choosing, rather, to use the affectionate nickname of "Boz." The emotion, tinged with melancholy, which these old reminiscences call up, gives us of a younger generation some inkling of the enthusiasm that inspired the hearts of thousands when the monthly instalments in their blue covers (great rarities, now) arrived at English homes. At such times, my old Dickensian told me, people would walk a long way to meet the postman when a fresh number was due, so impatient were they to read what Boz had to tell. . . . How could they be expected to wait patiently until the letter-carrier, lumbering along on an old nag, would arrive with the solution of these burning problems? When the appointed hour came round, old and young would sally forth, walking two miles and more to the post office merely to have the issue sooner. On the way home they would start reading, those who had not the luck of holding the book looking over the shoulder of the more fortunate mortal; others would set about reading aloud as they walked; only persons with a genius for self-sacrifice would defer a purely personal gratification, and would scurry back to share the treasure with wife and child.

In every village, in every town, in the whole of the British Isles, and far beyond, away in the remotest parts of the earth where the English-speaking nations had gone to settle and colonize, Charles Dickens was loved. People loved him from the first moment when (through the medium of print) they made his acquaintance until his dying day. . . .[4]

Dickens's tours as a reader gave final proof of public affection for him, both at home and abroad. By nine o'clock on the morning that tickets for his lecture course were placed on sale in New York, there were two lines of buyers, each more than three-quarters of a mile in length:

The tickets for the course were all sold before noon. Members of families relieved each other in the queues; waiters flew across the streets and squares from the neighboring restaurant, to serve parties who were taking their breakfast in the open December air; while excited men offered five and ten dollars for the mere permission to exchange places with other persons standing nearer the head of the line! [5] *

Isn't this atmosphere similar to that of Chaplin's tour through Europe, or the triumphant visit to Moscow of "Doug" and "Mary," or the excited anticipation around the première of *Grand Hotel* in New York, when an airplane service assisted ticket buyers on the West Coast? The immense popular success of Dickens's novels in his own time can be equaled in extent only by that whirlwind success which is now enjoyed by this or that sensational film success.

Perhaps the secret lies in Dickens's (as well as cinema's) creation of an extraordinary plasticity. The observation in the novels is extraordinary—as is their optical quality. The characters of Dickens are rounded with means as plastic and slightly exaggerated as are the screen heroes of today. The screen's heroes are engraved on the senses of the spectator with clearly visible traits, its villains are remembered by certain facial expressions, and all are saturated in the peculiar, slightly unnatural radiant gleam thrown over them by the screen.

It is absolutely thus that Dickens draws his characters—this is the faultlessly plastically grasped and pitilessly sharply

---

* Dickens himself witnessed a modern by-product of popular success—speculators: "At Brooklyn I am going to read in Mr. Ward Beecher's chapel: the only building there available for the purpose. You must understand that Brooklyn is a kind of sleeping-place for New York, and is supposed to be a great place in the money way. We let the seats pew by pew! the pulpit is taken down for my screen and gas! and I appear out of the vestry in canonical form! . . . The sale of tickets there was an amazing scene. The noble army of speculators have now furnished (this is literally true, and I am quite serious) each man with a straw mattress, a little bag of bread and meat, two blankets, and a bottle of whisky. . . . It being severely cold at Brooklyn, they made an immense bonfire in the street—a narrow street of wooden houses—which the police turned out to extinguish. A general fight then took place; from which the people furthest off in the line rushed bleeding when they saw any chance of ousting others nearer the door, put their mattresses in the spots so gained, and held on by the iron rails. . . ."[6]

sketched gallery of immortal Pickwicks, Dombeys, Fagins, Tackletons, and others.

Just because it never occurred to his biographers to connect Dickens with the cinema, they provide us with unusually objective evidence, directly linking the importance of Dickens's observation with our medium.

[John] Forster speaks of Dickens's recollections of his childhood sufferings, and notes, as he could hardly fail to note, Dickens's amazingly detailed memory. He does not note, as he should, how this super-acuteness of physical vision contributed a basic element to Dickens's artistic method. For with that acuteness of physical vision, and that unerring recollection of every detail in the thing seen, went an abnormally complete grasp of the thing in the totality of its natural connections. . . .

And if ever a man had the gift of the eye—and not merely of the eye but of the ear, and of the nose—and the faculty of remembering with microscopic accuracy of detail everything ever seen, or heard, or tasted, smelled, or felt, that man was Charles Dickens. . . . The whole picture arises before us in sight, sound, touch, taste, and pervading odour, just exactly as in real life, and with a vividness that becomes positively uncanny.

To readers less sensitive than Dickens, this very vividness with which he visualizes plain things in plain everyday life appears to be "exaggeration." It is no such thing. The truth is that Dickens always sees instantly, and in every last, least, tiny detail, *all* that there is to be seen; while lesser mortals see only a part, and sometimes a trifling part at that.[7]

Zweig continues the case:

He cuts through the fog surrounding the years of childhood like a clipper driving through the waves. In *David Copperfield*, that masked autobiography, we are given reminiscences of a two-year-old child concerning his mother with her pretty hair and youthful shape, and Peggotty with no shape at all; memories which are like silhouettes standing out from the blank of his infancy. There are never any blurred contours where Dickens is concerned; he does not give us hazy visions, but portraits whose every detail is sharply defined. . . . As he himself once said, it is the little things that give meaning to life. He is, therefore, perpetually on the watch for tokens, be they never so slight; a spot of grease on a dress, an awkward gesture caused by shyness, a strand of reddish hair peeping from beneath a wig if its wearer happens to lose his temper. He captures all the nuances of a handshake, knows what the pressure of each finger signifies; detects the shades of meaning in a smile.

Before he took the career of a writer, he was parliamentary reporter for a newspaper. In this capacity he became proficient in the art of summary, in compressing long-winded discussions; as shorthand writer he conveyed a word by a stroke, a whole sentence by a few curves and dashes. So in later days as an author he invented a kind of shorthand to reality, consisting of little signs instead of lengthy descriptions, an essence of observation distilled from the innumerable happenings of life. He has an uncannily sharp eye for the detection of these insignificant externals; he never overlooks anything; his memory and his keenness of perception are like a good camera lens which, in the hundredth part of a second, fixes the least expression, the slightest gesture, and yields a perfectly precise negative. Nothing escapes his notice. In addition, this perspicacious observation is enhanced by a marvellous power of refraction which, instead of presenting an object as merely reflected in its ordinary proportions from the surface of a mirror, gives us an image clothed in an excess of characteristics. For he invariably underlines the personal attributes of his characters. . . .

This extraordinary optical faculty amounted to genius in Dickens. . . . His psychology began with the visible; he gained his insight into character by observation of the exterior—the most delicate and fine minutiae of the outward semblance, it is true, those utmost tenuosities which only the eyes that are rendered acute by a superlative imagination can perceive. Like the English philosophers, he does not begin with assumptions and suppositions, but with characteristics. . . . Through traits, he discloses types: Creakle had no voice, but spoke in a whisper; the exertion cost him, or the consciousness of talking in that feeble way, made his angry face much more angry, and his thick veins much thicker. Even as we read the description, the sense of terror the boys felt at the approach of this fiery blusterer becomes manifest in us as well. Uriah Heep's hands are damp and cold; we experience a loathing for the creature at the very outset, as though we were faced by a snake. Small things? Externals? Yes, but they invariably are such as to recoil upon the soul.[8]

The visual images of Dickens are inseparable from aural images. The English philosopher and critic, George Henry Lewes,[9] though puzzled as to its significance, recorded that "Dickens once declared to me that every word said by his characters was distinctly *heard* by him. . . ."

We can see for ourselves that his descriptions offer not only absolute *accuracy of detail*, but also an absolutely *accurate drawing of the behavior* and actions of his characters. And this is just as true for the most trifling details of behavior—even gesture, as it is for the basic generalized characteristics of the image. Isn't this piece of description of Mr. Dombey's behavior actually an exhaustive regisseur-actor directive?

He had already laid his hand upon the bell-rope to convey his usual summons to Richards, when his eye fell upon a writing-desk, belonging to his deceased wife, which had been taken, among other things, from a cabinet in her chamber. It was not the first time that his eye had lighted on it. He carried the key in his pocket; and he brought it to his table and opened it now—having previously locked the room door—with a well-accustomed hand.[10]

Here the last phrase arrests one's attention: there is a certain awkwardness in its description. However, this "inserted" phrase: *having previously locked the room door*, "fitted in" as if recollected by the author in the middle of a later phrase, instead of being placed where it apparently should have been, in the consecutive order of the description, that is, before the words, *and he brought it to his table*, is found exactly at this spot for quite *un*fortuitous reasons.

In this deliberate "montage" displacement of the time-continuity of the description there is a brilliantly caught rendering of the *transient thievery* of the action, slipped between the preliminary action and the act of reading another's letter, carried out with that absolute "correctness" of gentlemanly dignity which Mr. Dombey knows how to give to any behavior or action of his.

This very (montage) arrangement of the phrasing gives an exact direction to the "performer," so that in defining this decorous and confident opening of the writing-desk, he must "play" the closing and locking of the door with a hint of an entirely different shade of conduct. And it would be this "shading" in which would also be played the unfolding of the letter; but in this part of the "performance" Dickens makes this shading more precise, not only with a significant arrangement of the words, but also with an exact description of characteristics.

From beneath a heap of torn and cancelled scraps of paper, he took one letter that remained entire. Involuntarily holding his breath as he opened this document, and 'bating in the stealthy action something of his arrogant demeanour, he sat down, resting his head upon one hand, and read it through.

The reading itself is done with a shading of absolutely gentlemanly cold decorum:

He read it slowly and attentively, and with a nice particularity to every syllable. Otherwise than as his great deliberation seemed unnatural, and perhaps the result of an effort equally great, he allowed no sign of emotion to escape him. When he had read it through, he folded and refolded it slowly several times, and tore it carefully into fragments. Checking his hand in the act of throwing these away, he put them in his pocket, as if unwilling to trust them even to the chances of being reunited and deciphered; and instead of ringing, as usual, for little Paul, he sat solitary all the evening in his cheerless room.

This scene does not appear in the final version of the novel, for with the aim of increasing the tension of the action, Dickens cut out this passage on Forster's advice; in his biography of Dickens Forster preserved this passage to show with what mercilessness Dickens sometimes "cut" writing that had cost him great labor. This mercilessness once more emphasizes that sharp clarity of representation towards which Dickens strove by all means, endeavoring with purely cinematic laconism to say what he considered necessary. (This, by the way, did not in the least prevent his novels from achieving enormous breadth.)

I don't believe I am wrong in lingering on this example, for one need only alter two or three of the character names and change Dickens's name to the name of the hero of my essay, in order to impute literally almost everything told here to the account of Griffith.

From that steely, observing glance, which I remember from my meeting with him, to the capture *en passant* of key details or tokens—indications of character, Griffith has all this in as much a Dickens-esque sharpness and clarity as Dickens, on his part, had cinematic "optical quality," "frame composition," "close-up," and the alteration of emphasis by special lenses.

Analogies and resemblances cannot be pursued too far—they lose conviction and charm. They begin to take on the air of machination or card-tricks. I should be very sorry to lose the conviction of the affinity between Dickens and Griffith, allowing this abundance of common traits to slide into a game of anecdotal semblance of tokens.

All the more that such a gleaning from Dickens goes beyond the limits of interest in Griffith's individual cinematic craftsmanship and widens into a concern with film-craftsmanship in general. This is why I dig more and more deeply into the film-indications of Dickens, revealing them through Griffith—for the use of future film-exponents. So I must be excused, in leafing through Dickens, for having found in him even—a "dissolve." How else could this passage be defined—the opening of the last chapter of *A Tale of Two Cities:*

Along the Paris streets, the death-carts rumble, hollow and harsh. Six tumbrils carry the day's wine to La Guillotine. . . .

Six tumbrils roll along the streets. Change these back again to what they were, thou powerful enchanter, Time, and they shall be seen to be the carriages of absolute monarchs, the equipages of feudal nobles, the toilettes of flaring Jezebels, the churches that are not my Father's house but dens of thieves, the huts of millions of starving peasants!

How many such "cinematic" surprises must be hiding in Dickens's pages!

However, let us turn to the basic montage structure, whose rudiment in Dickens's work was developed into the elements of film composition in Griffith's work. Lifting a corner of the veil over these riches, these hitherto unused experiences, let us look into *Oliver Twist*. Open it at the twenty-first chapter. Let's read its beginning:

Chapter XXI *

1. It was a cheerless morning when they got into the street; blowing and raining hard; and the clouds looking dull and stormy.

The night had been very wet: for large pools of water had collected in the road: and the kennels were overflowing.

There was a faint glimmering of the coming day in the sky; but it rather aggravated than relieved the gloom of the scene: the sombre light only serving to pale that which the street lamps afforded, without shedding any warmer or brighter tints upon the wet housetops, and dreary streets.

There appeared to be nobody stirring in that quarter of the town; for the windows of the houses were all closely shut; and the streets through which they passed, were noiseless and empty.

2. By the time they had turned into the Bethnal Green Road, the day had fairly begun to break. Many of the lamps were already extinguished;

a few country waggons were slowly toiling on, towards London;

and now and then, a stage-coach, covered with mud, rattled briskly by:

the driver bestowing, as he passed, an admonitory lash upon the heavy waggoner who, by keeping on the wrong side of the road, had endangered his arriving at the office, a quarter of a minute after his time.

The public-houses, with gas-lights burning inside, were already open.

By degrees, other shops began to be unclosed; and a few scattered people were met with.

* For demonstration purposes I have broken this beginning of the chapter into smaller pieces than did its author; the numbering is, of course, also mine.

Then, came straggling groups of labourers going to their work;
then, men and women with fish-baskets on their heads:
donkey-carts laden with vegetables;
chaise-carts filled with live-stock or whole carcasses of meat;
milk-women with pails;
and an unbroken concourse of people, trudging out with various
supplies to the eastern suburbs of the town.

3. As they approached the City, the noise and traffic gradually
increased;
and when they threaded the streets between Shoreditch and
Smithfield, it had swelled into a roar of sound and bustle.
It was as light as it was likely to be, till night came on again; and
the busy morning of half the London population had begun. . . .

4. It was market-morning.
The ground was covered, nearly ankle-deep, with filth and mire;
and a thick steam, perpetually rising from the reeking bodies of
the cattle,
and mingling with the fog,
which seemed to rest upon the chimney-tops, hung heavily
above. . . .
Countrymen,
butchers,
drovers,
hawkers,
boys,
thieves,
idlers,
and vagabonds of every low grade,
were mingled together in a dense mass;

5. the whistling of drovers,
the barking of dogs,
the bellowing and plunging of oxen,
the bleating of sheep,
the grunting and squeaking of pigs;
the cries of hawkers,
the shouts, oaths and quarrelling on all sides;
the ringing of bells
and roar of voices, that issued from every public-house;

the crowding, pushing, driving, beating,
whooping and yelling;
the hideous and discordant din that resounded from every corner of the market;
and the unwashed, unshaven, squalid, and dirty figures constantly running to and fro, and bursting in and out of the throng;
rendered it a stunning and bewildering scene, which quite con-
founded the senses.

How often have we encountered just such a structure in the
work of Griffith? This austere accumulation and quickening
tempo, this gradual play of light: from burning street-lamps,
to their being extinguished; from night, to dawn; from dawn,
to the full radiance of day (*It was as light as it was likely to be,
till night came on again*); this calculated transition from purely
visual elements to an interweaving of them with aural elements:
at first as an indefinite rumble, coming from afar at the second
stage of increasing light, so that the rumble may grow into a
roar, transferring us to a purely aural structure, now concrete
and objective (section 5 of our break-down); with such scenes,
picked up *en passant*, and intercut into the whole—like the
driver, hastening towards his office; and, finally, these magnificently typical details, the reeking bodies of the cattle, from
which the steam rises and mingles with the over-all cloud of
morning fog, or the close-up of the legs in the almost ankle-
deep filth and mire, all this gives the fullest cinematic sensation
of the panorama of a market.

Surprised by these examples from Dickens, we must not forget one more circumstance, related to the creative work of
Dickens in general.

Thinking of this as taking place in "cozy" old England, we
are liable to forget that the works of Dickens, considered not
only against a background of English literature, but against a
background of world literature of that epoch, as well, were
produced as the works of a city artist. He was the first to
bring factories, machines, and railways into literature.

But indication of this "urbanism" in Dickens may be found
not only in his thematic material, but also in that head-spinning

tempo of changing impressions with which Dickens sketches
the city in the form of a dynamic (montage) picture; and this
montage of its rhythms conveys the sensation of the limits of
speed at that time (1838), the sensation of a rushing—stage-
coach!

As they dashed by the quickly-changing and ever-varying objects, it was curious to observe in what a strange procession they
passed before the eye. Emporiums of splendid dresses, the materials
brought from every quarter of the world; tempting stores of everything to stimulate and pamper the sated appetite and give new
relish to the oft-repeated feast; vessels of burnished gold and silver,
wrought into every exquisite form of vase, and dish, and goblet;
guns, swords, pistols, and patent engines of destruction; screws and
irons for the crooked, clothes for the newly-born, drugs for the
sick, coffins for the dead, church-yards for the buried—all these
jumbled each with the other and flocking side by side, seemed
to flit by in motley dance. . . .[11]

Isn't this an anticipation of a "symphony of a big city"? *
But here is another, directly opposite aspect of a city, out-
distancing Hollywood's picture of the City by eighty years.

It contained several large streets all very like one another, inhab-
ited by people equally like one another, who all went in and out
at the same hours, with the same sound upon the same pavements,
to do the same work, and to whom every day was the same as
yesterday and tomorrow, and every year the counterpart of the
last and the next.[12]

Is this Dickens's Coketown of 1853, or King Vidor's *The
Crowd* of 1928?

If in the above-cited examples we have encountered proto-
types of characteristics for Griffith's *montage exposition*, then
it would pay us to read further in *Oliver Twist*, where we can
find another montage method typical for Griffith—the method
of a *montage progression of parallel scenes, intercut into each
other.*

* A reference to the Ruttmann-Freund film, *Berlin: Die Sinfonie der
Grosstadt* (1927).

For this let us turn to that group of scenes in which is set forth the familiar episode of how Mr. Brownlow, to show faith in Oliver in spite of his pick-pocket reputation, sends him to return books to the book-seller, and of how Oliver again falls into the clutches of the thief Sikes, his sweetheart Nancy, and old Fagin.

These scenes are unrolled absolutely à la Griffith: both in their inner emotional line, as well as in the unusual sculptural relief and delineation of the characters; in the uncommon full-bloodedness of the dramatic as well as the humorous traits in them; finally, also in the typical Griffith-esque montage of parallel interlocking of all the links of the separate episodes. Let us give particular attention to this last peculiarity, just as unexpected, one would think, in Dickens, as it is characteristic for Griffith!

Chapter XIV

COMPRISING FURTHER PARTICULARS OF OLIVER'S STAY AT MR. BROWN-LOW'S, WITH THE REMARKABLE PREDICTION WHICH ONE MR. GRIM-WIG UTTERED CONCERNING HIM, WHEN HE WENT OUT ON AN ERRAND.

. . . "Dear me, I am very sorry for that," exclaimed Mr. Brownlow; "I particularly wished those books to be returned tonight."

"Send Oliver with them," said Mr. Grimwig, with an ironical smile; "he will be sure to deliver them safely, you know."

"Yes; do let me take them, if you please, Sir," said Oliver. "I'll run all the way, Sir."

The old gentleman was just going to say that Oliver should not go out on any account; when a most malicious cough from Mr. Grimwig determined him that he should; and that, by his prompt discharge of the commission, he should prove to him the injustice of his suspicions: on this head at least: at once.

[Oliver is prepared for the errand to the bookstall-keeper.]

"I won't be ten minutes, Sir," replied Oliver, eagerly.

[Mrs. Bedwin, Mr. Brownlow's housekeeper, gives Oliver the directions, and sends him off.]

"Bless his sweet face!" said the old lady, looking after him. "I can't bear, somehow, to let him go out of my sight."

At this moment, Oliver looked gaily round, and nodded before

he turned the corner. The old lady smilingly returned his salutation, and, closing the door, went back to her own room.

"Let me see; he'll be back in twenty minutes, at the longest,"
said Mr. Brownlow, pulling out his watch, and placing it on the
table. "It will be dark by that time."

"Oh! you really expect him to come back, do you?" inquired
Mr. Grimwig.

"Don't you?" asked Mr. Brownlow, smiling.

The spirit of contradiction was strong in Mr. Grimwig's breast,
at the moment; and it was rendered stronger by his friend's confident smile.

"No," he said, smiting the table with his fist, "I do not. The boy
has a new suit of clothes on his back; a set of valuable books under
his arm; and a five-pound note in his pocket. He'll join his old
friends the thieves, and laugh at you. If ever that boy returns to
this house, Sir, I'll eat my head."

With these words he drew his chair closer to the table; and there
the two friends sat, in silent expectation, with the watch between
them.

This is followed by a short "interruption" in the form of a
digression:

It is worthy of remark, as illustrating the importance we attach
to our own judgments, and the pride with which we put forth our
most rash and hasty conclusions, that, although Mr. Grimwig was
not by any means a bad-hearted man, and though he would have
been unfeignedly sorry to see his respected friend duped and de-
ceived, he really did most earnestly and strongly hope, at that
moment, that Oliver Twist might not come back.

And again a return to the two old gentlemen:

It grew so dark, that the figures on the dial-plate were scarcely
discernible; but there the two old gentlemen continued to sit, in
silence: with the watch between them.

Twilight shows that only a little time has passed, but the
close-up of the watch, already twice shown lying between the
old gentlemen, says that a great deal of time has passed already.
But just then, as in the game of "will he come? won't he
come?", involving not only the two old men, but also the

kind-hearted reader, the worst fears and vague forebodings of
the old housekeeper are justified by the cut to the new scene—
Chapter XV. This begins with a short scene in the public-
house, with the bandit Sikes and his dog, old Fagin and Miss
Nancy, who has been obliged to discover the whereabouts of
Oliver.

"You are on the scent, are you, Nancy?" inquired Sikes, proffer-
ing the glass.

"Yes, I am, Bill," replied the young lady, disposing of its contents; "and tired enough of it I am, too. . . ."

Then, one of the best scenes in the whole novel—at least
one that since childhood has been perfectly preserved, along
with the evil figure of Fagin—the scene in which Oliver,
marching along with the books, is suddenly

startled by a young woman screaming out very loud, "Oh, my
dear brother!" And he had hardly looked up, to see what the
matter was, when he was stopped by having a pair of arms thrown
tight round his neck.

With this cunning maneuver Nancy, with the sympathies
of the whole street, takes the desperately pulling Oliver, as
her "prodigal brother," back into the bosom of Fagin's gang
of thieves. This fifteenth chapter closes on the now familiar
montage phrase:

The gas-lamps were lighted; Mrs. Bedwin was waiting anxiously
at the open door; the servant had run up the street twenty times
to see if there were any traces of Oliver; and still the two old
gentlemen sat, perseveringly, in the dark parlour: with the watch
between them.

In Chapter XVI Oliver, once again in the clutches of the
gang, is subjected to mockery. Nancy rescues him from a
beating:

"I won't stand by and see it done, Fagin," cried the girl. "You've
got the boy, and what more would you have? Let him be—let him
be, or I shall put that mark on some of you, that will bring me
to the gallows before my time."

By the way, it is characteristic for both Dickens and Griffith to have these sudden flashes of goodness in "morally degraded" characters and, though these sentimental images verge on hokum, they are so faultlessly done that they work on the most skeptical readers and spectators!

At the end of this chapter, Oliver, sick and weary, falls "sound asleep." Here the physical time unity is interrupted—an evening and night, crowded with events; but the montage unity of the episode is not interrupted, tying Oliver to Mr. Brownlow on one side, and to Fagin's gang on the other.

Following, in Chapter XVIII, is the arrival of the parish beadle, Mr. Bumble, in response to an inquiry about the lost boy, and the appearance of Bumble at Mr. Brownlow's, again in Grimwig's company. The content and reason for their conversation is revealed by the very title of the chapter: OLIVER'S DESTINY CONTINUING UNPROPITIOUS, BRINGS A GREAT MAN TO LONDON TO INJURE HIS REPUTATION . . .

"I fear it is all too true," said the old gentleman sorrowfully, after looking over the papers. "This is not much for your intelligence; but I would gladly have given you treble the money, if it had been favourable to the boy."

It is not at all improbable that if Mr. Bumble had been possessed of this information at an earlier period of the interview, he might have imparted a very different coloring to his little history. It was too late to do it now, however; so he shook his head gravely; and, pocketing the five guineas, withdrew. . . .

"Mrs. Bedwin," said Mr. Brownlow, when the housekeeper appeared; "that boy, Oliver, is an impostor."

"It can't be, Sir. It cannot be," said the old lady energetically. . . . "I never will believe it, Sir. . . . Never!"

"You old women never believe anything but quack-doctors, and lying story-books," growled Mr. Grimwig. "I knew it all along. . . ."

"He was a dear, grateful, gentle child, Sir," retorted Mrs. Bedwin, indignantly. "I know what children are, Sir; and have done these forty years; and people who can't say the same, shouldn't say anything about them. That's my opinion!"

This was a hard hit at Mr. Grimwig, who was a bachelor. As

it extorted nothing from that gentleman but a smile, the old lady tossed her head, and smoothed down her apron preparatory to another speech, when she was stopped by Mr. Brownlow.

"Silence!" said the old gentleman, feigning an anger he was far from feeling. "Never let me hear the boy's name again. I rang to tell you that. Never. Never, on any pretence, mind! You may leave the room, Mrs. Bedwin. Remember! I am in earnest."

And the entire intricate montage complex of this episode is concluded with the sentence:

There were sad hearts in Mr. Brownlow's that night.

It was not by accident that I have allowed myself such full extracts, in regard not only to the composition of the scenes, but also to the delineation of the characters, for in their very modeling, in their characteristics, in their behavior, there is much typical of Griffith's manner. This equally concerns also his "Dickens-esque" distressed, defenseless creatures (recalling Lillian Gish and Richard Barthelmess in *Broken Blossoms* or the Gish sisters in *Orphans of the Storm*), and is no less typical for his characters like the two old gentlemen and Mrs. Bedwin; and finally, it is entirely characteristic of him to have such figures as are in the gang of "the merry old Jew" Fagin.

In regard to the immediate task of our example of Dickens's montage progression of the story composition, we can present the results of it in the following table:

1. *The old gentlemen.*
2. Departure of Oliver.
3. *The old gentlemen and the watch. It is still light.*
4. Digression on the character of Mr. Grimwig.
5. *The old gentlemen and the watch. Gathering twilight.*
6. Fagin, Sikes and Nancy in the public-house.
7. Scene on the street.
8. *The old gentlemen and the watch. The gas-lamps have been lit.*
9. Oliver is dragged back to Fagin.
10. Digression at the beginning of Chapter XVII.

11. The journey of Mr. Bumble.
12. *The old gentlemen* and Mr. Brownlow's command to forget Oliver forever.

As we can see, we have before us a typical and, for Griffith, a model of parallel montage of two story lines, where one (the waiting gentlemen) emotionally heightens the tension and drama of the other (the capture of Oliver). It is in "rescuers" rushing along to save the "suffering heroine" that Griffith has, with the aid of parallel montage, earned his most glorious laurels!

Most curious of all is that in the *very center* of our breakdown of the episode, is wedged another "interruption"—a whole digression at the beginning of Chapter XVII, on which we have been purposely silent. What is remarkable about this digression? It is Dickens's own "treatise" on the principles of this montage construction of the story which he carries out so fascinatingly, and which passed into the style of Griffith. Here it is:

It is the custom on the stage, in all good murderous melodramas, to present the tragic and the comic scenes, in as regular alternation, as the layers of red and white in a side of streaky well-cured bacon. The hero sinks upon his straw bed, weighed down by fetters and misfortunes; and, in the next scene, his faithful but unconscious squire regales the audience with a comic song. We behold, with throbbing bosoms, the heroine in the grasp of a proud and ruthless baron: her virtue and her life alike in danger; drawing forth her dagger to preserve the one at the cost of the other; and just as our expectations are wrought up to the highest pitch, a whistle is heard: and we are straightway transported to the great hall of the castle: where a grey-headed seneschal sings a funny chorus with a funnier body of vassals, who are free of all sorts of places from church vaults to palaces, and roam about in company, carolling perpetually.

Such changes appear absurd; but they are not so unnatural as they would seem at first sight. The transitions in real life from well-spread boards to death-beds, and from mourning-weeds to holiday garments, are not a whit less startling; only, there, we are busy actors, instead of passive lookers-on; which makes a vast difference. The actors in the mimic life of the theatre, are blind to violent transitions and abrupt impulses of passion of feeling, which, presented before the eyes of mere spectators, are at once condemned as outrageous and preposterous.

As sudden shiftings of the scene, and rapid changes of time and place, are not only sanctioned in books by long usage, but are by many considered as the great art of authorship: an author's skill in his craft being, by such critics, chiefly estimated with relation to the dilemmas in which he leaves his characters at the end of every chapter: this brief introduction to the present one may perhaps be deemed unnecessary. . . .

There is another interesting thing in this treatise: in his own words, Dickens (a life-long amateur actor) defines his direct relation to the theater melodrama. This is as if Dickens had placed himself in the position of a connecting link between the future, unforeseen art of the cinema, and the not so distant (for Dickens) past—the traditions of "good murderous melodramas."

This "treatise," of course, could not have escaped the eye of the patriarch of the American film, and very often his structure seems to follow the wise advice, handed down to the great film-maker of the twentieth century by the great novelist of the nineteenth. And Griffith, hiding nothing, has more than once acknowledged his debt to Dickens's memory.

We have already seen that the first screen exploitation of such a structure was by Griffith in *After Many Years*, an exploitation for which he held Dickens responsible. This film is further memorable for being the first in which the close-up was *intelligently* used and, chiefly, *utilized.**

Lewis Jacobs has described Griffith's approach to the close-up, three months earlier, in *For Love of Gold*, an adaptation of Jack London's *Just Meat:*

* Close shots of heads and objects were not so rare in the pre-Griffith film as is generally assumed; close shots can be found used solely for novelty or trick purposes by such inventive pioneers as Méliès and the English "Brighton School" (as pointed out by Georges Sadoul).

The climax of the story was the scene in which the two thieves begin to distrust each other. Its effectiveness depended upon the audience's awareness of what was going on in the minds of both thieves. The only known way to indicate a player's thoughts was by double-exposure "dream balloons." This convention had grown out of two misconceptions: first, that the camera must always be fixed at a viewpoint corresponding to that of a spectator in a theatre (the position now known as the long shot); the other, that a scene had to be played in its entirety before another was begun. . . .

Griffith decided now upon a revolutionary step. He moved the camera closer to the actor, in what is now known as the full shot (a larger view of the actor), so that the audience could observe the actor's pantomime more closely. No one before had thought of changing the position of the camera in the middle of a scene. . . .

The next logical step was to bring the camera still closer to the actor in what is now called the close-up. . . .

Not since Porter's *The Great Train Robbery*, some five years before, had a close-up been seen in American films. Used then only as a stunt (the outlaw was shown firing at the audience), the close-up became in *Enoch Arden* [*After Many Years*] the natural dramatic complement of the long shot and full shot. Going further than he had ventured before, in a scene showing Annie Lee brooding and waiting for her husband's return Griffith daringly used a large close-up of her face.

Everyone in the Biograph studio was shocked. "Show only the head of a person? What will people say? It's against all rules of movie making!" . . .

But Griffith had no time for argument. He had another surprise, even more radical, to offer. Immediately following the close-up of Annie, he inserted a picture of the object of her thoughts—her husband, cast away on a desert isle. This cutting from one scene to another, without finishing either, brought a torrent of criticism down upon the experimenter.[13]

And we have read how Griffith defended his experiment by calling on Dickens as a witness.

If these were only the first intimations of that which was to bring glory to Griffith, we can find a full fruition of his

new method in a film made only a year after he began to direct
films—*The Lonely Villa*. This is told in Iris Barry's monograph
on Griffith:

> By June, 1909, Griffith was already gaining control of his mate-
> rial and moved to further creative activity: he carried Porter's
> initial method * to a new stage of development in *The Lonely
> Villa*, in which he employed cross-cutting to heighten suspense
> throughout the parallel scenes where the burglars are breaking in
> upon the mother and children while the father is rushing home to
> the rescue. Here he had hit upon a new way of handling a tried
> device—the last-minute rescue—which was to serve him well for
> the rest of his career. By March, 1911, Griffith further developed
> this disjunctive method of narration in *The Lonedale Operator*,
> which achieves a much greater degree of breathless excitement
> and suspense in the scenes where the railwayman-hero is racing
> his train back to the rescue of the heroine attacked by hold-up
> men in the depot.[15]

Melodrama, having attained on American soil by the end of
the nineteenth century its most complete and exuberant ripe-
ness, at this peak must certainly have had a great influence on
Griffith, whose first art was the theater, and its methods must
have been stored away in Griffith's reserve fund with no little
quantity of wonderful and characteristic features.

What was this period of American melodrama, immediately
preceding the appearance of Griffith? Its most interesting
aspect is the close scenic entwining of *both* sides that are characteristic for the future creation of Griffith; of those *two
sides*, typical for Dickens's writing and style, about which we
spoke at the beginning of this essay.

This may be illustrated by the theatrical history of the
original *Way Down East*. Some of this history has been preserved for us in the reminiscences of William A. Brady. These

---

* Miss Barry had previously pointed out that "Edwin S. Porter in
The Great Train Robbery had taken a vital step by introducing parallel
action through a rough form of cross-cutting. . . ."[14]

are particularly interesting as records of the emergence and popularizing of that theatrical genre known as the "homespun" melodrama of locale. Certain features of this tradition have been preserved to our own day. The successes of such keenly modern works as Erskine Caldwell's *Tobacco Road* and John Steinbeck's *The Grapes of Wrath* (in their original and film versions) contain ingredients common to this popular genre. These two works complete a circle of rural poesy, dedicated to the American countryside.

Brady's reminiscences are an interesting record of the scenic embodiment of these melodramas on the stages of that era. For purely as staging, this scenic embodiment in many cases literally anticipates not only the themes, subjects and their interpretations, but even those staging methods and effects, which always seem to us so "purely cinematic," without precedent and . . . begotten by the screen! *

A variety actor named Denman Thompson in the late 'seventies was performing a sketch on the variety circuits called *Joshua Whitcomb*. . . . It happened that James M. Hill, a retail clothier from Chicago, saw *Joshua Whitcomb*, met Thompson, and persuaded him to write a four-act drama around Old Josh.[16]

Out of this idea came the melodrama, *The Old Homestead*, financed by Hill. The new genre caught on slowly, but skillful advertising did its work—recalling sentimental dreams and memories of the good old, and alas! deserted hearth-side; of life in good old rural America, and the piece played for twenty-five years, making a fortune for Mr. Hill.

Another success from the same formula was *The County Fair* by Neil Burgess:

* For this reason immediately after the facts on the circumstances and arrangement that brought success to the play of *Way Down East* in the 'nineties, I shall offer a description, in no less bold relief, of the scenic effects in the melodrama *The Ninety and Nine*, a success in the New York theater of 1902.

He introduced in the play, for the first time on any stage, a horse race on tread-mills. He patented the device and collected royalties the world over when it was used in other productions. *Ben Hur* used it for twenty years. . . .

The novelty and attraction of this thematic material cast in scenic devices of this sort quickly made it popular everywhere and "homespun dramas sprung up on every side. . . ."

Another long-lived earthy melodrama was *In Old Kentucky*, which with its Pickaninny Band made a couple of millions in ten years for its owner, Jacob Litt. . . . Augustus Thomas tried his hand writing a trio of rurals—*Alabama, Arizona,* and *In Missouri.*

An energetic all-round entrepreneur like Brady was sure to be drawn towards this new money-making dramatic form:

All through the 'nineties, I was a very busy person in and around Broadway. I tackled anything in the entertainment line— melodramas on Broadway or the Bowery, prize fights, bicycle races—long or short, six days, twenty-four hours, or sprints—league baseball. . . . Broadsword fights, cake-walks, tugs of war, wrestling matches—on the level and made to order. Masquerade balls for all nations at Madison Square Garden. Matching James J. Corbett against John L. Sullivan and winning the world's heavyweight championship. This put me on the top of the world, and so I had to have a Broadway theatre.

Brady leased the Manhattan Theatre with "a young fellow named Florenz Ziegfeld, Jr." and went looking for something to put into it.

A booking agent of mine named Harry Doel Parker brought me a script called *Annie Laurie* [by his wife, Lottie Blair Parker]. I read it, and saw a chance to build it up into one of those rural things that were cleaning up everywhere. . . . I told him that the play had the makings, and we finally agreed on an outright purchase price of ten thousand dollars, he giving me the right to call in a play doctor. I gave the job to Joseph R. Grismer, who rechristened the play *Way Down East. . . .* *

---

* Elsewhere, William A. Brady has given more detail on Grismer's contribution: "During the trial-and-error period at one time or another we had used every small town in the United States as dog for *Way*

. . . We booked it at our Broadway theater, where it ran seven months, never knowing a profitable week. The critics tore it to pieces. . . . During its Broadway run we used every trick known to the barnstormer to pull them in, but to no avail. . . . We depended on "snow"—sloughing New York and its suburbs with "Pass 2's."

One night a well-known minister dropped in and he wrote us a nice letter of appreciation. That gave us a cue. We sent out ten thousand "minister tickets" and asked them all for tributes and got them. They all said it was a masterpiece—made long speeches from the stage to that effect—and followed it up with sermons from their pulpits. I hired the big electric sign on the triangle building at Broadway and Twenty-third Street (the first big one in New York). It cost us a thousand dollars a month. How it did make the Rialto talk! In one of our weekly press notices, which *The Sun* printed, it stated that *Way Down East* was better than *The Old Homestead*. That gave us a slogan which lasted twenty years. . . .

The manager of the Academy of Music, the home of *The Old Homestead*, was asked to put *Way Down East* into his theater.

He was willing, but insisted that the show and its production was too small for his huge stage. Grismer and I put our heads together and decided on a huge production, introducing horses, cattle, sheep, all varieties of farm conveyances, a monster sleigh drawn by four horses for a sleigh-ride, an electric snowstorm, a double quartette singing at every opportunity the songs that mother loved —forming, all in all, a veritable farm circus. It went over with a bang, and stayed in New York a full season, showing profits exceeding one hundred thousand dollars. After that, it was easy

Down East, and no two of them ever saw the same version. . . . Grismer lived, slept and ate it. He certainly earned that credit-line which always ran in the program: 'Elaborated by Joseph R. Grismer.' Why, the mechanical snowstorm used in the third act, which had no small part in making the play a memorable success, was specially invented by him for the production and then patented. One of his inspirations was laying hands on a vaudeville actor named Harry Seamon, who had a small-time hick act, breaking his routine into three parts and running him into *Way Down East.*" [17]

going. I launched a half-dozen touring companies. They all cleaned up.

The show was a repeater and it took twenty-one years to wear it out. The big cities never seemed to grow tired of it. . . .

The silent movie rights of *Way Down East* were purchased by D. W. Griffith for one hundred and seventy thousand dollars, twenty-five years after its first stage production.

In the fall of 1902, exactly a year before the production of *The Great Train Robbery*, a moralistic melodrama entitled *The Ninety and Nine* (the title derives from a familiar hymn by Sankey) opened at the same Academy of Music. Under a striking photo of the climactic scene in the production, *The Theatre Magazine* printed this explanatory caption:

A hamlet is encircled by a raging prairie fire and three thousand people are threatened. At the station, thirty miles away, scores of excited people wait as the telegraph ticks the story of peril. A special is ready to go to the rescue. The engineer is absent and the craven young millionaire refuses to take the risk to make the dash. The hero springs forward to take his place. Darkness, a moment of suspense, and then the curtain rises again upon an exciting scene. The big stage is literally covered with fire. Flames lick the trunks of the trees. Telegraph poles blaze and the wires snap in the fierce heat. Sharp tongues of fire creep through the grass and sweep on, blazing fiercely. In the midst of it all is the massive locomotive, full sized and such as draw the modern express trains, almost hidden from view in the steam or smoke. Its big drive wheels spin on the track, and it rocks and sways as if driven at topmost speed. In the cab is the engineer, smoke-grimed and scarred, while the fireman dashes pails of water on him to protect him from the flying embers.*

Further comment seems superfluous: here too is the tension of parallel action, of the race, the chase—the necessity to get

---

* In his accompanying review, Arthur Hornblow gives us some idea of how this effect was achieved: "This scene, which is the 'sensation' of the production, is one of the most realistic effects of machinery ever seen on any stage. . . . Tissue paper streamers, blown by concealed electric fans, on which brilliant red and yellow lights play, represent the flames, while the motion of the on-rushing locomotive is simulated by revolving the forest background in an inverse direction."

there in time, to break through the flaming barrier; here too is the moral preachment, capable of inflaming a thousand ministers; here too, answering the "modern" interests of the audience, is HOME in all its "exotic fullness"; here too are the irresistible tunes, connected with memories of childhood and "dear old mother." In short, here is laid out the whole arsenal with which Griffith later will conquer, just as irresistibly.

But if you should like to move the discussion from general attitudes of montage over to its more *narrowly specific* features, Griffith might have found still other "montage ancestors" for himself—and on his own grounds, too.

I must regretfully put aside Walt Whitman's huge montage conception. It must be stated that Griffith did not continue the Whitman *montage tradition* (in spite of the Whitman lines on "out of the cradle endlessly rocking," which served Griffith unsuccessfully as a refrain shot for his *Intolerance;* but of that later).

It is here that I wish, in connection with montage, to refer to one of the gayest and wittiest of Mark Twain's contemporaries—writing under the *nom de plume* of John Phoenix. This example of montage is dated October 1, 1853 (!), and is taken from his parody on a current novelty—illustrated newspapers.

The parody newspaper is entitled "Phoenix's Pictorial and Second Story Front Room Companion," and was first published in the San Diego *Herald*.[18] Among its several items, ingeniously illustrated with the miscellaneous "boiler-plate" found in any small-town newspaper print-shop of the time, there is one item of particular interest for us:

Fearful accident on the Princeton Rail Road!
Terrible loss of life!!

"By all the rules of the art" of montage, John Phoenix "conjures up the image." The montage method is obvious: the play of *juxtaposed detail*-shots, which in themselves are immutable and even unrelated, but from which is created the desired *image of the whole*. And particularly fascinating here is the "close-up" of the false teeth, placed next to a "long-shot" of the overturned railway coach, but both given in *equal size*, that is, exactly as if they were being shown on "a full screen"!

Curious also is the figure of the author himself, hiding beneath the pseudonym of Phoenix the honored name of Lieutenant George Horatio Derby, of the United States Army Engineers, wounded at Serro Gordo in 1846, a conscientious surveyor, reporter and engineer till his death in 1861. Such was one of the first American ancestors of the wonder-working method of montage! He was one of the first important American humorists of a new type, who belongs as well to the indubitable forerunners of that "violent" humor, which has achieved its wildest flourish in films, for example, in the work of the Marx Brothers.*

I don't know how my readers feel about this, but for me personally it is always pleasing to recognize again and again the fact that our cinema is not altogether without parents and without pedigree, without a past, without the traditions and rich cultural heritage of the past epochs. It is only very thoughtless and presumptuous people who can erect laws and an esthetic for cinema, proceeding from premises of some incredible virgin-birth of this art!

Let Dickens and the whole ancestral array, going back as far as the Greeks and Shakespeare, be superfluous reminders that both Griffith and our cinema prove our origins to be not

---

* Sufficient evidence of this lies in the anecdote by John Phoenix in which Tushmaker's new tooth-pulling machine "drew the old lady's skeleton completely and entirely from her body, leaving her a mass of quivering jelly in her chair! Tushmaker took her home in a pillowcase. She lived seven years after that, and they called her the 'India-Rubber Woman.' She had suffered terribly with the rheumatism, but after this occurrence, never had a pain in her bones. The dentist kept them in a glass case. . . ." [19]

solely as of Edison and his fellow inventors, but as based on an enormous cultured past; each part of this past in its own moment of world history has moved forward the great art of cinematography. Let this past be a reproach to those thoughtless people who have displayed arrogance in reference to literature, which has contributed so much to this apparently unprecedented art and is, in the first and most important place: the art of viewing—not only the *eye*, but *viewing*—both meanings being embraced in this term.

This esthetic growth from the *cinematographic eye* to the *image of an embodied viewpoint on phenomena* was one of the most serious processes of development of our Soviet cinema in particular; our cinema also played a tremendous rôle in the history of the development of world cinema as a whole, and it was no small rôle that was played by a basic understanding of the principles of film-montage, which became so characteristic for the Soviet school of film-making.

None the less enormous was the rôle of Griffith also in the evolution of the system of Soviet montage: a rôle as enormous as the rôle of Dickens in forming the methods of Griffith. Dickens in this respect played an enormous rôle in heightening the tradition and cultural heritage of preceding epochs; just as on an even higher level we can see the enormous rôle of those social premises, which inevitably in those pivotal moments of history ever anew push elements of the montage method into the center of attention for creative work.

The rôle of Griffith is enormous, but our cinema is neither a poor relative nor an insolvent debtor of his. It was natural that the spirit and content of our country itself, in themes and subjects, would stride far ahead of Griffith's ideals as well as their reflection in artistic images.

In social attitudes Griffith was always a liberal, never departing far from the slightly sentimental humanism of the good old gentlemen and sweet old ladies of Victorian England, just as Dickens loved to picture them. His tender-hearted film morals go no higher than a level of Christian accusation of human injustice and nowhere in his films is there sounded a protest against social injustice.

In his best films he is a preacher of pacifism and compromise with fate (*Isn't Life Wonderful?*) or of love of mankind "in general" (*Broken Blossoms*). Here in his reproaches and condemnations Griffith is sometimes able to ascend to magnificent pathos (in, for example, *Way Down East*).

In the more thematically dubious of his works—this takes the form of an apology for the Dry Law (in *The Struggle*) or for the metaphysical philosophy of the eternal origins of Good and Evil (in *Intolerance*). Metaphysics permeates the film which he based on Marie Corelli's *Sorrows of Satan*. Finally, among the most repellent elements in his films (and there are such) we see Griffith as an open apologist for racism, erecting a celluloid monument to the Ku Klux Klan, and joining their attack on Negroes in *The Birth of a Nation*.*

Nevertheless, nothing can take from Griffith the wreath of one of the genuine masters of the American cinema.

But montage thinking is inseparable from the general content of thinking as a whole. The structure that is reflected in the concept of Griffith montage is the structure of bourgeois society. And he actually resembles Dickens's "side of streaky, well-cured bacon"; in actuality (and this is no joke), he is woven of irreconcilably alternating layers of "white" and "red"—rich and poor. (This is the eternal theme of Dickens's novels, nor does he move beyond these divisions. His mature work, *Little Dorrit*, is so divided into two books: "Poverty" and "Riches.") And this society, perceived *only as a contrast between the haves and the have-nots*, is reflected in the consciousness of Griffith no deeper than the image of an intricate race between two parallel lines.

Griffith primarily is the greatest master of the most graphic form in this field—a master of *parallel montage*. Above all else,

* In all instances the craftsmanship of Griffith remains almost unaltered in these films, springing as it does from profound sincerity and a full conviction in the rightness of their themes, but before all else I am noting the themes themselves and their ideological aims.

Griffith is a great master of montage constructions that have been created in a direct-lined quickening and *increase of tempo* (chiefly in the direction of the higher forms of parallel montage).

The school of Griffith before all else is a school of *tempo*. However, he did not have the strength to compete with the young Soviet school of montage in the field of expression and of relentlessly affective *rhythm,* the task of which goes far beyond the narrow confines of tempo tasks.

It was exactly this feature of *devastating rhythm* as distinguished from effects of *tempo* that was noted at the appearance of our first Soviet films in America. After recognizing the themes and ideas of our works it was this feature of our cinema that the American press of 1926-27 remarked.

But true rhythm presupposes above all organic *unity*.

Neither a successive mechanical alternation of cross-cuts, nor an interweaving of antagonistic themes, but above all a unity, which in the play of inner contradictions, through a shift of the play in the direction of tracing its organic pulse— that is what lies at the base of rhythm. This is not an outer unity of story, bringing with it also the classical image of the chase-scene, but that inner unity, which can be realized in montage as an entirely different system of construction, in which so-called parallel montage can figure as one of the highest or particularly personal variants.

And, naturally, the montage concept of Griffith, as a primarily parallel montage, appears to be a copy of his dualistic picture of the world, running in two parallel lines of poor and rich towards some hypothetical "reconcilation" where . . . the parallel lines would cross, that is, in that infinity, just as inaccessible as that "reconciliation."

Thus it was to be expected that our concept of montage had to be born from an entirely different "image" of an understanding of phenomena, which was opened to us by a world-view both monistic and dialectic.

For us the microcosm of montage had to be understood as a unity, which in the inner stress of contradictions is halved, in order to be re-assembled in a new unity on a new plane, qualitatively higher, its imagery newly perceived.

I attempted to give theoretical expression to this *general tendency* of our understanding of montage, and advanced this in 1929, thinking least of all at that time to what degree our method of montage both generically and in principle was in opposition to the montage of Griffith.

This was stated in the form of a definition of the *stages* of relationship between the shot and montage. Of the thematic unity of content in a film, of the "shot," of the "frame," I wrote:

The shot is by no means an *element* of montage.
The shot is a montage *cell*.
Just as cells in their division form a phenomenon of another order, the organism or embryo, so, on the other side of the dialectical leap from the shot, there is montage.

Montage is the expansion of intra-shot conflict (or, contradiction) at first in the conflict of two shots standing side by side:

Conflict within the shot is potential montage, in the development of its intensity shattering the quadrilateral cage of the shot and exploding its conflict into montage impulses *between* the montage pieces.

Then—the threading of the conflict through a whole system of planes, by means of which ". . . we newly collect the disintegrated event into one whole, but in *our* aspect. According to the treatment of our relation to the event." *

Thus is broken up a *montage unit*—the cage—into a multiple chain, which *is anew gathered into a new unity—in the montage phrase, embodying the concept of an image of the phenomenon.*

It is interesting to watch such a process moving also through the history of language in relation to the word (the "shot")

* See "The Cinematographic Principle and the Ideogram," pages 34-38.

and the sentence (the "montage phrase"), and to see just such a primitive stage of "word-sentences" later "foliating" into the sentence, made up of separately independent words.

V. A. Bogoroditzky writes that ". . . in the very beginning mankind expressed his ideas in single words, which were also primitive forms of the sentence." [20] The question is presented in more detail by Academician Ivan Meshchaninov:

> Word and sentence appear as the product of history and are far from being identified with the whole lengthy epoch of gutturals. They are antedated by an unfoliated state, till this day undetected within the materials of incorporated languages.*
>
> Broken up into their component parts, word-sentences show a unity between the original words and their combination into the syntactic complex of the sentence. This gains a diversity of possibilities in expressive word-combinations. . . .
>
> The embryos of syntax, previously laid down, were in a latent form of incorporated word-sentences, then, later during its decomposition, projected outward. The sentence appeared to have been broken down to its chief elements, that is, the sentence is created as such with its laws of syntax. . . .[21]

We have previously stated the particularity of *our* attitude towards montage. However, the distinction between the American and our montage concepts gains maximum sharpness and clarity if we glance at such a difference in principle of the understanding of another innovation, introduced by Griffith into cinematography and, in the same way, receiving at our hands an entirely different understanding.

We refer to the *close-up*, or as we speak of it, the "large scale."

This distinction in principle begins with an essence that exists in the term itself.

We say: an object or face is photographed in "large scale," i.e., *large*.

---

* This is a term for those modern languages, preserving this character up to the present day, for example, the languages of the Chukchi, the Yukagirs and the Gilyaks. A full account for those of us especially interested in these languages may be found in Professor Meshchaninov's work.

The American says: *near,* or "close-up." *

We are speaking of the *qualitative* side of the phenomenon, linked with its meaning (just as we speak of a *large* talent, that is, of one which stands out, by its significance, from the general line, or of *large* print [bold-face] to emphasize that which is particularly essential or significant).

Among Americans the term is attached to *viewpoint.*

Among us—to *the value of what is seen.*

We shall see below what a profound distinction in principle is here, after we have understood the system which, both in method and in application, uses the "large scale" in our cinema in a way distinguished from the use of the "close-up" by the American cinema.

In this comparison immediately the first thing to appear clearly relating to the principal function of the close-up in our cinema is—not only and not so much to *show* or to *present,* as to *signify,* to *give meaning,* to *designate.*

In our own way we very quickly realized the very nature of the "close-up" after this had been hardly noticed in its sole capacity as a means of showing, in American cinema practice.

The first factor that attracted us in the method of the close-up was the discovery of its particularly astonishing feature: to create *a new quality of the whole from a juxtaposition of the separate parts.*

Where the isolated close-up in the tradition of the Dickens kettle was often a determining or "key" detail in the work of Griffith, where the alternation of close-ups of faces was an anticipation of the future synchronized dialogue (it may be apropos here to mention that Griffith, in his sound film, did not freshen a single method then in use)—there we advanced the idea of a *principally new qualitative fusion,* flowing out of the process of *juxtaposition.*

---

* Griffith himself, in his famous announcement in *The New York Dramatic Mirror* of December 3, 1913, employed both designations: "The large or close-up figures. . . ." But it is characteristic that in habitual American film usage it should be the latter term, "close-up," that has been retained.

For example, in almost my first spoken and written declarations of the 'twenties, I designated the cinema as above all else an "art of juxtaposition."

If Gilbert Seldes is to be believed, Griffith himself came to the point of seeing "that by dovetailing the ride of the rescuers and the terror of the besieged in a scene, he was multiplying the emotional effect enormously; the whole was infinitely greater than the sum of its parts," [22] but this was also insufficient for us.

For us this *quantitative accumulation* even in such "multiplying" situations was not enough: we sought for and found in juxtapositions more than that—*a qualitative leap.*

The leap proved beyond the *limits of the possibilities* of the stage—a leap beyond the *limits of situation:* a leap into the field of montage *image,* montage *understanding,* montage as a means before all else of revealing the *ideological conception.*

By the way, in another of Seldes's books there appears his lengthy condemnation of the American films of the 'twenties, losing their spontaneity in pretensions towards "artiness" and "theatricality."

It is written in the form of "An Open Letter to the Movie Magnates." It begins with the juicy salutation: "Ignorant and Unhappy People," and contains in its conclusion such remarkable lines as these:

. . . and then the new film will arrive without your assistance. For when you and your capitalizations and your publicity go down together, the field will be left free for others. . . . Presently it will be within the reach of artists. With players instead of actors and actresses, with fresh ideas (among which the idea of making a lot of money may be absent) these artists will give back to the screen the thing you have debauched—imagination. They will create with the camera, and not record . . . it is possible and desirable to create great epics of American industry and let the machine operate as a character in the play—just as the land of the West itself, as the corn must play its part. The grandiose conceptions of Frank Norris are not beyond the reach of the camera. There are painters willing to work in the medium of the camera and architects and photographers. And novelists, too, I fancy, would find much of interest in the scenario as a new way of expression. There is no end to what we can accomplish.

. . . For the movie is the imagination of mankind in action. . . .[23]

Seldes expected this bright film future to be brought by some unknown persons who were to reduce the cost of films, by some unknown "artists," and by epics, dedicated to American industry or American corn. But his prophetic words justified themselves in an entirely different direction: they proved to be a prediction that in these very years (the book appeared in 1924) on the other side of the globe were being prepared the first Soviet films, which were destined to fulfill all his prophecies.

For only a new social structure, which has forever freed art from narrowly commercial tasks, can give full realization to the dreams of advanced and penetrating Americans!

In technique also, montage took on a completely new meaning at this time.

To the parallelism and alternating close-ups of 'America we offer the contrast of uniting these in fusion; the MONTAGE TROPE.

In the theory of literature a *trope* is defined thus: "a figure of speech which consists in the use of a word or phrase in a sense other than that which is proper to it," [24] for example, a *sharp* wit (normally, a *sharp* sword).

Griffith's cinema does not know this type of montage construction. His close-ups create atmosphere, outline traits of the characters, alternate in dialogues of the leading characters, and close-ups of the chaser and the chased speed up the tempo of the chase. But Griffith at all times remains on a level of *representation and objectivity* and nowhere does he try through the *juxtaposition* of shots to shape *import and image*.

However, within the practice of Griffith there was such an attempt, an attempt of huge dimensions—*Intolerance*.

Terry Ramsaye, a historian of the American film, has definitively called it "a giant metaphor." No less definitively has he called it also "a magnificent failure." For if *Intolerance*—in its modern story—stands unsurpassed by Griffith himself, a brilliant model of his method of montage, then at the same time, along the line of a desire to get away from the *limits of story* towards *the region of generalization* and metaphorical allegory, the picture is overcome completely by failure. In explaining the failure of *Intolerance* Ramsaye claims:

> Allusion, simile and metaphor can succeed in the printed and spoken word as an aid to the dim pictorial quality of the word expression. The motion picture has no use for them because it itself is the event. It is too specific and final to accept such aids. The only place that these verbal devices have on the screen is in support of the sub-title or legends. . . .[25]

But Terry Ramsaye is not correct in denying to cinematography *all possibility in general of imagistic story-telling*, in not permitting the assimilation of simile and metaphor to move, in its best instances, beyond the text of the sub-titles!

The reason for this failure was of quite another nature; particularly, in Griffith's misunderstanding, that the region of metaphorical and imagist writing appears in the sphere of *montage juxtaposition*, not of *representational montage pieces*.

Out of this came his unsuccessful use of the repeated refrain shot: Lillian Gish rocking a cradle. Griffith had been inspired to translate these lines of Walt Whitman,

> . . . endlessly rocks the cradle, Uniter of Here and Hereafter.*

not in the structure, nor in *the harmonic recurrence of montage expressiveness*, but in *an isolated picture*, with the result that the cradle could not possibly be *abstracted into an image of eternally reborn epochs* and remained inevitably simply a *life-like cradle*, calling forth derision, surprise or vexation in the spectator.

We know of a nearly analogous blunder in our films, as well: the "naked woman" in Dovzhenko's *Earth*. Here is another

* This is Griffith's editing of two Whitman phrases, actually twenty lines apart: "Out of the cradle endlessly rocking . . ." ". . . uniter of here and hereafter."

example of a lack of awareness that for *imagist* and *extra-life-like* (or *sur*realist) "manipulation" of film-shots there must be *an abstraction of the lifelike representation.*

Such an abstraction of the lifelike may in certain instances be given by the *close-up.*

A healthy, handsome woman's body may, actually, be heightened to *an image of a life-affirming beginning,* which is what Dovzhenko had to have, to clash with his montage of the funeral in *Earth.*

A skillfully leading montage creation with *close-ups,* taken in the "Rubens manner," isolated from naturalism and abstracted in the necessary direction, could well have been lifted to such a "sensually palpable" image.

But the whole structure of *Earth* was doomed to failure, because in place of such montage material the director cut into the funeral *long shots* of the interior of the peasant hut, and the naked woman flinging herself about there. And the spectator could not possibly separate out of this concrete, lifelike woman that generalized sensation of blazing fertility, of sensual life-affirmation, which the director wished to convey of all nature, as a pantheistic contrast to the theme of death and the funeral!

This was prevented by the ovens, pots, towels, benches, tablecloths—all those details of everyday life, from which the woman's body could easily have been freed by *the framing of the shot,*—so that *representational* naturalism would not interfere with the embodiment of the *conveyed metaphorical* task.

But to return to Griffith—

If he made a blunder because of non-montage thinking in the treatment of a recurring "wave of time" through an unconvincing plastic idea of a rocking cradle, then at the opposite pole—in the gathering together of all four motifs of the film along the same principle of his montage, he made another blunder.

This weaving of four epochs was magnificently conceived.*

---

* It was Porter (again) who earlier explored, in film, this parallel thematic linking of unconnected stories. In *The Kleptomaniac* (1905), "The story told of two women, one poor and the other rich, who are

Griffith stated:

> . . . the stories will begin like four currents looked at from a hilltop. At first the four currents will flow apart, slowly and quietly. But as they flow, they grow nearer and nearer together, and faster and faster, until in the end, in the last act, they mingle in one mighty river of expressed emotion.[26]

But the effect didn't come off. For again it turned out to be a combination of *four different stories*, rather than *a fusion of four phenomena* in *a single imagist generalization*.

Griffith announced his film as "a drama of comparisons." And that is what *Intolerance* remains—a drama of comparisons, rather than *a unified, powerful, generalized image*.

Here is the same defect again: an inability to abstract a phenomenon, without which it cannot expand beyond the *narrowly representational*. For this reason we could not resolve any "*supra*-representational," "conveying" (metaphorical) tasks.

Only by dividing "hot" from a *thermometer reading* may one speak of "a sense of heat."

Only by abstracting "deep" from *meters and fathoms* may one speak of "a sense of depth."

Only by disengaging "falling" from *the formula of the accelerated speed of a falling body* ($mv^2/2$) may one speak of "a sensation of falling!"

However, the failure of *Intolerance* to achieve a true "mingling" lies also in another circumstance: the four episodes chosen by Griffith are actually un-collatable. The *formal failure* of their mingling in *a single image* of Intolerance is only *a reflection of a thematic and ideological error*.

Is it possible that a tiny general feature—a general and superficially metaphysical and vague viewpoint towards Intolerance

caught shoplifting and are arrested. The rich one is freed; the poor one is jailed. The story's effectiveness depended on the paralleling of the causes of the actions and fates of the two women." (Jacobs) Griffith's most ambitious pre-*Intolerance* trial of this multiple story form seems to have been made in *Home, Sweet Home* (1914).

(with a capital *I!*)—can really unite in the spectator's consciousness such obvious historically uncollated phenomena as
the religious fanaticism of St. Bartholomew's Eve with labor's
struggle in a highly developed capitalist state! And the bloody
pages of the struggle for hegemony over Asia with the complicated process of conflict between the colonial Hebrew people
and enslaving Mother Rome?

Here we find a key to the reason why the problem of abstraction is not once stumbled upon by Griffith's montage
method. The secret of this is not professional-technical, but
ideological-intellectual.

It is not that representation cannot be raised with correct
presentation and treatment to the structure of metaphor, simile,
image. Nor is it that Griffith here altered his method, or his
professional craftsmanship. But that he made no attempt at a
genuinely thoughtful abstraction of phenomena—at an *extraction of generalized conclusions* on historical phenomena from
a wide variety of historical data; that is the core of the fault.

In history and economics it was necessary for the gigantic
work of Marx and the continuers of his teaching to aid us in
understanding *the laws of the process* that stand behind miscellaneous *separate data*. Then science could succeed in abstracting *a generalization from the chaos of separate traits* characteristic for the phenomena.

In the practice of American film studios there is a splendid
professional term—"limitations." Such a director is "limited"
to musical comedies. The "limits" of a certain actress are
within fashionable rôles. Beyond these "limitations" (quite
sensible in most cases) this or that talent cannot be thrust.
Risking departure from these "limitations" sometimes results
in unexpected brilliance, but ordinarily, as in commonplace
phenomena, this leads to failure.

Using this term, I would say that in the realm of *montage
imagery* the American cinema wins no laurels for itself; and it
is ideological "limitations" that are responsible for this.

This is not affected by technique, nor by scope, nor by dimensions.

The question of montage imagery is based on a definite structure and system of thinking; it derives and has been derived only through collective consciousness, appearing as a reflection of a new (socialist) stage of human society and as a thinking result of ideal and philosophic education, inseparably connected with the social structure of that society.

We, our epoch—*sharply ideal* and *intellectual*—could not read the content of a shot without, before all else, having read its ideological nature, and therefore find in the *juxtaposition of shots an arrangement of a new qualitative element*, a new *image*, a new *understanding*.

Considering this, we could not help rushing into sharp excesses in this direction.

In *October* we cut shots of harps and balalaikas into a scene of Mensheviks addressing the Second Congress of Soviets. And these harps were shown not as harps, but as an imagist symbol of the mellifluent speech of Menshevik opportunism at the Congress. The balalaikas were not shown as balalaikas, but as an image of the tiresome strumming of these empty speeches in the face of the gathering storm of historical events. And placing side by side the Menshevik and the harp, the Menshevik and the balalaika, we were *extending the frame of parallel montage into a new quality, into a new realm:* from the sphere of *action* into the sphere of *significance.**

The period of such rather naive juxtapositions passed swiftly enough. Similar solutions, slightly "baroque" in form, in many ways attempted (and not always successfully!) with the available palliative means of the silent film to anticipate that which is now done with such ease by the music track in the sound-film! They quickly departed from the screen.

However, the chief thing remained—an understanding of montage as not merely a means of producing effects, but above all as a means of *speaking*, a means of *communicating* ideas, of communicating them by way of a special film language, by way of a special form of film *speech*.

* Further analysis of this error can be found on page 58.—EDITOR.

The arrival at an understanding of normal film-speech quite naturally went through this *stage of excess in the realm of the trope and primitive metaphor.* It is interesting that in this direction we were covering methodological ground of great antiquity. Why, for example, the "poetic" image of the centaur is nothing more than a combination of man and horse with the aim of expressing *the image of an idea, directly un-representable by a picture* (but its exact meaning was that people of a certain place were "high speed"—swift in the race).

Thus the very production of simple meanings rises as a process of juxtaposition.

Therefore *the play of juxtaposition* in montage also has such a deep background of influence. On the other hand, it is exactly through elementary *naked juxtaposition* that must be worked out a system of the complicated inner (the outer no longer counts) juxtaposition that exists in each phrase of ordinary normal literate montage speech.

However, this same process is also correct for the production of *any kind of speech* in general, and above all *for that literary speech,* of which we are speaking. It is well known that the metaphor is an abridged simile.

And in connection with this Mauthner has very acutely written about our language:

Every metaphor is witty. A people's language, as it is spoken today, is the sum total of a million witticisms, is a collection of the points of a million anecdotes whose stories have been lost. In this connection one must visualize the people of the language-creating period as being even wittier than those present-day wags who live by their wits. . . . Wit makes use of distant similes. Close similes were captured immediately into concepts or words. A change in meaning consists in the conquest of these words, in the metaphorical or witty extension of the concept to distant similes. . . .[27]

And Emerson says of this:

As the limestone of the continent consists of infinite masses of the shells of animalcules, so language is made up of images, or tropes, which now, in their secondary use, have long ceased to remind us of their poetic origin.[28]

At the threshold of the creation of language stands the simile, the trope and the image.

All meanings in language are imagist in origin, and each of these may, in due time, lose its original imagist source. Both these states of words—imagery and non-imagery—are equally natural. If the non-imagery of a word was considered derivative as something elementary (which it is always), that derives from the fact that it is a temporary latency of thought (which imagery is its new step), but movement attracts more attention and is more provocative of analysis than is latency.

The calm observer, reviewing a prepared transferred expression of a more complicated poetic creation, may find in his memory a corresponding non-imagist expression, more imagistically corresponding to his (the observer's) mood of thought. If he says that this non-imagery is *communis et primum se offerens ratio* then he attributes his own condition to the creator of imagist expression. This is as if one were to expect that in the midst of a heated battle it is possible thus calmly to deliberate, as at a chess-board, with an absent partner. If one should transfer into the condition of the speaker himself, that would easily reverse the assertion of the cold observer and he would decide that *primum se offerens,* even if not *communis,* is exactly imagist. . . .[29]

In Werner's work on the metaphor he thus places it in the very cradle of language, although for other motives—he links it not with the tendency to *perceive* new regions, familiarizing the unknown through the known, but, on the contrary, with the tendency to *hide,* to substitute, to replace in customary usage that which lies under some oral ban—and is "tabu." [30]

It is interesting that the "fact word" itself is *naturally* a rudiment of the poetic trope:

Independently from the connection between the primary and derivative words, any word, as an aural indication of meaning, based on the combination of sound and meaning in simultaneity or succession, consequently, is metonymy.[31]

And he who would take it into his head to be indignant and rebel against this would inevitably fall into the position of the pedant in one of Tieck's stories, who cried out:

". . . When a man begins to compare one object with another, he lies directly. 'The dawn strews roses.' Can there be any thing more silly? 'The sun sinks into the sea.' Stuff! . . . 'The morning wakes.' There is no morning, how can it sleep? It is nothing but the hour when the sun rises. Plague! The sun does not rise, that too is nonsense and poetry. Oh! If I had my will with language, and might properly scour and sweep it! O damnation! Sweep! In this lying world, one cannot help talking nonsense!" [32]

The *imagist* transference of thought to simple *representation* is also echoed here. There is in Potebnya a good comment on this:

The image is more important than the representation. There is a tale of a monk who, in order to prevent himself from eating roast suckling during Lent, carried on himself this invocation: "Suckling, transform thyself into a carp!" This tale, stripped of its satirical character, presents us with a universal historical phenomenon of human thought: word and image are the spiritual half of the matter, its essence.[33]

Thus or otherwise the primitive metaphor necessarily stands at the very dawn of language, closely linked with the period of the production of the first transfers, that is, the first words to convey meanings, and not merely *motor* and *objective* understanding, that is, with the period of the birth of the first tools, as the first means of "transferring" the functions of the body and its actions from man himself to the tool in his hands. It is not astonishing, therefore, that the period of the birth of articulate montage speech of the future had also to pass through a sharply metaphorical stage, characterized by an abundance, if not a proper estimation, of "plastic sharpness"!

However, these "sharpnesses" very soon became sensed as excesses and twistings of some sort of a "language." And attention was gradually shifted from curiosity *concerning excesses* towards an interest in *the nature of this language itself.*

Thus the secret of the structure of montage was gradually revealed as a secret of *the structure of emotional speech*. For the very principle of montage, as is the entire individuality of its formation, is the substance of *an exact copy of the language of excited emotional speech.*

It is enough to examine the characteristics of similar speech, in order to be convinced, with no further commentary, that this is so.

Let us open to the appropriate chapter in Vendryes' excellent book, *Language:*

The main difference between affective and logical language lies in the construction of the sentence. This difference stands out clearly when we compare the written with the spoken tongue. In French the two are so far removed from each other that a Frenchman never speaks as he writes and rarely writes as he speaks. . . .

. . . The elements that the written tongue endeavours to combine into a coherent whole seem to be divided up and disjointed in the spoken tongue: even the order is entirely different. It is no longer the logical order of present-day grammar. It has its logic, but this logic is primarily affective, and the ideas are arranged in accordance with the subjective importance the speaker gives to them or wishes to suggest to his listener, rather than with the objective rules of an orthodox process of reasoning.

In the spoken tongue, all idea of meaning in the purely grammatical sense, disappears. If I say, *L'homme que vous voyez la-bas assis sur la greve est celui que j'ai rencontre hier à la gare* (The man that you see sitting down there on the beach is he whom I met yesterday at the station), I am making use of the processes of the written tongue and form but one sentence. But in speaking, I should have said: *Vous voyez bien cet homme-la-bas—il est assis sur la greve—eh bien! je l'ai rencontre hier, il etait à la gare.* (You see that man, down there—he is sitting on the beach—well! I met him yesterday, he was at the station.) How many sentences have we here? It is very difficult to say. Imagine that I pause where the dashes are printed: the words *la-bas* in themselves would form one sentence, exactly as if in answer to a question—"Where is this man?—*Down there.*" And even the sentence *il est assis sur la greve* easily becomes two if I pause between the two component parts: "*il est assis*," [*il est*] "*sur la greve*" (or "[*c'est*] *sur la greve* [*qu'*] *il est assis*"). The boundaries of the grammatical sentence are here so elusive that we had better give up all attempts to determine them. In a certain sense, there is but one sentence. The verbal image is one though it follows a kind of kinematical development. But whereas in the written tongue it is presented as a whole, when spoken it is cut up into short sections whose number and intensity correspond to the speaker's impressions, or to the necessity he feels for vividly communicating them to others.[34]

Isn't this an exact copy of what takes place in montage? And doesn't what is said here about "written" language seem a duplication of the clumsy "long shot," which, when it attempts to present something *dramatically*, always hopelessly looks like a florid, awkward phrase, full of the subordinate clauses, participles and adverbs of a "theatrical" *mise-en-scène*, with which it dooms itself?!

However, this by no means implies that it is necessary to chase at any cost after "montage hash." In connection with this one may speak of the *phrase* as the author of "A Discussion of Old and New Style in the Russian Language," the Slavophile Alexander Shishkov wrote of *words:*

In language both long and short words are necessary; for without short ones language would sound like the long-drawn-out moo of the cow, and without long ones—like the short monotonous chirp of a magpie.[35]

Concerning "affective logic," about which Vendryes writes and which lies at the base of spoken speech, montage very quickly realized that "affective logic" is the chief thing, but for finding all the fullness of its system and laws, montage had to make further serious creative "cruises" through the "inner monologue" of Joyce, through the "inner monologue" as understood in film, and through the so-called "intellectual cinema," before discovering that a fund of these laws can be found in a third variety of speech—not in *written*, nor in *spoken* speech, but in *inner speech*, where the affective structure functions in an even more full and pure form. But the formation of this *inner speech* is already inalienable from that which is enriched by *sensual thinking*.

Thus we arrived at the primary source of those interior principles, which already govern not only the formation of montage, but the inner formation of all works of art—of those basic *laws of the speech of art in general*—of those general *laws of form*, which lie at the base not only of works of film art, but of all and all kinds of arts in general. But of that—at another time.

Let us return now to that historical stage when montage in our field realized itself as a *montage trope*, and let us follow that path of development which it performed in the field of creating a unity of work, inseparable from that process, in which it became conscious of itself as an independent language.

Thus, in its way, montage became conscious of itself among us with the very first, not imitative, but independent steps of our cinema.

It is interesting that even in the interval between the old cinema and our Soviet cinema, researches were conducted exactly along the line of *juxtaposition*. And it is even more interesting that at this stage they naturally are known as . . . *contrasts*. Therefore on them above all else lies the imprint of *"contemplative dissection"* instead of an *emotional fusion* in some "new quality," as were already characterizing the first researches in the field of the Soviet cinema's own language. Such a speculative play of contrasts fills, for example, the film *Palace and Fortress* as if to carry the principle of contrast from its title into the very style of the work. Here are still constructions of a type of *un-crossed* parallelism: "here and there," "before and now." It is completely in the spirit of the posters of the time, split into two halves, showing on the left, a landlord's house *before* (the master, serfdom, flogging) and on the right—*now* (a school in the same building, a nursery). It is completely such a type of colliding shots that we find in the film: the "points" of a ballerina (the *Palace*) and the shackled legs of Beidemann (the *Fortress*). Similarly speculative in the *order of parallelism* is given also in the combination of shots—Beidemann behind bars and . . . a caged canary in the jailer's room.*

In these and other examples there is nowhere any further tendency towards *a union of representations in a generalized image:* they are united neither by a unity of composition nor by the chief element, emotion: they are presented in an even narrative, and not in that degree of emotional excitement when it is only natural for an imagist turn of speech to *arise*.

But pronounced without a corresponding emotional degree, without corresponding emotional preparation, the "image" inevitably sounds absurd. When Hamlet tells Laertes:

> I loved Ophelia; forty thousand brothers
> Could not, with all their quantity of love,
> Make up my sum. . . .

this is very pathetic and arresting; but try taking from this the expression of heightened emotion, transfer it to a setting of ordinary lifelike conversation, that is, consider the immediate objective content of this image, and it will evoke nothing but laughter!

Strike (1924) abounded in "trials" of this new and independent direction. The mass shooting of the demonstrators in the finale, interwoven with bloody scenes at the municipal slaughter-house, merged (for that "childhood" of our cinema this sounded fully convincing and produced a great impression!) in a film-metaphor of "a human slaughter-house," absorbing into itself the memory of bloody repressions on the part of the autocracy. Here already were not the simple "contemplative" *contrasts* of *Palace and Fortress*, but already—though still crude and still "hand-made"—a consistent and conscious attempt at *juxtaposition*.

Juxtaposition, striving to tell about an execution of workers

---

* This motif was placed on a considerably higher stage of meaning—in an image of Hopelessness—as it was later used by Pudovkin in *Mother* in the scene of the conversation between the mother and son in the prison, interrupted by shots of a cockroach pushed back into the sticky mass by the sentry's finger.

not only in representations, but further also through a generalized "plastic turn of speech," approaching a verbal image of "a bloody slaughter-house."

In *Potemkin* three *separate* close-ups of three different marble lions in different attitudes were merged into *one* roaring lion and, moreover, in another *film-dimension*—an embodiment of a metaphor: "*The very stones roar!*"

Griffith shows us an ice-break rushing along. Somewhere in the center of the splintering ice lies, unconscious, Anna (Lillian Gish). Leaping from ice-cake to ice-cake comes David (Richard Barthelmess) to save her.

But the parallel *race of the ice-break* and of *the human actions* are nowhere brought together by him in a unified image of "*a human flood*," a mass of people bursting their fetters, a mass of people rushing onward in an all-shattering inundation, as there is, for example, in the finale of *Mother*, by Gorky-Zarkhi-Pudovkin.

Of course, on this path excesses also occur, and also bald failures; of course, in more than a few examples these were good intentions defeated by shortcomings in compositional principles and by insufficient reasons for them in the context: then, in place of a flashing unity of image, a miserable trope is left on the level of an unrealized fusion, on the level of a mechanical pasting together of the type of "Came the rain and two students."

But thus or otherwise the dual *parallel rows* characteristic of Griffith ran in our cinema on the way to realizing themselves in the future *unity of the montage image* at first as a whole series of plays of montage comparisons, montage metaphors, montage puns.

These were more or less stormy floods, all serving to make clearer and clearer the final main task in the montage side of creative work—the creation in it of an inseparable domination of the *image*, of *the unified montage image*, of *the montage-built image, embodying the theme*, as this was achieved in the "Odessa steps" of *Potemkin*, in the "attack of the Kappel Division" of *Chapayev*, in the hurricane of *Storm Over Asia*, in the

Dnieper prologue of *Ivan*, more weakly—the landing of *We Are from Kronstadt*, with new strength in "Bozhenko's funeral" in *Shchors*, in Vertov's *Three Songs About Lenin*, in the "attack of the knights" in *Alexander Nevsky*. . . . This is the glorious *independent* path of the Soviet cinema—the path of the creation of the *montage image-episode*, the *montage image-event*, the *montage image-film in its entirety*—of equal rights, of equal influence and equal responsibility in the perfect film—on an equal footing with the *image of the hero*, with the *image of man, and of the people.*

Our conception of montage has far outgrown the classic dualistic montage esthetic of Griffith, symbolized by the two never-convergent parallel racers, interweaving the thematically variegated strips with a view towards the mutual intensification of entertainment, tension and tempi.

For us montage became a means of achieving *a unity of a higher order*—a means *through the montage image of achieving an organic embodiment of a single idea conception, embracing all elements, parts, details of the film-work.*

And thus understood, it seems considerably broader than an understanding of narrowly cinematographic montage; thus understood, it carries much to fertilize and enrich our understanding of art methods in general.

And in conformity with this principle of our montage, *unity and diversity* are both sounded as principles.

Montage removes its last contradictions by abolishing dualist contradictions and mechanical parallelism between the realms of sound and sight in what we understand as audio-visual ("vertical") montage.*

It finds its final artistic unity in the resolution of the problems of the unity of audio-visual synthesis—problems that are now being decided by us, problems that are not even on the agenda of American researches.

Stereoscopic and color film are being realized before our eyes.

* See *The Film Sense*, particularly Chapters II-IV.

And the moment is drawing near when, not only through the method of montage, but also through the synthesis of *idea, the drama of acting man, the screen picture, sound, three-dimension and color*, that same great law of *unity and diversity*—lying at the base of our thinking, at the base of our philosophy, and to an equal degree penetrating the montage method from its tiniest link to the fullness of montage imagery in the film as a whole—passes into *a unity of the whole screen image*.

[1944]

APPENDIX A

A STATEMENT

THE DREAM of a sound-film has come true. With the invention of a practical sound-film, the Americans have placed it on the first step of substantial and rapid realization. Germany is working intensively in the same direction. The whole world is talking about the silent thing that has learned to talk.

We who work in the U.S.S.R. are aware that with our technical potential we shall not move ahead to a practical realization of the sound-film in the near future. At the same time we consider it opportune to state a number of principle premises of a theoretical nature, for in the accounts of the invention it appears that this advance in films is being employed in an incorrect direction. Meanwhile, a misconception of the potentialities within this new technical discovery may not only hinder the development and perfection of the cinema as an art, but also threatens to destroy all its present formal achievements.

At present, the film, working with visual images, has a powerful affect on a person and has rightfully taken one of the first places among the arts.

It is known that the basic (and only) means that has brought the cinema to such a powerfully affective strength is MONTAGE. The affirmation of montage, as the chief means of effect, has become the indisputable axiom on which the world-wide culture of the cinema has been built.

The success of Soviet films on the world's screens is due, to a significant degree, to those methods of montage which they first revealed and consolidated.

Therefore, for the further development of the cinema, the

important moments will be only those that strengthen and broaden the montage methods of affecting the spectator. Examining each new discovery from this viewpoint, it is easy to show the insignificance of the color and the stereoscopic film in comparison with the vast significance of SOUND.

Sound-recording is a two-edged invention, and it is most probable that its use will proceed along the line of least resistance, i.e., along the line of *satisfying simple curiosity*.

In the first place there will be commercial exploitation of the most saleable merchandise, TALKING FILMS. Those in which sound-recording will proceed on a naturalistic level, exactly corresponding with the movement on the screen, and providing a certain "illusion" of talking people, of audible objects, etc.

A first period of sensations does not injure the development of a new art, but it is the second period that is fearful in this case, a second period that will take the place of the fading virginity and purity of this first perception of new technical possibilities, and will assert an epoch of its automatic utilization for "highly cultured dramas" and other photographed performances of a theatrical sort.

To use sound in this way will destroy the culture of montage, for every ADHESION of sound to a visual montage piece increases its inertia as a montage piece, and increases the independence of its meaning—and this will undoubtedly be to the detriment of montage, operating in the first place not on the montage pieces, but on their JUXTAPOSITION.

ONLY A CONTRAPUNTAL USE of sound in relation to the visual montage piece will afford a new potentiality of montage development and perfection.

THE FIRST EXPERIMENTAL WORK WITH SOUND MUST BE DIRECTED ALONG THE LINE OF ITS DISTINCT NON-SYNCHRONIZATION WITH THE VISUAL IMAGES. And only such an attack will give the necessary palpability which will later lead to the creation of an ORCHESTRAL COUNTERPOINT of visual and aural images.

This new technical discovery is not an accidental moment in film history, but an organic way out of a whole series of impasses that have seemed hopeless to the cultured cinematic avant-garde.

The FIRST IMPASSE is the sub-title and all the unavailing attempts to tie it into the montage composition, as a montage piece (such as breaking it up into phrases and even words, increasing and decreasing the size of type used, employing camera movement, animation, and so on).

The SECOND IMPASSE is the EXPLANATORY pieces (for example, certain inserted close-ups) that burden the montage composition and retard the tempo.

The tasks of theme and story grow more complicated every day; attempts to solve these by methods of "visual" montage alone either lead to unsolved problems or force the director to resort to fanciful montage structures, arousing the fearsome eventuality of meaninglessness and reactionary decadence.

Sound, treated as a new montage element (as a factor divorced from the visual image), will inevitably introduce new means of enormous power to the expression and solution of the most complicated tasks that now oppress us with the impossibility of overcoming them by means of an imperfect film method, working only with visual images.

The CONTRAPUNTAL METHOD of constructing the sound-film will not only not weaken the INTERNATIONAL CINEMA, but will bring its significance to unprecedented power and cultural height.

Such a method for constructing the sound-film will not confine it to a national market, as must happen with the photographing of plays, but will give a greater possibility than ever before for the circulation throughout the world of a filmically expressed idea.

> (signed by) S. M. EISENSTEIN
> V. I. PUDOVKIN
> G. V. ALEXANDROV

[Note: This historic collective "Statement," generally assumed to have been initiated and composed by the first of its three signatories and endorsed by the other two, first appeared in the Leningrad magazine, *Zhizn Iskusstva*, on August 5, 1928. All previous English texts have been translated from a German publication of the statement later in that month. The above is the first direct translation into English from the original Russian text. As predicted by the Statement, progress in the technical development of the Soviet sound-film was slow. In September of that year, the Shorin sound-system was first tested in Leningrad, and these tests were exhibited in March of the following year; in Moscow the Tager system was tried out in July 1929. In August the Leningrad studio of Sovkino constructed the first sound-stage, which was first used for the synchronization of recently completed films. Following the release of *Old and New* in October, arrangements were made for Eisenstein, Alexandrov, and Tisse to go abroad to study the sound-film.]

APPENDIX B

NOTES FROM A DIRECTOR'S LABORATORY

(DURING WORK ON *Ivan the Terrible*)

1. The First Vision

THE MOST important thing is to have the vision. The next is to grasp and hold it. In this there is no difference whether you are writing a film-script, pondering the plan of the production as a whole, or thinking out a solution for some particular detail.

You must see and feel what you are thinking about. You must see and grasp it. You must hold and fix it in your memory and senses. And you must do it at once.

When you are in a good working mood, images swarm through your busy imagination. Keeping up with them and catching them is very much like grappling with a run of herring.

You suddenly see the outline of a whole scene and, rising simultaneously before this same inner eye, a close-up in full detail: a head nesting on a great white ruff.

Just as you are seizing from the passing figures in your imagination a characteristic bend of Tzar Ivan's back in the confessional, you must drop your pencil and take up your pen to sketch the dialogue for this scene, and before the ink of this is dry, your pencil is once more making a note of an image that came to you during the dialogue—of the priest's long white hair descending like a canopy over the Tzar's graying head. Before this mood has finished, you find yourself drawing with your pen and penciling notes for the dialogue—on the sheets of drawings.

Directions become drawings; the voices and intonations of various characters are drawn as series of facial expressions. Whole scenes first take shape as batches of drawings before they take on the clothing of words.

In this way mountains of folders, stuffed with drawings, accumulate around the writing of the script—these multiply as the production plans are conceived—and they become a storage problem as the details of sequences and *mises-en-scène* are worked out.

These are nothing more than attempts to grasp stenographically the features of those images that flash through your mind in thinking about the individual details of your film. These drawings cannot claim to be more than this, nor can they possibly make any claim as drawings!

But neither can they claim less than this! For in them are secured the principal, initial elements of those ideas that will later have to be worked on, developed and realized in the course of the coming weeks and months: through the work of the designer who will have to transform rough sketches into a system of blueprints for the settings, through the work of the make-up man who will have to fuss for hours with greasepaint and wigs to achieve the same effect on the screen that the light pressure of a pencil indicated so freely on paper.

For days we will struggle with the stubborn cloth, cutting and draping it to capture that rhythm of folds that suddenly struck me when I closed my eyes over that bit of brocade and envisioned a procession of boyars in heavy robes moving slowly to the chambers of the dying Tzar.

And Cherkasov's incomparably lithe and flexible body will practice long and tiringly to produce the tragic bend of Tzar Ivan's figure so spontaneously fixed on paper as camera set-ups. In intent these drawings are no more (but also no less) than those Japanese paper toys that, when cast into warm water, unfold and develop stems, leaves and flowers of fantastic and surprising shape.

Altogether, to change the image, they are no more than the corner of a veil lifted from the creative kitchen of film production.

Here a viewpoint on that suddenly rising head and ruff is calculated.

Here the characteristic position of fingers and hands in El Greco's paintings is analyzed.

And here is a trial for the most effective intersection of the curve of an arch by a tall, dark figure in the foreground.

Sometimes the hint fixed on paper will be developed and transferred to the screen. Sometimes it will be scrapped. Sometimes the contribution of an actor, or some unforeseen possibility (or more frequently, impossibility) of lighting, or any kind of production circumstance will alter or revise your first vision. But even here, by other means and methods, you will strive to convey in the finished work that invaluable seed that was present in your first vision of what you hoped to see on the screen.

2. Facing the Camera

The dream becomes reality.

It is no longer pen and pencil, notebooks, scraps torn from envelopes, backs of telegrams, announcements, invitations—all completely covered with sketches and notes—that lie before one.

The dream has grown up to be an unwieldy, massive thing.

The words of the script on the capture of Kazan have grown into a military camp.

The rays of the sun are so scorching that we are all compelled to wear sun helmets. No second under this sun can be spent in dream or fantasy. Fancy is now in harness.

The earlier free play of fantasy has now become depth of focus, choice of the properly dense filters for the lens, the clicking of the footage meter.

The cold glass of the lens looks out mercilessly on the hot chaos of tents, reflectors, armor and umbrellas—paying attention to nothing but that which has been called into being by the innocent pages of the script.

From the sun-scorched plains of Kazan the cameras move to the sound-stage. No longer do we face the dust of hundreds of galloping horses.

Now Tzar Ivan is swearing his vow over the coffin of his poisoned wife. At this moment he would seem to be absolutely alone with her body.

Nothing of the sort. The fearful steel cameras are recording his every movement, every trace of emotion on his face.

Eyes are watching him intently from every corner of the sound-stage: to make sure that he does not slide out of the compositional margins, that he does not slip out of focus, or out of the laboriously set lighting, that he does not raise his voice beyond the level that the sound-engineers have prepared for. . . .

A few days later in the same cathedral where the aging Tzar wept over the coffin of his Tzaritza, the same man, but now fifteen years younger, is being crowned Tzar!

It requires a great effort of creative will and imagination on the part of Cherkasov to transform himself from a mature man weighed down by cares, into an impassioned youth full of hope and boldly looking towards a glorious future.

And with the ruthlessness of H. G. Wells' "time machine," the same camera boom is wheeled into position to record, with the same objectivity and accuracy as for the stern words of the graying Tzar, the youthful speech and gestures of the newly crowned Tzar.

One of the absorbing aspects of film-making, compensating for much that is irksome, difficult and unpleasant, is the constant variety and novelty of the subject matter.

Today you film a record-breaking harvest. Tomorrow a

matador in the bull-ring. The next day, the Patriarch blessing the new Tzar.

And each subject requires its own peculiar and strict technique.

That the scythe may be more effective in the fields of the collective-farm, it must be handled with no less strict an observance of rule than that observed by the matador preparing his muleta and sword for the kill.

Equally strict is the ritual in the ceremonies and customs of the past which you resurrect when you bring the people of that past to the screen of today.

And so Father Pavel Tzvetkov, one of the deans of Moscow, himself dressed in civilian clothes, patiently teaches the actor who plays the rôle of the Metropolitan, the proper performance of the ritual of blessing of the Tzar. At the same time he instructs the young Tzar how to conduct himself at this solemn moment, in accordance with the ancient canons.

And here, in a deep bass (how deep, and what a bass!) the words of the prayer for the young Tzar's health pass from the pages of the script onto the sound-track.

Not only have we selected the best bass in our country, that of People's Artist Mikhailov, but we have also selected that version of the "Long Life" prayer that best suits the atmosphere of our sequence—the solemn coronation of the first Russian Autocrat—Tzar Ivan Vasilyevich IV.

[Note: These "Notes" were originally written to accompany sketches and production stills made during the preparation and filming of *Ivan the Terrible*.]

NOTES ON TEXTS AND TRANSLATIONS

"Through Theatre to Cinema" (Srednaya iz trekh, 1924-1929). Originally printed in *Sovyetskoye kino*, November-December 1934 (Moscow). The present translation, by the editor and Paya Haskelson, has been previously published in *Theatre Arts Monthly*, New York, September 1936.

"The Unexpected" (Nezhdannyi styk). Originally printed in *Zhizn iskusstva*, 19 August 1928 (Leningrad). The present translation is the first appearance in English of this essay.

"The Cinematographic Principle and the Ideogram" (Za kadrom). An afterword to *Yaponskoye kino*, by N. Kaufman (Moscow, 1929). Translated by Ivor Montagu and S. S. Nolbandov and revised by the author and Ivor Montagu, published as "The Cinematographic Principle and Japanese Culture (with a digression on montage and the shot)" in *Transition*, June 1930 (Paris). The present text employs this translation, with alterations based on the original Russian text.

"A Dialectic Approach to Film Form." The original German manuscript, deposited in the Eisenstein Collection at the Museum of Modern Art Film Library, New York, has been newly translated for this edition by John Winge. Only the first half of this essay has been previously translated by Ivor Montagu as "The Principles of Film Form," *Close Up*, September 1931 (London).

"The Filmic Fourth Dimension" (Kino chetyrekh izmerenii). Originally printed in *Kino*, 27 August 1929 (Moscow). Previously translated by W. Ray as "The Fourth Dimension in the Kino," *Close Up*, March 1930 (Territet). The translation for this edition has been newly made from the original Russian text.

"Methods of Montage," written in London to supplement the preceding essay, this essay was translated by W. Ray as "The Fourth Dimension in the Kino: II," *Close Up*, April 1930 (Territet). The present text is a revision of Miss Ray's translation.

"A Course in Treatment" (Odolzhaites!). Originally printed in *Proletarskoye kino*, No. 17-18, 1932 (Moscow). Previously translated by W. Ray as "Cinematography *with* Tears," *Close Up*, March 1933, and "An American Tragedy," *Close Up*, June 1933 (London). The translation for this edition has been newly made from the original Russian text, restoring omitted passages.

"Film Language" ("E!" o chistotye kinoyazyka). Originally printed in *Sovyetskoye kino*, May 1934 (Moscow). The present translation is the first appearance in English of this essay. (The portion of analysis was quoted in Vladimir Nilsen's *The Cinema as a Graphic Art*, translated by Stephen Garry, London, 1936.)

"Film Form: New Problems." The full text of this speech at the All-Union Creative Conference of Workers in Soviet Cinematography, Moscow, 8-13 January 1935, was published in *Za bolshoye kinoiskusstvo* (Moscow, 1935). The greater part of the speech was translated by Ivor Montagu as "Film Form, 1935—New Problems," *Life and Letters Today*, September-December 1935 (London). The present text employs this translation, with alterations based on the original Russian text.

"The Structure of the Film" (O stroyenii veshchei). Originally printed in *Iskusstvo kino*, June 1939 (Moscow). The present translation is the first appearance in English of this essay. A detailed mathematical analysis of ideal proportions (in relation to the inter-related parts of *Potemkin*), employing illustrations from the practice of architecture, poetry, and painting, has been omitted in this translation.

"Achievement" (Gordost). Originally printed in *Iskusstvo kino*, January-February 1940 (Moscow). Previously translated as "Pride," *International Literature*, April-May, 1940 (Moscow). The translation for this edition has been newly made from the original Russian text.

"Dickens, Griffith, and the Film Today" (Dikkens, Griffit i myi). An essay in *Amerikanskaya kinematografiya: D. U. Griffit*, Volume I in *Materialy po istorii mirovogo kinoiskusstva* (Moscow, 1944). The present translation has been made for this edition.

"Statement" (Zayavleniye). Originally printed in *Zhizn iskusstva*, 5 August 1928 (Leningrad). Previously translated from a German text in the New York *Herald Tribune* (September 21, 1928), the New York *Times* (October 7, 1928), and *Close Up* (October 1928). The present translation has been made for this edition from the original Russian text.

"Notes from a Director's Laboratory." Written for the VOKS *Film Chronicle*, February 1945 (Moscow), and published as "In a Regisseur's Laboratory." The present text is an adaptation of the earlier translation, based on the original Russian text.

SOURCES

"THROUGH THEATER TO CINEMA"

1. Gustave Flaubert, *Madame Bovary*, translated by Eleanor Marx-Aveling. New York, Alfred A. Knopf, 1929.
2. Andrei Belyi (Boris Nikolayevich Bugayev), *Masterstvo Gogolya.* Moscow, 1934.

"THE UNEXPECTED"

1. Quoted in *Haiku Poems, Ancient and Modern*, translated and annotated by Miyamori Asatarō. Tokyo, Maruzen Company, 1940.
2. From a collection of anecdotes about Vasili Ignatyevich Givochini.
3. "Montage of Attractions," *LEF*, 3, 1923; a translated excerpt appears in Appendix 2 of *The Film Sense*.
4. Zoë Kincaid, *Kabuki, The Popular Stage of Japan.* London, Macmillan and Co., 1925, pp. 199-200.
5. J. Ingram Bryan, *The Literature of Japan.* London, Thornton Butterworth Ltd., 1929, pp. 33-34.
6. Julius Kurth, *Japanische Lyrik*, p. iv.
7. Heinrich von Kleist, "Über das Marionettentheater," translated by Eugene Jolas, in *Vertical*. New York City, Gotham Book Mart, 1941.

"THE CINEMATOGRAPHIC PRINCIPLE AND THE IDEOGRAM"

1. Jean Pierre Abel Rémusat, *Recherches sur l'origine et la formation de l'écriture chinoise*. Paris.
2. Translation by Miyamori, op. cit.
3. Translation by Frederick Victor Dickins, in *Primitive & Mediaeval Japanese Texts*. Oxford, Clarendon Press, 1906.
4. Yone Noguchi, *The Spirit of Japanese Poetry*. London, John Murray, 1914, p. 53.
5. Julius Kurth, *Sharaku*. München, R. Piper, 2nd edition, 1922, pp. 78-79. The Sharaku print referred to is that numbered 24 in the catalogue by Harold G. Henderson and Louis V. Ledoux, *The Surviving Works of Sharaku*. Published by E. Weyhe, in behalf of the Society for Japanese Studies, 1939.
6. George Rowley, *Principles of Chinese Painting*. Princeton University Press, 1947, p. 56.
7. Ibid., p. 66.
8. Lev Kuleshov, *Iskusstvo Kino*. Leningrad, 1929.
9. Illustration No. 12, "How to choose composition," in *Jinjo Shogaku Shintei Gaten Dai Roku Gaku Nen Dan Sei Yo* (Elementary Grade Drawing Manual for Sixth Grade Boys). Tokyo, Board of Education, 1910.

"A DIALECTIC APPROACH TO FILM FORM"

1. In *Conversations with Eckermann* (5 June 1825), translated by John Oxenford.
2. Razumovsky, *Theory of Historical Materialism*, Moscow, 1928.
3. Ludwig Klages, *The Science of Character*, translated by W. H. Johnston, London, George Allen & Unwin Ltd., 1929.
4. Graham Wallas, *The Great Society, A Psychological Analysis.* Macmillan, 1928, p. 101.
5. In *Conversations with Eckermann* (23 March 1829).
6. In the preface to Baudelaire's *Les fleurs du mal*, illustrated by Auguste Rodin, Paris, Limited Editions Club, 1940.
7. Renoir's manifesto for *La Société des Irrégularistes* (1884) is thus synopsized by Lionello Venturi in his *Painting and Painters*, New York, Scribners, 1945; the original text can be consulted in *Les archives de l'Impressionisme*, edited by Lionello Venturi, Paris, Durand-Ruel, 1939, I, pp. 127-129.
8. Charles Baudelaire, *Intimate Journals* (13 May 1856), translated by Christopher Isherwood. New York, Random House, 1930.

"THE FILMIC FOURTH DIMENSION"

1. Albert Einstein, *Relativity, the Special and General Theory*, translated by Robert W. Lawson. Peter Smith, p. 65.

"METHODS OF MONTAGE"

1. *Memoirs of Goldoni*, translated by John Black, New York, Alfred A. Knopf, 1926.
2. Vladimir Ilyich Lenin, *Filosofskiye tetradi*. Moscow, Ogiz, 1947, pp. 192-193.

"A COURSE IN TREATMENT"

1. James Joyce, *Ulysses*, New York, Random House, 1934, p. 425.
2. Nikolai Gogol, "The Story of the Quarrel between Ivan Ivanovich and Ivan Nikiforovich."
3. "What 'The Friends of the People' Are," in Lenin, *Sochineniya*, Moscow, 1929.
4. Quoted in Herbert Gorman, *The Incredible Marquis.* New York, Farrar & Rinehart, 1929, p. 441.
5. Jean Lucas-Dubreton, *The Fourth Musketeer, the Life of Alexander Dumas*, translated by Maida Castelhun Darnton, New York, Coward-McCann, 1928, p. 145.
6. Ibid., p. 148.
7. Ibid., pp. 141-142.
8. "Maupaussant" by Isaac Babel.
9. See *Last Plays of Maxim Gorky*, translated by Gibson-Cowan. New York, International Publishers, 1937.
10. Friedrich Engels, *Socialism: Utopian and Scientific*, translated by Edward Aveling. New York, International Publishers, 1935. Introduction, p. 18.

11. Theodore Dreiser, *An American Tragedy*, New York, Boni and Liveright, 1925, II, p. 78. (Note: Eisenstein's copy of this work, used in the preparation of his film treatment, is in the Eisenstein Collection of the Museum of Modern Art, New York.)
12. Translated by Stuart Gilbert as *We'll to the Woods No More*, Cambridge, New Directions, 1938.
13. See, particularly, René Bizet, *La double vie de Gérard de Nerval*. Paris, Plon, 1928.

"FILM LANGUAGE"

1. From a speech, "Soviet Literature," delivered at the First Soviet Writers' Congress. Proceedings published as *Problems of Soviet Literature*. New York, International Publishers, 1934.
2. Belyi, op. cit.
3. Book V, Chap. XXV of *Gargantua and Pantagruel*, "How We Disembarked at the Isle of Hodes, Where the Roads a-Roading Go," in *All the Extant Works of François Rabelais*, translated by Samuel Putnam. New York, Covici-Friede, 1929.
4. Translation by Miyamori, op. cit.
5. Emile Zola, *Germinal*, translated by Havelock Ellis. New York, Boni & Liveright, 1924.
6. Sebastien Mercier, *Paris pendant la Revolution* . . . Paris, Poulet-Malassis, 1862, I, p. 88.

"FILM FORM: NEW PROBLEMS"

1. "The Actor and the Image," in *Proceedings of the Moscow Club of Art Craftsmen*, No. 1, Moscow, 1934.
2. Wilhelm Wundt, *Elements of Folk Psychology*, translated by Edward Leroy Schaub. New York, Macmillan, 1928, p. 72.
3. This illustration, employed by Lévy-Bruhl in *Les fonctions mentales dans les sociétés inférieures*, is taken from *The Klamath Language*, by A. Gatschet (Contributions to *North American Ethnology*, ii, I); the previous illustration from the Bororo tribe, used by Lévy-Bruhl in the same work, is taken from *Unter den Naturvölkern Zentralbräsiliens*, by K. von den Steinen.
4. "The Philosophy of Style," in *Essays: Scientific, Political, and Speculative*. New York and London, D. Appleton and Co., 1916.
5. Engels, op. cit.
6. Engels, op. cit., p. 48.

"THE STRUCTURE OF THE FILM"

1. Maxim Gorky, essay on "Man."
2. Franz Kafka, "Reflections on Sin, Pain, Hope, and the True Way," in *The Great Wall of China*, translated by Willa and Edwin Muir. New York, Schocken Books, 1947.
3. Johann Nicolaus Forkel, "On Johann Sebastian Bach's Life, Genius, and Works," translated by Mr. Stephenson. In *The Bach Reader*, edited by Hans T. David and Arthur Mendel. New York, W. W. Norton & Company, 1945.

4. *The Works of Leo Tolstoy,* Oxford University Press, London, 1937 (Centenary Edition). *The Kreutzer Sonata,* translated by Louise and Aylmer Maude, Chap. XXIII.
5. Ibid., Vol. 9, *Anna Karenina,* translated by Louise and Aylmer Maude, Part II, Chap. XI.
6. V. Veresayev (Smidovich), *Vospominaniya* (second edition). Moscow, 1938.
7. *The Kreutzer Sonata,* ed. cit., Chap. XIII.
8. Ibid., Chap. XVI.
9. Lenin, loc. cit., Vol. XIII, pp. 302-303.
10. See Notes for *L'Assommoir* as described in the appendix to Matthew Josephson, *Zola and His Time,* New York, Macaulay, 1928; the full notes have been printed by Henri Massis in *Comment Zola composait ses Romans,* 1906.
11. Victor Shklovsky, *Ikh nastoyashcheye.* Moscow, Kinopechat, 1927.
12. See "P-R-K-F-V," Eisenstein's introduction to *Sergei Prokofiev,* by Israel Nestyev, New York, Alfred A. Knopf, 1945.

"ACHIEVEMENT"

1. Quoted in Léon Moussinac, *La décoration théâtrale.* Paris, F. Rieder, 1922, p. 13.
2. A. Gvozdëv, *Zapadno-yevropeiskii teatre na rubezhe XIX i XX stoletii.* Leningrad, Iskusstvo, 1939.
3. Quoted in Moussinac, op. cit., pp. 12, 14.
4. Gvozdëv, op. cit.
5. Moussinac, op. cit., p. 16.
6. Gvozdëv, op. cit.
7. The context of these opening titles can be found in the printed treatment of *Old and New,* in *Film Writing Forms,* edited by Lewis Jacobs. New York, Gotham Book Mart, 1934.
8. In *Novi Zritel,* No. 35, 1926.

"DICKENS, GRIFFITH, AND THE FILM TODAY"

1. George Bernard Shaw, *Back to Methuselah* (Preface). London, 1921.
2. Gilbert Keith Chesterton, *Charles Dickens, The Last of the Great Men.* New York, The Readers Club, 1942, p. 107.
3. Mrs. D. W. Griffith, *When the Movies Were Young.* New York, E. P. Dutton & Company, 1925, p. 66.
4. Stefan Zweig, *Three Masters: Balzac, Dickens, Dostoyevsky,* translated by Eden and Cedar Paul. New York, The Viking Press, 1930, pp. 51-53.
5. A Philadelphia newspaper, New York correspondent, December 1867.
6. Letters of January 5 and 9, 1868; quoted in John Forster, *The Life of Charles Dickens.* London, Chapman and Hall, 1892.
7. T. A. Jackson, *Charles Dickens; The Progress of a Radical.* New York, International Publishers, 1938, pp. 250-251, 297-298.
8. Zweig, op. cit.

9. George Henry Lewes, "Dickens in Relation to Criticism," *The Fortnightly Review*, February 1, 1872, p. 149.
10. Quoted in Forster, op. cit., p. 364.
11. Charles Dickens, *Nicholas Nickleby*, Chap. XXXII.
12. Charles Dickens, *Hard Times*, Book I, Chap. V.
13. Lewis Jacobs, *The Rise of the American Film*. New York, 1939, pp. 101-103.
14. Iris Barry, *D. W. Griffith, American Film Master*. New York, The Museum of Modern Art, 1940, p. 15.
15. Ibid., pp. 16-17.
16. This, and the following citations from Brady's reminiscences are quoted from his "Drama in Homespun," *Stage*, January 1937, pp. 98-100.
17. William A. Brady, *Showman*. New York, E. P. Dutton & Co., 1937.
18. This entire issue has been reproduced in *Phoenixiana*, edited by Francis P. Farquhar, San Francisco, The Grabhorn Press, 1937.
19. "Phoenix at Benicia" (first printed in the *Pioneer*, July 1855), ibid., p. 175.
20. V. A. Bogoroditzky, *General Course in Russian Grammar*. Moscow-Leningrad, 1935, p. 203.
21. Ivan I. Meshchaninov, *General Linguistics*. Leningrad, 1940.
22. Gilbert Seldes, *The Movies Come from America*. New York, Scribner's, 1937, pp. 23-24.
23. Gilbert Seldes, *The Seven Lively Arts*. New York, Harper & Brothers, 1924.
24. *The Shorter Oxford English Dictionary*.
25. Terry Ramsaye, *A Million and One Nights*. New York, Simon and Schuster, 1926.
26. Robert Edgar Long, *David Wark Griffith*. D. W. Griffith Service, 1920.
27. Fritz Mauthner, *Beitrage zu einer Kritik der Sprache: Zweiter Band, Zur Sprachwissenschaft*. Leipzig, Felix Meiner, 1923, pp. 487-488.
28. Ralph Waldo Emerson, "The Poet." In *Essays: Second Series*.
29. A. A. Potebnya, *From Notes on a Theory of Literature*. Kharkov, 1905.
30. Richard Maria Werner [?].
31. Potebnya, op. cit., p. 203.
32. Johann Ludwig Tieck, *Die Gemälde;* cited translation published London, 1825.
33. Potebnya, op. cit., p. 490.
34. Joseph Vendryes, *Language, A Linguistic Introduction to History*, translated by Paul Radin. New York, Alfred A. Knopf, 1925, pp. 145-146.
35. Alexander Semyonovich Shishkov, *Collected Works and Translations*. St. Petersburg, 1825, Part 5, p. 229.

INDEX

273